MW00426488

THE EXISTENCE
AND UNITY OF GOD

THE EXISTENCE AND UNITY OF GOD

Three Treatises Attributed to
Moses Maimonides

Translated and annotated
from the Hebrew editions

by

FRED ROSNER, M.D.

with bibliographies by
JACOB I. DIENSTAG

JASON ARONSON INC.
Northvale, New Jersey
London

Copyright © 1990 by Fred Rosner

10 9 8 7 6 5 4 3 2 1

All rights reserved. Printed in the United States of America. No part of this book may
be used or reproduced in any manner whatsoever without written permission from
Jason Aronson Inc. except in the case of brief quotations in reviews for inclusion in a
magazine, newspaper, or broadcast.

Library of Congress Cataloging-in-Publication Data

The Existence and unity of God : three treatises attributed to Moses
  Maimonides / translated and annotated from the Hebrew editions by
  Fred Rosner; with bibliographies by Jacob I. Dienstag.
    p. cm.
  Translation of: Ma'amar ha-yihud; Sefer ha-nimtsah;Tish' ah perakim mi-yihud.
    "The Ma'amar Hayichud . . . may well have been authored by
    Maimonides . . . Sefer Hanimtzah is probably spurious, and the Nine
    Chapters were certainly not written by Maimonides"—Pref.
    Includes bibliographical references.
    ISBN 0-87668-805-9
    1. God (Judaism)—Early works to 1800. 2. God—Simplicity—Early
    works to 1800.   I. Rosner, Fred. II. Maimonides, Moses,
    1135–1204. Ma 'amar ha-yihud. English. 1990. III. Sefer ha
    —nimtsah. English. 1990. IV. Tish' ah perakim mi–yihud. English.
    1990.
BM610.E95   1990
296.3'11—dc20
DNL.M/DLC
for Library of Congress
                                      90-15
                                        CIP

Manufactured in the United States of America. Jason Aronson Inc. offers books and
cassettes. For information and catalog write to Jason Aronson Inc., 230 Livingston
Street, Northvale, New Jersey 07647.

CONTENTS

PREFACE

For many years I have been involved in the translation of nearly all of Maimonides' ten authentic medical writings, most of which have been published in English by the Maimonides Research Institute in Haifa, Israel.

My interest in Maimonides is not limited to his medical writings but extends to his philosophical and theological works. The first extensive commentary to the entire Mishnah was written by Maimonides. It is broader than that of Rashi as it contains lengthy digressions to propound general principles of rabbinic law and Judaic religious practices and fundamental tenets of the Jewish faith. Although such discourses of varying lengths are found throughout Maimonides' Mishnah Commentary, there are three sections that deserve special attention on account of the lengthy discussions of some of the most fundamental topics contained therein. The first is the General Introduction to the Commentary, which I translated into English many years ago (*Maimonides' Commentary on the Mishnah*, Feldheim, New York, 1975). This introduction contains a lengthy excursus into prophethood, discussions concerning the value and necessity of homiletical exposition, as well as a protracted dissertation on knowledge and wisdom and the understanding of the existence of living and inanimate things, the purpose of the world and all that is contained therein. The second is his *Introduction to Tractate Avot*, known as the *Eight Chapters* (critical edition by Joseph Gorfinkle, Columbia University Press, New York, 1912) in which Maimonides again departs from conciseness to make lengthy excursions into discussions of ethics, psychology, theology, and philosophy.

The third and perhaps most important section of Maimonides' Mishnah Commentary is the Commentary on Tractate Sanhedrin, which I also translated into English (*Maimonides' Commentary on the Mishnah, Tractate Sanhedrin*, Sepher-Hermon, New York, 1981) and which includes the widely read tenth chapter called *Perek Chelek*. In his lengthy commentary to this chapter, he discusses the basic tenets of the Jewish faith, such as the existence, unity, eternity, and incorporeality of God, prophethood in general and the prophecy of Moses in particular, reward and punishment, the messianic age, and the resurrection of the dead.

I then published an English translation of Maimonides' *Treatise on Resurrection* (Ktav, New York, 1982), which is an extended controversial discussion of the problems of God's Unity, the messianic age, resurrection, and the world to come. Two years later, I extracted medically related pronouncements from the *Mishneh Torah*, Maimonides' monumental codification of biblical and talmudic law, and organized them in a lucid, systematic, and logical manner in a book entitled *Medicine in the Mishneh Torah of Maimonides* (Ktav, New York, 1984).

The present work is the culmination of my search for additional Maimonidean writings. Many treatises have been falsely attributed to Maimonides for a variety of reasons. Although probably spurious, these works are important for the reader interested in medieval Judaism in general and Moses Maimonides in particular. The three works attributed to Maimonides in the present book deal with the existence and Unity of God and are, therefore, presented in a single volume. *Ma'amar Hayichud* (Treatise on the Unity of God) may well have been authored by Maimonides himself, *Sefer Hanimtzah* (Treatise on the One Who Exists) is probably spurious, and *Tishah Perakim Miyichud* (Nine Chapters on the Unity of God) were certainly not written by Maimonides. The evidence to support this assertion is described in the introductions to each of the three works.

Acknowledgment

I am indebted to: Professor Jacob Dienstag of New York City for the bibliographies, Rabbi Moshe Greenes, Mr. Louis Gross, Rabbi Dr. David Novak, Rabbi Yonah Munk, and Mr. William Wolf for reviewing the manuscript and offering helpful suggestions, and to Sophie Falk, Miriam Regenworm, and Annette Carbone for secretarial assistance.

Once again, I affirm my love and devotion to my wife, Saranne, and to my cherished children Mitchel and Lydia, Miriam and Motty, Aviva and Michael, and Shalom, and thank them for their infinite patience during the long hours of painstaking work. I ask their forgiveness for having spent so much time on Maimonidean and pseudo-Maimonidean translations rather than with them.

FOREWORD

The reading public is indebted to Dr. Fred Rosner for his continued toil in the Maimonidean vineyards. His years of intensive study and research have enriched Jewish literature with yet another classic, *The Existence and Unity of God: Three Treatises Attributed to Moses Maimonides*, now published in English for the first time.

Dr. Rosner has not only earned our gratitude but, I believe, also the appreciation of Maimonides. Of his three classical works, only the *Yad Hachazakah* (*Code of Maimonides* or *Mishneh Torah*) was written in Hebrew, while his *Peirush Ha-Mishnah* (*Commentary on the Mishnah*) and *Moreh N'Vuchim* (*Guide of the Perplexed*) were both written in Arabic, as were his many short essays, or "letters," such as *Iggeret Taiman* (*Epistle to the Yemenite Communities*) and his many known Responsa. Maimonides' motive for this choice of language was not any particular attraction to or love of the Arabic language, for nowhere in his voluminous writings do we find any indication, or even trace, of "Arabophilia." It was simply that he wanted to open Torah learning—especially *Torah Sheh-B'al-Peh* (the *Oral Torah*), of which *Mishnah* is the core around which all branches of talmudic law are built—to the masses who were not fluent enough in Hebrew to study it in the original.

Likewise, Maimonides wanted to enhance the *Hashkafa*, or Torah viewpoint, of these same masses who had a limited understanding of the breadth and depth of Torah and who were forced to seek their intellectual and spiritual nourishment at the murky springs of philosophies alien to the teachings of the Torah.

In Maimonides' day, the *lingua franca* of the vast majority of Jews was Arabic, just as it was French for the *Tosafists* and Yiddish for the prewar Eastern Europeans. He, therefore, chose Arabic as the vehicle through which to reach the non-learned, or semilearned, Jew. In our days this role is being filled by English, and were Maimonides alive today, he possibly would choose that language for his *Peirush Hamishnah, Moreh N'vuchim,* and *Sefer HaMitzvot* (perhaps written in the Hebrew alphabet, as Yiddish is German-based and Ladino Spanish-based but written in the Hebrew *aleph, bet, gimmel,* rather than the Roman a,b,c). But that is another premise that cannot be adequately elaborated within this short foreword. It is thus not unreasonable to assume that Maimonides, reposing in his heavenly abode, is pleased to see his Arabic works rendered in English.

I cannot close without a word of recognition for my dear friend, Dr. Fred Rosner. Reviewing his published works, which include such masterpieces as *Maimonides' Introduction to the Mishnah* (1975), *Maimonides' Glossary of Drug Names* (1979), *Maimonides' Commentary on Tractate Sanhedrin* (1981), *Maimonides' Treatise on Resurrection* (1982), *Medicine in the Mishneh Torah of Maimonides* (1984), *Maimonides' Treatise on Poisons, Hemorrhoids, and Coitus* (1984), *Maimonides' Commentary on the Aphorisms of Hippocrates* (1987), *Maimonides' Medical Aphorisms* (1990), and *Maimonides' Treatises on the Regimen of Health* (1990) (aside from several important not yet published manuscripts) and the two volumes now being presented, one would have the impression that we have here a cloistered scholar confined to a secluded *Kolel,* or perhaps a university library, spending his life poring over medieval manuscripts and obscure nineteenth-century Torah research papers long overlooked by modern scholars. When one realizes that Dr. Rosner is a practicing physician and one of the United States's leading hematologists with many accomplishments in that field, and at the same time a popular and much sought-after lecturer on both medical and Judaic topics, one must look with awe upon this prolific, many-faceted personality.

May God grant him many more years of good health and his usual good cheer to continue his fruitful work, Amen.

Rabbi Moshe Greenes

Book I

MA'AMAR HAYICHUD
TREATISE ON THE UNITY OF GOD

INTRODUCTION

In his famous work on the Arabic literature of the Jews[1] Steinschneider describes a Maimonidean treatise entitled *Ma'-amar Hayichud*[2] or *Treatise on the Unity of God*, which is actually a synopsis of the basic philosophical and ethical principles enun-

---

[1] *Die Arabische Literatur Der Juden* (Frankfurt A.M.: J. Kauffmann, 1902), pp. 208–209.

[2] The Hebrew word *Yichud* in relation to God can be translated as "Oneness" or "Unity." Yeshiva University's Rabbi Yosef Dov Soloveitchik has also used the terms "singularity" and "uniqueness" in lectures that he delivered on this subject. According to Rabbi David Novak, although Unity is the usual translation of *Yichud*, it implies a synthesis of particular elements. For Maimonides in the present treatise, continues Novak, *Yichud* is a simple Oneness. This view was pointed out by Hermann Cohen in his essay "Einheit oder Einzigheit Gottes?" (*Jüdische Schriften*, Vol. 1). The use of "Einheit" by Steinschneider and "Unity" by Kalisch, concludes Novak, is therefore incorrect. Most Hebraists with whom I have spoken feel that *Treatise on the Unity of God* is a more appropriate translation of Maimonides' *Ma'amar Hayichud* than *Treatise on the Oneness of God* although both are probably acceptable. Numerous works, including Wolfson's *Crescas' Critique of Aristotle*, *Philosophy of Spinoza*, and other reference books also use the term "Unity" rather than "Oneness." Hence, I have chosen to translate *Ma'amar Hayichud* as "Treatise on the Unity of God."

ciated by Maimonides in the first two books of his *Mishneh Torah*. In the original Arabic version, probably known as *Makalah fi Al-Tachid*, biblical citations were not cited directly but paraphrased and these paraphrases were translated as such into Hebrew by Isaac ben Nathan in the middle of the fourteenth century. Only four manuscripts are known and are described in Steinschneider's German foreword.

In 1846 Steinschneider edited this brief Maimonidean treatise using the title *Ma'amar Hayichud* from Duke's copy of Hamburg Manuscript 256. Very few copies of this edition were printed. A year later, Steinschneider's edition was reprinted under the title *Sefer Sh'nay Hame'oroth* or *The Book of Two Luminaries* and included not only Maimonides' *Ma'amar Hayichud* but three responsa of Abraham Ibn Ezra. Hence, Maimonides and Ibn Ezra represent the two luminaries from which the title of the 1847 Steinschneider edition was derived. In his Hebrew foreword, Steinschneider describes his difficulty in getting *Ma'amar Hayichud* published and the reason he combined it with the responsa of Ibn Ezra into a single booklet, *The Two Luminaries*. In both the 1846 and 1847 editions, Steinschneider provides the reader not only with notes on the Isaac ben Nathan Hebrew translation of Maimonides' *Ma'amar Hayichud* but also Hebrew and German forewords, a German summary, and a letter of commentaries and corrections by Rabbi Shlomo Yehudah Rapoport of Prague. Steinschneider's copious notes primarily cite parallel passages in the *Mishneh Torah* or deal with linguistic or technical Arabic terms or phrases. The only differences between the 1846 and 1847 editions are the inclusion in the latter of additional corrections and notes by Steinschneider in a lengthy addendum to his Hebrew foreword and different prefaces by the two publishers of the 1846 and 1847 editions. All these are translated into English in the present work.

Maimonides' *Ma'amar Hayichud* is not very well known, in part because of the scarcity of both Steinschneider's 1846 and 1847 editions. I have not even found mention of the *Ma'amar Hayichud* in over 100 books dealing with the life and works of

Maimonides except for a brief footnote in one book.[3] In 1928, Isidor Kalisch published a book on his own selected writings and included an English translation of the *Ma'amar Hayichud*,[4] although his English rendition of the *Ma'amar Hayichud* had previously appeared in the *Israelite* (Vol. 9, numbers 49, 50, 51 and Vol. 10, numbers 1, 2, 3, 6, 7, and 11). Kalisch's translation is extremely free and faulty and does not convey the flavor of the original work. Numerous phrases and whole sentences are totally omitted in his version. Most of Chapter 3 of the *Ma'amar Hayichud* was totally bypassed by Kalisch, and in addition, his work is without introduction, analysis, or annotations.

The *Ma'amar Hayichud* was written later than the *Guide of the Perplexed* since Maimonides quotes the *Guide* in the *Ma'amar Hayichud*. The reason Maimonides wrote this work, as suggested by Steinschneider, was to provide a booklet on basic Jewish theology, philosophy, and ethics for the non-Jewish reader. If this suggestion is correct, one can ask: why did Maimonides write another treatise essentially paraphrasing parts of the first two volumes of his *Mishneh Torah*, and why did Maimonides not quote biblical verses in their original phrases but rather paraphrased them in flowery language? One cannot conclude simply from the fact that *Ma'amar Hayichud* was originally written in Arabic that it was intended for a non-Jewish audience since all of Maimonides' writings including his *Commentary on the Mishnah*, his *Guide of the Perplexed*, his *Book of Logic*, his *Letter to Yemen*, his *Treatise on Resurrection*, his *Responsa*, and his ten medical books were all written in Arabic, the vernacular of the Jews of Egypt, where Maimonides lived. The only exception is the *Mishneh Torah*, which was written in a beautiful Mishnaic Hebrew.

A second possible explanation as to why Maimonides wrote the *Ma'amar Hayichud* is offered by Rapoport who states that

---

[3]A. Cohen, *The Teachings of Maimonides* (New York: Ktav, 1968), p. 325, note 2.

[4]"Maimonides' 'Ma'amar Hayichud': Treatise on the Unity of God" in *Studies in Ancient and Modern Judaism* (New York: Dobsevage, 1928), pp. 135–163.

Maimonides' intent was to teach in Arabic that which he had
already taught in Hebrew. Apparently the Hebrew translator of
the *Ma'amar Hayichud*, Isaac ben Nathan, attempted to preserve
the flowery paraphrasing of biblical verses cited by Maimonides. Although Steinschneider considered this phenomenon of paraphrasing scriptural citations not to be a rare
occurrence, Rapoport criticizes the translator for having done
so since the reader may have difficulty in correctly identifying
the source of the scriptural verses. Isaac ben Nathan, according
to both Steinschneider and Rapoport, also translated Arabic
comments on certain parts of the *Guide of the Perplexed*.

The name of the *Ma'amar Hayichud* or *Treatise on the Unity of
God* is the subject of some controversy since the treatise does
not, strictly speaking, devote itself to the Unity of God but, as
already stated, to a paraphrasing of major sections of the first
two books of the *Mishneh Torah*. *Ma'amar Hayichud* discusses
various subjects including the Unity and Immutability of God,
the creation of the world, the different levels and types of
angels, the spheres and stars and constellations of the heavens,
the four fundamental elements (fire, air, water, and earth), the
human soul and its immortality, prophets and prophecy, human physical and emotional constitutions and temperaments,
and a regimen of health including hygienic and medical
principles for the preservation of one's health. Steinschneider,
however, points out that Maimonides wished to teach incisively
the monotheistic approach of Judaism as its most fundamental
tenet—hence the title *Ma'amar Hayichud*.

On the other hand, Rapoport feels that the *Ma'amar Hayichud*
is identical to another treatise attributed to Maimonides, the
Sefer Hanimtzah or *Book of Him that Exists* and states that the
latter name is more appropriate because of the character of
Ma'amar Hayichud in which Maimonides speaks more of the
existence of the world than the Unity of God. Steinschneider is
puzzled by Rapoport's suggestion because it raises many problems. Steinschneider had already written[5] against the opinion

---

[5]*Oesterreiche Blätter für Litteratur*, Vol. 2, p. 110.

of those who equate *Ma'amar Hayichud* with *Sefer Hanimtzah*. In fact, Steinschneider believes *Sefer Hanimtzah* to be a spurious work.[6-7] If it is not a forgery and if it is identical with *Sefer Hanimtzah*, why did the translator render the original Arabic into *Ma'amar Hayichud*? One must assume that Isaac ben Nathan faithfully translated the title. Furthermore, the word *Sefer* or book (Arabic: *kitab*) is less appropriate for such a small work than is *Ma'amar* or treatise. Finally, the published versions of the *Sefer Hanimtzah*[8-12] do not at all resemble the *Ma'amar Hayichud* except for the last section dealing with the regimen of health, which is found paraphrased from Chapter 4 of *Hilchot De'ot* of the *Mishneh Torah* in both *Ma'amar Hayichud* and *Sefer Hanimtzah*.

Although there is considerable debate about the authorship of *Sefer Hanimtzah*, there seems to be no challenge to the authenticity of *Ma'amar Hayichud* as a Maimonidean writing. It is cited as early as the thirteenth century by Rabbi Joseph ben Yitzchok ben Al Fawwal, translator from Arabic into Hebrew of Maimonides' Mishnah Commentary on *Seder Moed*. In his introduction to that translation, which is found in most standard editions of the Babylonian Talmud, Al Fawwal states that Maimonides composed many works including the *Mishneh Torah*, the *Guide of the Perplexed*, the *Book of Commandments*, a *Commentary on the Talmud*, the *Ma'amar Hayichud* and several other treatises and essays on matters of Torah, general wisdom, and other matters.

---

[6]Ibid., reference 1 above p. 218.

[7]*Die Hebraeischen Uebersetzungen Des Mittelters Und Die Juden Als Dolmetscher* (Berlin: Kommissionsverlag des Bibliographischen Bureaus, 1893), p. 774.

[8]Abraham ben Shlomo Akara, *Sefer Hanimtzah of Maimonides* in *Sefer Amarot Tehorot* by R. Abraham Chayun appended to the commentary on Lamentations of R. Shmuel ben Chabib Di Vidash. Salonika 5356 (1596), pp. 59–70.

[9]Gabriel Polak, "Notiz Ueber das Sefer Ha Nimza von Mose ben Maimun," *Literaturblatt des Orients* (1849), Vol. 10, pp. 273–279, 293–298.

[10]Gabriel Polak, *Sefer Hanimtzah of Maimonides* in *Sefer Ben Geroni* (Amsterdam 5611 [1851]), pp. I–XVII. Reprinted in Jerusalem by *Kedem* in 1971.

[11]Y. L. Maimon, *Sefer Hanimtzah of Maimonides* in *HaRam BeMazal* (Jerusalem: Mossad Harav Kook, 1955), pp. 7–17.

[12]Y. L. Maimon, *Sefer Hanimtzah of Maimonides* in *Sinai* (Jerusalem: Mossad Harav Kook, Teveth 5715 [1955]), Vol. 36, 4, pp. 201–211.

Another problem is the nature of the additional or final chapter in the *Ma'amar Hayichud* that, according to the manuscript, was written to one of Maimonides' friends. Who was this friend? What relationship does this final chapter have to the rest of the work? It seems not to fit smoothly with the first three chapters. It also does not paraphrase from the *Mishneh Torah* as does the remainder of the treatise. This problem remains unresolved.

Another difficulty is the inclusion in the *Ma'amar Hayichud* of paraphrases of certain chapters but total omission of other chapters from the first two books of the *Mishneh Torah*. Why did Maimonides paraphrase chapters 1, 2, 3, 4, and 7 of *Hilchot Yesodei Hatorah* and totally neglect chapters 5, 6, 8, 9, and 10? Why did Maimonides paraphrase chapters 1, 2, and 4 of *Hilchot De'ot* and completely omit chapters 3, 4, 5, 6, and 7? This question also remains unanswered. I hope that future research and study may provide insight into these problems.

The present translation is based entirely on Steinschneider's 1846 and 1847 Hebrew editions. I have attempted to render as closely as possible the flavor and sense of the original work. Although involved in the translation of Maimonidean medical and rabbinic writings for many years, I found the present work extremely difficult to translate. I can only echo the words of Steinschneider, who, in his Hebrew foreword to this work, said: "Who would believe the effort and toil and sweat that I exerted in . . . such a small . . . book?" The meanings of some words and phrases still remain unclear to me. Even Steinschneider marks certain difficult passages with a parenthetical question mark.

To facilitate understanding of the *Ma'amar Hayichud*, I have also translated the publishers' forewords from both 1846 and 1847 editions, Steinschneider's German and Hebrew forewords, his German summary and the letter he received about the work from Rabbi S. Y. Rapoport of Prague. I have not translated in their entirety all of Steinschneider's copious footnotes, which he described as "perhaps excessively detailed," since most of the notes deal with technical, philological, and linguistic discussions of Arabic terminology. Pertinent notes, however, have been translated. Words in brackets in the text are my own additions to facilitate understanding of the material.

After I had completed the English translation of *Ma'amar Hayichud*, Professor Jacob Dienstag pointed out that Rabbi Samuel David Luzzatto, known as *Shadal*, wrote a letter dated December 15, 1846, to Steinschneider commenting on the latter's Hebrew edition of *Ma'amar Hayichud*. Luzzatto's letter was published in his book *Iggrot Shadal*.[13] He praises Steinschneider for his edition of the *Ma'amar Hayichud* but points out two errors that had escaped both Steinschneider and Rapoport. First is the word *katzuv*, found several times in the Hebrew text (see page 10, line 4 and page 12, line 5 of the Hebrew text and footnotes 102 and 112 in my English translation). Luzzatto points out that the Hamburg manuscript of the *Ma'amar Hayichud* was written by a German scribe who, as was customary in the fourteenth century, wrote the Hebrew letters *tzadi* and *ayin* so that they resembled each other to the point that the reader would sometimes have difficulty distinguishing them. Thus, the letter *tzadi* in the Hebrew word *katzuv* should really be an *ayin* and the correct word is *ka'or* meaning concave. The second comment of Luzzatto concerns the Hebrew word *asiyah* which should correctly be *asiri* (see footnote 127 in my English translation).

I must accept full responsibility for any errors in the translation and/or in my interpretative footnotes. May God grant illumination to our minds and understanding to our intellects to allow us to fully appreciate the genius of the author of *Ma'amar Hayichud* about whom it is said: "From Moses [ben Amram] to Moses [ben Maimon], there never arose a man like Moses," and none has since.

---

[13]S. D. Luzzatto, *Iggrot Shadal*, (Crakow: S.I. Greber, 5651 [1894]), Vol. 7, Number 50, pp. 1007–1008.

Publisher's Preface to the 1846 Edition

King Solomon, may he rest in peace, said, "Remember then thy Creator in the days of thy youth, before the evil days come, and the years draw high, when thou shalt say: I have no pleasure in them" [Ecclesiastes 12:1]. The wise [Solomon] warns a person as long as the breath of the spirit of life is still in his nostrils[1] to remember the covenant and the oath that his soul accepted when it came out from the heavenly[2] world where it had honorable repose—before the word of the Most Supreme King[3]—who has the right to say "return unto thy rest, [O my soul]."[4] When I pondered about this matter,[5] I said to myself: Let us search and examine[6] the deeds of the days of my life that have long since passed to see whether these [deeds] were for the benefit of my Creator[7] or that of my own inclination.[8]

I reviewed most of my actions from my youth until now; and I did not find that I had rest and peace that I could consider [as fulfillment of] my obligations to the Creator in relation to serving Him and His Torah. I have not been relieved [of this obligation] to toil and to labor and to bother, and I burned the midnight oil.[9] I said to myself: what will you answer before the Most Supreme King concerning your obligation to serve Him and His Torah which you neglected,[10] and King Solomon, may he rest in peace, said, "For God shall bring every work into the judgment concerning every hidden thing" (Ecclesiastes 12:14). Please look and see the weakness of your strength and your

---

[1] Allusion to Genesis 7:22.
[2] Literally: upper.
[3] Literally: King of all Kings, that is, God.
[4] Allusion to Psalm 116:7.
[5] Literally: when I raised this matter into my memory.
[6] Allusion to Lamentations 3:40.
[7] Hebrew: *yotzri*.
[8] Hebrew: *yitzri*.
[9] Literally: and the night shineth as the day. Allusion to Psalm 139:12.
[10] Literally: you hid or concealed yourself.

constitution: The teeth have ceased [to function] and the eyes
have dimmed in the windows.[11] Lift up your eyes and look[12]
upon the hairs on your head[13] and your beard. White-colored
ones have budded and blossomed until you reached hoariness
and this will also be for you a sign and a remembrance.[14] And
a person will observe this [sign of hoariness] and a living
person will take to heart [15] the closeness of the day of his
demise.[16]

And if you neglected [your divine duty] during the days
already passed, do not abstain during remaining days allotted
to you to ponder about the divine obligations which are upon
you. And do not say "as it happeneth to the fool, so will it
happen to me"[17] because you will be prosecuted[18] according to
the talent with which the Creator endowed you. Consider
preparing provisions[19] for the long way[20] and a gift to bring
before the Most Supreme King when He asks you for an
accounting. No one can flee or escape from before Him. And
let not any matter occupy you saying "tomorrow" because life[21]
rushes by and constantly flows onwards.

I said to myself, come what may upon me,[22] during the
remaining days of my life that are allocated to me by the One
who allocates life to all living beings,[23] I will bring an offering
to God in that I will occupy myself with holy servitude and with
His Torah. And may the Lord be a help unto me for he who

---

[11]Allusion to Ecclesiastes 12:3.
[12]Allusion to Genesis 13:14 and 31:12.
[13]Allusion to Song of Songs 7:3.
[14]Allusion to Exodus 13:9.
[15]Allusion to Ecclesiastes 7:2.
[16]Allusion to Lamentations 4:18.
[17]Allusion to Ecclesiastes 2:15.
[18]Literally: summoned, that is judged.
[19]That is, Good deeds.
[20]Allusion to Deuteronomy 19:3.
[21]Literally: the journey.
[22]Allusion to Job 13:13.
[23]Allusion to the *Chol Ma'aminim* prayer recited on Rosh Hashanah and
Yom Kippur.

comes to be purified is assisted from above,[24] and I will engage
in holy work. And the Creator is the beginning of all beginnings
and the cause of all causes, for there is no restraint to the Lord
to assist, etc.[25]

Behold, that which I agreed to do and was engraved[26] and
carved out in my heart was to search and to investigate the
words of our ancient Sages of blessed memory which are still in
manuscript form. And when I was detained here in Berlin for
several months on my return from the hot baths, it became
known to me that the wise and eminent sage and rabbinic
scholar, Moshe Steinschneider, had in his possession an ancient
manuscript, a treatise small in size but large in quality, the
Ma'amar Hayichud of Moses Maimonides of blessed memory,
which had never been published. And I said to myself: perhaps
this is what God has prepared in response to my request. And
I went to him.[27] And when I saw the preciousness of that
treatise I rejoiced because the name of the author is known
throughout Jewish circles and we live by the words of his
mouth.

This aforementioned scholar has also crowned this work with
the crown[28] of enlightening notes for places that are difficult to
understand and for foreign words. And he refined it and
purified it[29] of all errors as is explained in his introduction at
the beginning of the book. He had already prepared this
booklet for publication. And when I asked him to allow me to
publish it at my expense to thereby serve as a mediator of a
good deed[30] but not to seek glory, he answered in his generous
spirit: yes. In the depths[31] of my heart are hidden and
concealed blessings and praises for his goodheartedness and

---

[24] Allusion to *Shabbat* 104a, *Yoma* 38b, and elsewhere including Maimonides'
Mishneh Torah, Hilchot Teshuvah 6:5.

[25] Allusion to I Samuel 14:6.

[26] ?Allusion to Exodus 32:16 and Jeremiah 17:1.

[27] That is Steinschneider.

[28] ?Allusion to Song of Songs 3:11.

[29] Literally: distilled.

[30] Literally: messenger or envoy to perform a commandment or good deed.

[31] Literally: chambers.

may they be fulfilled from heaven. I said: it is clearly evident
that God has, in response to my request, prepared this booklet
whose praise waits in silence[32] and which speaks of antiquity
and of the Unity of God, which is the fundamental axiom of
our faith and by which the believer is separated from the
heretic.

And we are obligated to investigate and to examine the Unity
of the Creator through intellectual reflection, each according to
his perception.[33] This is ordained by the intellect and the
Torah and tradition. The faith of the believer is not complete if
he does not know them and do them; that is to say, if he does
not understand them first. (*Chovat Halvovot* in the introduction,
and in *Sha'ar Hayichud*, chapter 3.)

It appears to me that the words of the prophet[34] had this in
mind: "Seek ye the Lord while He may be found, call ye upon
Him while He is near." This means: inquire into and investigate
His existence and then call upon Him when He is near, namely,
according to your perception.

And this is what I have begun to do[35] with this booklet; that
which will awaken the slumberer from the sleep of his unconsciousness, to his work. And let the discerning become
aroused—those who love the words of our ancient sages, of
blessed memory. And may they help me to be able to raise my
hands to publish other ancient things which are hidden,[36]
namely the words of the Torah and of wisdom and of morality.
Let the wise man hear and increase in learning.[37] In my naïveté
I supported myself and relied upon the rabbinic statement:
the one who sacrifices a lot (and the one who sacrifices a little)
have the same merit, provided that the heart is directed to
heaven.[38] And direct your deeds[39] toward heaven and you will

---

[32]Allusion to Psalm 65:2.
[33]Literally: attainment, that is capacity or ability.
[34]Isaiah 55:6.
[35]Allusion to Esther 9:23.
[36]Literally: imprisoned.
[37]Allusion to Proverbs 1:5.
[38]*Berachot* 5b and *Menachot* 110b.
[39]Literally: take your business.

be blessed by your deeds and have longevity and [many] years of life.

These are the words of the publisher.

Berlin, Elul 4, 5606 (1846)
Tzvi Hirsh ben Mordechai Zev of Kolvaria

Behold before you a letter from the Grand Rabbi S. Y. Rapoport that is full of wisdom and moral instruction. It clarifies profound matters in this booklet. There is not enough space[40] to speak at length about it and to make heard all its praises because it reached us at the completion of the printing.

The aforementioned Tzvi

Publisher's Preface to the 1847 Edition

Thus states the publisher:

To you the remnants of the people of God[1] to whom the word of God and the honor of rabbinical scholars is still dear,[2] I hereby offer before you today a new offering,[3] which is this composition, small in quantity but large in quality. Its name *Two Luminaries* is derived from two Jewish luminaries and is comprised of *Ma'amar Hayichud* (which includes divine philosophy) by the great luminary Rabbi Moses Maimonides, may his memory be blessed, and a letter on astronomy by the great luminary Rabbi Abraham Ibn Ezra. These were in manuscript form for the past seven hundred years until today. And now I offer before you today this "offering of the poor" which is being published for the first time. Indeed, I muzzle my mouth—far be it from me to set my heart to speak in praise of this composition and about the esteem of its authors, because they

---

[40]Literally: the couch is too narrow to stretch out on. See Isaiah 28:20.
[1]Probably an allusion to Jeremiah 31:1.
[2]Probably an allusion to 1 Samuel 3:1.
[3]Probably an allusion to Leviticus 23:16.

need no praise. If a blind man such as I would say that light is good,[4] it would be laughable.

However, it should be said in the presence of all my people[5] that these two luminaries will enlighten you, and you will derive pleasure from their light and will bless Him who makes those great lights.[6] I also know that the new light that shines from the footnotes of this composition[7] will be to you like a light of sweetness to the soul and for that I offer the following blessing: Blessed be He Who fashioned you; blessed be He Who made you; blessed be He Who owns you.[8]

And it should come to pass that just as I have been privileged to offer you this small composition, so may I be privileged, within a short time period, to place before you a much larger work, both in quantity and even more so in quality. There you will find novellae and hidden secrets and responsa of earlier scholars that have been concealed in manuscript form for the past one-thousand years. And may the graciousness of God be upon me and upon you.[9] These are the words of your servant, this lowest and poorest man among men.

Aryeh Leib, son of my father and teacher Dov, of blessed memory, Zarenzanski, born in Poland. Written here in Berlin on the third day of the week, the second day of *Rosh Chodesh* (the new moon) of Tammuz, 5607.

Steinschneider's German Foreword

The study of our ancient literature is neither handyman's work, nor a vocation, neither military nor diplomatic service, al-

---

[4]Probably an allusion to Genesis 1:4.

[5]Probably an allusion to Psalm 116:18.

[6]Probably an allusion to Psalm 136:7.

[7]Probably an allusion to the daily morning prayer. See S. R. Hirsch, *The Hirsch Siddur* (New York: Feldheim, 1978), pp. 110–111.

[8]Quoted from the blessing recited monthly on viewing the New Moon. See *The Hirsch Siddur, op. cit.*, pp. 740–741.

[9]Probably an allusion to Psalm 90:17.

though it has recently been branded and degraded as such for various and even conflicting reasons. Because I bring to attention a previously almost totally unknown, but in some respects interesting, writing by the most deserving and renowned Jewish scholar, I deeply regret, because of unforeseen circumstances, among them personal indisposition, not being able to provide a proper introduction to this brief work although I actually intended to do so to the best of my ability. One portion of the materials gathered for this purpose will, I hope, be incorporated in the soon-to-be-published first volume of a *Jewish-Arabic Library*. In the following inadequate but indispensable notes, he who misses the "profundity, comprehension, critical and logical sharpness, scientific and philosophical tact, inspired prophetic vision, exceptional ability of representation, and their like," and the whole apparatus of endlessly rehashed phrases as in Proverbs 26:11—warns his followers to stay away from the Communist literature factories which, without a solar microscope, portray a rich infusorial life, and which have recently specifically recruited those "pious" screamers and scribblers to whom "this so-called Science" is no longer too low to get a sinecure—according to the noteworthy summary of our author who is, in that respect, particularly admirable.[1]

The present work, written later than the *Guide* [*of the Perplexed*], is a compendium of the philosophy of religion and ethics. It is, in fact, a type of paraphrase of the first two volumes of the Hebrew work *Mishneh Torah* with omission of the special legal matter or *halachah*.[2] Also characteristic is the paraphrasing of biblical and talmudic citations, even including certain Hebrew technical terms such as *Ma'ase Bereshit*, which, in their literal Hebrew translation, have an unrecognizable appearance. Nevertheless, this phenomenon is not totally isolated. In a thirteenth-century Arabic copy of the *Guide* in Arabic letters,

---

[1]Compare the letters to Joseph Aknin in the R.G.A. (?) and in Munk's "Notice sur Joseph ben Yehudah."

[2]I edited the health regimen in chapter 3 according to the *halachot* (chapter 4 of *Hilchot De'ot*).

Munk found the biblical passages in Arabic.[3] It thus seems a reasonable presumption that our booklet, [the *Ma'amar Hayichud*] was originally intended as, or later transformed into, a work for the non-Jewish reader. Perhaps one should also take into consideration the fact that the Hebrew translator of our booklet, Rabbi Isaac ben Nathan, also translated the commentary of the Mohammedan Tebrizi on one part of the *Guide*.[4]

I do not even dare to enunciate a hypothesis concerning the concluding chapter [of the *Ma'amar Hayichud*] and its relationship to the work as a whole.

The title [*Ma'amar Hayichud*], which, translated back into the Arabic, would be known as *Makalah Al Tochid*, does not appear to be sufficiently explicit; it here also denotes (see note 6 below) one of the fundamental concepts of Judaism, which considers the abolition of all independence of attributes to be an extremely basic concept of the Unity of God, as was especially asserted by Saadiah against Christianity and the Mohammedan Szifatites and Moteschebbihites. This strict monotheism not only has its advocate within Islam, but is also found in its earlier philosophical precursors up to the extravagance of the Mu'atthilites. Indeed, in comparison with the Bible, even the Koran characterizes itself as a type of syllogistic representation of monotheism. It is thus hardly thinkable that Maimonides' understanding of a "Book of Monotheism" should be, as perhaps that of today's "theologians," a "Compendium of Jewish Beliefs and Ethics." It is, however, in the perception of our author and, as such, as far as is known, the last and concise representation of his whole system, which is, in any case, of a higher interest. I am not familiar with the mention of this book by other authors.

Two other manuscripts in the Vatican have the same title [*Ma'amar Hayichud*], namely, No. 170:3 with the same peculiar

---

[3]See Frankel's *Zeitschrift*, Vol. 2, p. 112.

[4]To be sure, one can hardly think of proselytes such as Rabbi Obadiah (*Kerem Chemed*, Vol. 5, p. 104). An epigraph of an Arabic manuscript in Oxford (Nicoll, p. 227) provides interesting disclosures about Maimonides' personal relationship with Mohammedan scholars.

beginning and the epigraph, and No. 171:10, written by Rabbi Isaac Papat (?) in Kandia in 1493 (not 1296).[5] Wolf[6] had a 1476 manuscript, probably the same, which is now in the Municipal Library in Hamburg as Codex 310 in 4. I received a copy of the latter in the year 1841—in exchange for one of my copies of the *Iggeret Ha-Petiraby Abubekr Ibn es Szaigh*[7]—from my learned friend Mr. L. Dukes, and delivered it for a short time into the hands of Rabbi Rapoport to obtain his gracious comments which, with his well-known willingness, he promised me for this work which I intended to publish soon. He had already partly prepared them when various circumstances induced me to hand over the manuscript to the Austro-Hungarian censor and to bring it with me here during my move to this city. Yet, it appears that extraordinary circumstances have hindered the fulfillment of my recently renewed request to Rabbi Rapoport. In any case, I must, therefore, together with the public, deplore this loss.

I am especially sorry because elsewhere[8] I already wrote about the orally expressed opinion of that renowned literary historian, namely, that our work [the *Ma'amar Hayichud*] is identical with the *Sefer Hanimtzah*. I, therefore, all the more deeply regret not to have more precise proof because even that path to the elucidation of this question failed. Wolf (Vol. 1, p. 864) and Azulai (*Vaad* Vol. 1:5, 1) assert that this alleged medical-ascetic work was printed together with the (rare) book *Amarot Tehorot* by Abraham Chajun in Thessaloniki [Salonica] in 1596. (Azulai also adds thereto the commentary to the lamentation of Samuel de Vidash.)

I did not find this work of Maimonides [*Sefer Hanimtzah*] in the printed catalogue of the Oppenheim Library but did find it among the manuscripts in the possession of Dr. Zunz.[9] On the other hand, in response to an inquiry from the latter to the

---

[5]In *Hebrew Bibliography*, Vol. 1, p. 1261, Wolf cites the copyist as an author.
[6]*Ibid.*, Vol. 4, p. 919.
[7]See provisionally Frankel's *Zeitschrift*, Vol. 3, p. 274, note 13.
[8]*Oesterreiche Blätter fur Litteratur*, Vol. 2, p. 110.
[9]Concerning this same Zunz, see *Zur Geschichte und Litteratur*, p. 137.

current owner of the famous library of the late H. Michael in Hamburg, it was reported that the *Sefer Hanimtzah* was not present in their copy of *Amarot Tehorot*.

In my Hebrew foreword, I describe the condition of my text. In the perhaps excessively detailed footnotes—which, for preparing for the print, took me twice as much time as R. Kalonymous in his translation of the *Iggeret Ba'ale Chayim*—I was particularly motivated by two related considerations: on the one hand philology, through parallel substantiated explanations of Arabic terms—which may include the scientific Hebrew terminology[10]—so that in this manner specific materials for a comprehensive dictionary of modern Hebrew would be assembled. On the other hand, [I was motivated] by the relationship of Jewish scholasticism to that of the Mohammedans which, like a large part of the history of scholasticism in general, is mirrored by certain linguistic types, figures, and metaphors.

Naturally, completeness could not be considered (an attainable goal) and, therefore, only specific viewpoints of the Maimonidean concept of prophecy are mentioned, as they are incisively articulated throughout his writings in opposition to the prophecy of Mohammed from the introduction to his *Commentary on the Mishnah* to the Letter to Yemen *(Iggeret Teman)*. A challenge to this lies in the recently repeated opinion of Munk that Maimonides, in Spain, where he wrote the introduction to his *Commentary on the Mishnah*, outwardly acknowledged Islam, and so forth.[11] When one otherwise deduces the system of a person from his character, one must certainly, in the case of a man like Maimonides, not neglect the opposite. For this reason we salute Scheyer's *Psychology of Maimonides*. Although it does not sufficiently separate the individual personality from the general work, it is an important advance in the works concerning the knowledge and assessment of a man whose vast interests alone justify the attention accorded him.

---

[10]See my *Fremdsprachliche Elemente*, etc., p. 26.
[11]See Frankel's *Zeitschrift*, Vol. 2, p. 115; where I, however, erroneously placed P. Beer among the forerunners of Munk.

I conclude with the wish that inferior works such as Bukofzer's *Maimonides*, etc.—in which a strict critic such as my learned friend L. could still discover "good intentions," and that deceptive works such as the alleged "Materials" of a Mr. Chw. should rapidly and forever give way to sound and honest works.

Berlin, August 1846

M. Steinschneider

Note: This foreword was already in press when the awaited missive from Rabbi Rapoport arrived. According to his wish, I transmitted it to the printer unchanged. The conjecture enunciated therein that *Nimtzah* is another translation for [*Ma'amar*] *Hayichud* raises a variety of difficulties in regard to the title, since our translator probably faithfully also translated the title, and even if we assume that the other translator had before him in the original Arabic the reading *Mogod* for *Tochid*, the word *Sefer* (Arabic: *kitab*) is less appropriate for such a small treatise than *Ma'amar*. Accordingly, *Sefer Hanimtzah* should be rendered "Discovered Book."[12]

Steinschneider's Hebrew Foreword

In my opening remarks in the German foreword I spoke about the matters that pertain to this treatise published here for the first time, Moses Maimonides' *Treatise on the Unity of God*. Therefore, there is no need here to expand on these matters. I will only add a brief comment about the character of the manuscript from which this book was published and about the corrections and additions.

The understanding reader will observe from the corrections, which I simply note or which I dovetail with a brief explanation or proofs in my comments, that errors crept into the text at least in the translation from language to language or [in the copying] from one parchment to another. Therefore, do not be

---

[12]Contrary to my earlier opinion in *Oesterreiche Blätter, loc. cit.*

surprised that there remain unintelligible sections in certain matters, some of which I noted with a question mark. Others I did not mark at all because the deficiency is obvious.ᵪ

I have inserted biblical and talmudic citations and have added certain corrections in the text but have placed these in parentheses. Indeed [repeated] words such as *chalufi* and *tachlis* (in Chapter 1) are found in the manuscript but I considered them to be superfluous. Nevertheless, I did not change a single word from that written by the scribe, my friend, the translator and renowned scholar Dukes, except for obvious errors which are clearly apparent to all and they are the following:

[Steinschneider then lists about twenty spelling and other minor philological and linguistic errors in the Hebrew text and in his footnotes.]

Who would believe the effort and toil and sweat that I exerted in the printing and correction of such an apparently small book? And if it is not large enough for me to recite "Blessed be He who has freed me from this responsibility,"[1] let me at least say "Blessed is my Master for helping me complete this work."

Written by me here in Berlin, on Monday, the second day of the month of Elul, 5606.

The young Moshe, son of my revered and noble father Yaakov, may God watch over him.

After I completed [this work] I had great pleasure.[2]

The precious letter about which I have already spoken arrived from the venerable scholar and most expert among those who study antiquity [Rabbi S. Y. Rapoport]. With many thanks to his goodness and generosity, I rushed to present it to you unchanged and unedited.[3]

The aforementioned.[4]

---

[1] Recited by a father when his son has concluded the blessing after the reading of the Torah at his bar mitzvah.

[2] Allusion to Genesis 18:12.

[3] Literally: in its form and its image.

[4] In the 1846 edition, Steinschneider's Hebrew foreword ends here. In the 1847 edition, he added supplementary material describing the reprinting of the earlier version together with the responsa by Ibn Ezra. Steinschneider also added many more textual corrections in this additional material.

I will now relate an important matter to you, dear reader. There was an old man on whose behalf I toiled, but who was a nuisance and a hardship. He took several printed books but never paid the printer so that the latter despaired of ever collecting his due.[5] Furthermore, out of the goodness of his heart, the printer gave him several books that he [the old man] requested and which he circulated through a bookseller for monetary gain.[6] How can such a prisoner loosen the bonds of those who hope in the print shop?[7]

But behold, a "redeemer of bloods" has now come forward and he is the publisher of Responsa of *Ga'onim* which will shortly appear with a distinguished preface by the investigator and scholar Rabbi S. Y. Rapoport. He also brought with him another letter, short in length but great in quality, by the scholar Rabbi Abraham Ibn Ezra of blessed memory. This letter was sent by my friend, the renowned and famous good-hearted scholar Rabbi Samuel David Luzzatto to the scholar Goldberg, with comments and corrections enclosed in parentheses. (This treatise is already mentioned in *Kerem Chemed*, part 4, p. 174 and in *Alot Hamizrach*, 1846, p. 420.)

I said to myself: two are better than one.[8] The assembling of the "Two Great Luminaries"[9] will make the light of the moon like the light of the sun and give pleasure to the reader. And may the son of Meir [Abraham, son of Meir ibn Ezra], be like the author of *The Luminary*[10] and shine brightly[11] for the children of Israel in all their dwelling places.

And I here insert a few additional corrections and comments

---

[5]Literally: was forced to write a bill of divorce for the others.

[6]Literally: a loaf of bread.

[7]Allusion to the talmudic assertion in *Berachot* 5b, *Nedarim* 7b, and *Sanhedrin* 95a that a prisoner cannot release himself from prison. Steinschneider is decrying his inability to have his Hebrew edition of *Ma'amar Hayichud* published because of the meddling of this old man.

[8]Allusion to Ecclesiastes 4:9.

[9]The name of this book with writings of both Maimonides and Ibn Ezra.

[10]*The Luminary* is the original Arabic name of Maimonides' *Commentary on the Mishnah*

[11]Literally: light.

and additions to the *Ma'amar Hayichud*. And I will begin with a letter from my friend the eminent[12] scholar Samuel David Luzzatto, which he sent to me on the 26th of Kislev, 5607. The following are his precious words that pertain to our treatise:

[Steinschneider then quotes from Luzzatto's letter which lists numerous linguistic and philological corrections.]

And now I come to the final and concluding comments on the *Ma'amar Hayichud*. I saw by my honorable friend, the general scholar Dr. Zunz, a list of manuscripts belonging to the late Chayim Michael of blessed memory which had just come from the printer. On the list was No. 572: Maimonides' *Ma'amar Hayichud* and a Responsum by Maimonides[13] to one of the great scholars of his generation on the subject of antiquity and creation, and several essays regarding a commentary on the *Hagiograph* by Rabbi Joseph ben Chayun, and a treatise on the blessings of the Torah (Deuteronomy: 33). To my mind this is no more than another copy made from the Wolf manuscript in the city of Hamburg but in slightly different order. The above-cited responsum is the letter of Maimonides to Rabbi Chasdai Halevi, the Spaniard (see Maimonides' *Responsa*). It appears from the beginning as if it was copied by the scholar (section 4, p. 919). Similarly, the responsum on the creation of the world, which is listed in the Vatican as No. 270 with the name of the author, is the same aforementioned one.

I wish to inform the interested reader that at this very moment there is being published in English, in the city of London *The Story of Maimonides*[14] by my friend Rabbi Abraham Banesh. I sent him an accurate list of all the books of Maimonides to remove any errors and to give each item its proper place according to its time and its language and its subject matter.

And I will add a few additional comments to my notes: [Steinschneider then lists a few additional linguistic and philo-

---

[12]Literally: complete or perfect.
[13]Literally: the Rabbi.
[14]Hebrew: *Toldot HaRambam;* literally: the history, chronicles, or descendants of Maimonides.

logical corrections and few additional citations to his footnotes in the main text.]

And after all these matters and the truth, it is also up to me to conclude on a very positive note offering thanksgiving to God.

Berlin, Tuesday the second day of *Rosh Chodesh*[15]

Tammuz, 5607

Steinschneider's German Summary

The immutability of the First Being (God) includes the immutability of His actions, and absolute perfection of the existences that emanate from Him allow neither increase nor decrease. Scriptural expressions such as hand, foot, and their like, which give the impression of alluding to sensuality or mutability of God are, therefore, only guides and hints for the narrow-minded whose minds adhere to sensuality, according to the statement of the Sages: "The Bible uses the language of human beings." God used allegorical expressions when speaking to mankind, neglecting intelligent people in deference to the weaker-minded. Because of the variability of their mental capacity, God, in His all-embracing kindness, attempted to have every person in his own way reach the highest degree of bliss, that is to say, perfection through the knowledge of God. For the same reason, most of the prophets used such [allegorical] expressions according to the prevailing capacities of the people being addressed.

Since God is incorporeal, all corporeal properties such as composition and separation, space, time, quality, and their like, as well as all attributes of mutability such as movement and rest, anger and pleasure, and their like, are foreign to Him. Such scriptural expressions are thus to be understood metaphorically.

---

[15]New moon.

Chapter 1

The love of God, as commanded by Scripture, is brought about by reflecting upon all existences that emanated from Him, by contemplating about His dominion over the universe and His providence in relation to human beings, by pondering upon His gracious gifts of existence, intellect, revelation, and the promise associated therewith, and by continuous meditation that leads to the recognition of the incomprehensible perfection of God. Then, reflection upon one's own low level, one's insignificance and paltriness in relation to the beings such as the earth, sun, spheres, and their like, will fill one with reverence for the Highest Being [God].

Since one's knowledge of the Creator depends on one's knowledge of His works, I will make you aware of some of that which the Sages teach about the construction of the universe.

The created existences are of three types:

1. those composed of material and form, which are generated and which perish, such as animals, plants and minerals;
2. the same but with enduring form and with only subordinate accidental alterations such as changes in space; these are the spheres and the beings contained therein, whose prime matter is distinct from the four elements;
3. separate forms, that is to say, angels, who are totally incorporeal, so that their representation by the prophets is to be understood metaphorically, as is the use of similar portrayals of God Himself as well as the manifold manners of representing one and the same angel. They are, therefore, distinct from each other only through their rank, according to whether they stand closer or further away from God (but not in the sense of space) and accordingly were given various names. There are ten such types of angels, the lowest of whom are called *Ishim* and from whom originate the sublunary forms and prophetic communications. Their knowledge of God also corresponds to their rank. But only God knows Himself completely as well as the entire universe that emanated from Him; yet His knowledge is not separate from Him because this would assume that there is a plurality in Him, but our faith and our teaching are based upon His absolute Unity.

These extremely concisely discussed analyses are called "the divine secrets" by the Sages who inculcate the secrecy thereof only to exceptional minds [that is, to men of distinguished learning]. It is only the decline in knowledge and comprehension through the oppression of the nations that rule over us that motivated me to confer upon the worthy certain observations.

Chapter 2

The spheres have seven names corresponding to the seven planets; the eighth is the one of the fixed stars and the ninth encircles all and moves from East to West. They [the spheres] are all transparent—thus the stars, like in a single being, shine through—without any empty space or matter between them. Their substance lacks physical [or sensual] attributes: their blue color is produced by the air. They are completely round and their central point is the center of the earth, between which and them earth, water, air, and fire encircle one another concentrically. Some stars, however, are found in eccentric spheres. The constellation and movement of the stars show that there are eighteen concentric and eight eccentric [spheres] about which the Greek scholars [astronomers] wrote compositions.[1]

---

[1]Here Steinschneider offers the following footnote. According to the fragment of Philolaos, the Pythagoreans assumed that there are ten bodies in the universe: the heaven of the fixed stars, five planets, the sun, the moon, the earth, and the opposite earth, a type of metaphysical being, in order to preserve the sacredness of the Zehuzahl. Eudoxus maintains there are 40 (spheres or bodies), Callipus 34, and Aristotle 56. Later Greeks placed the eccentric and the epicyclic spheres, discovered by Appollonius of Pergamos, at a position that was still retained by Copernicus and first set aside by Keppler. Fracaster, a sixteenth-century physician, sought in his book to reactivate the Homocentrica system and required 77 spheres! See Ideler and Letronne, *Journal des Savants*, 1841, pp. 540 and 544 ff. Concerning the world construction of the Mohammedan Kabbala, see the interesting pronouncements of Hammer in *Wiener Jahrbuch*, Vol. 105, p. 135 ff.

The ninth sphere is divided into twelve divisions corresponding to the Zodiac although, since the deluge, they do not
correspond precisely anymore to each other.[2] Some stars are
smaller than the earth, some larger. The stars and the spheres
have a soul, but their knowledge is less than that of the angels.
Within the sphere of the moon, there is located one of the
various inanimate essences of spheres that directs the four
forms, the elements, the components of the essences to a
natural site, toward which they would strive following any
random displacement, for example, fire upward and the earth
downward. In the *Guide of the Perplexed*, I have already discussed at length the relationship between the sublunary and the
upper world that is alluded to in Jacob's ladder.

The sublunary beings also have a hierarchy that begins with
the elements out of which the higher beings are composed.
Because of their form, the highest level is occupied by angels in
human guise [*Ishim*] and among them are the prophets. Just as
in the material world, everlasting alterations between simple
and compound things take place without an existence perishing
or having something new added, so too the developed, rational
soul, the image of God, which no longer requires any material
substances for the acquisition of the nonmaterial intellect,
—when it separates from the body—returns to its site of origin
and there remains in everlasting spirituality or (if it remained
undeveloped) perishes.

Also the content of this concise chapter that the ancients
called "The Work of the Hand" (Creation) consists of lofty
secrets that are only communicated to exceptional people—to
be sure to a lesser degree than the content of the previous
chapter. The contemplation of the aforementioned, too, is
intended to increase one's love toward God, whose perfection
cannot be comprehended by human beings. This investigation
is called by the Sages, *Pardes*, as is known from the story of the
four scholars.[3]

---

[2]According to one opinion cited in the Jerusalem Talmud, *Pesachim* 1, the
Zodiac did not function during the deluge.

[3]See footnote 153 to the main text.

Among the principles of our faith is the belief in prophecy that, though a gift of grace from God, is accorded only to the worthy who prepare themselves for intellectual and moral perfection; the latter also leads to an association with the holy spirit and the level of angels called *Ishim*. Prophecy, too, has its hierarchy; some prophets remain only with the vision, whereas others interpret it. One means to prepare for prophethood is through music; the latter itself, as already mentioned, is a gracious act of Divine revelation, often combined with a mission to other people. Every prophet after Moses does not have to perform miracles as he did; rather, he [the prophet] only has to teach truth and justice. We are charged to obey him as long as he does not deviate from the basic principles—established elsewhere—of the Mosaic religion.

Chapter 3

The dispositions of people differ as do their temperaments and move between two extremes. The middle path is the correct one followed by the wise. One who leans in the direction of one of the extremes is considered to be a pious person. The soul, as the body, is susceptible to health and to illness. Assurance about the condition of the soul can be obtained by observing it and its own activities, as well as its activities in relation to the destiny of others.

Base characteristics are arrogance, haughtiness, and preoccupation with sensuality; lofty characteristics are modesty, generosity, and so forth as they are found among prophets and national leaders.

The ultimate recompense of [both] religious and Godless people in the world to come is a nonmaterial one—as already affirmed by the ancient Sages—and relates only to the soul.

Health of the body is a prerequisite for that of the soul. Hence, it seems appropriate to mention here certain general rules of dietetics. The maintenance of health requires that attention be paid to the type, time, and amount of food [to be consumed], with consideration also given to exercise, excretory function, and sleep. A proper meal should be preceded by softening [laxative] foods and followed by astringent foods. Light [to digest] nutrition should precede heavy foods. During the summer and in hot climates, cold foods are preferable; during the winter and in cold climates the reverse applies. Some foods, because of their heaviness, are absolutely harmful and should, therefore, not be consumed at all. Other, less harmful [foods] should be consumed in small amounts. Exercise and the avoidance of over-satiation soften nature and keep illness away even if one consumes harmful foods. A weekly bath also serves to soften [the stool] but one must pay attention to a variety of instructions [pertaining to bathing]. Bloodletting should only be resorted to for extreme need, and in the springtime. It should not be used at all for someone who has reached 50 years of age. Excessive emission of semen destroys the essence of the body. Therefore, one should indulge in coitus infrequently [literally: in small measures] and in specific ways.

Concluding chapter, addressed to a friend

Men of religion can be separated into two categories. One comprises those who are equally perfect in insight and piety; the other comprises those who are unintelligent, and who harm others, and even more so themselves. The Sages call the latter group "pious fools" and "world destroyers." People of the first category occupy themselves solely with their own duties, shun worldly affairs and the associated unpleasantnesses and burdens thereof, fulfill their obligations toward God in silence, and are, therefore, beloved by God and by human beings. People of the second category arrogantly meddle in the affairs of others, get involved in quarrels, arouse enmity, and cannot avoid anger, complaints, improper speech, and [evil] deeds. In their alleged zeal, they destroy their religion as well as their world through the hatred people have toward them.

The great scholars who recognized this, therefore, chose

seclusion and distanced themselves from courts of law and
devoted themselves exclusively to the study [of Torah].

May God lead us both to salvation in both worlds, and you, O
Master, consider this, and may God's verdict bring it to fruition.

Letter from Rabbi S. Y. Rapoport
Prague, Thursday, the fifth day of Elul 5606

To my friend, the accomplished scholar and honorable re-
searcher who interprets and delves into books of antiquity,
Moshe Steinschneider:

As one that findeth great spoil,[1] I rejoiced over the *Ma'amar
Hayichud* of our master Moses Maimonides which you hastened
to send me as soon as it came from the printer, even before it
was proofread to correct its typographical and editorial errors.

Blessed be the Lord who did not deprive us of a redeemer
such as yourself[2] who redeemed this day this book written by
this great man [Maimonides], from going down to rot in the
grave.[3] Although small in size, it was authored and established
by one of the great leaders of Israel.[4] Every letter that came
from his mouth, every word set down by his fingers, and every
investigation that emanated from his thoughts are more precious in our eyes than all the precious stones to be found in the
depths of the earth.[5]

Despite all the scholars and those who presume to be
scholars, and the pious and those who presume to be pious,
among our people in this era who attempted to dislodge this
giant from his lofty position, they did not succeed or [better
said] did not harm him at all. They did not touch his great

---

[1]Allusion to Psalm 119:162.
[2]Allusion to Ruth 4:14.
[3]Allusion to Isaiah 38:17.
[4]Allusion to 1 Samuel 15:17.
[5]Literally: hidden places, allusion to Psalm 95:4.

honor, which he truly deserves, by even the width of a hair.
These kinds of people are of three types. There are some who
are truly [God]-fearing and perfect who, in their own imagination, began to search for blemishes[6] in this sun of virtue.[7] They
did not rest nor repose in their continual search for any kind of
error[8] which is not in reality an error. The blemishes are only
in the visions, which they assemble to themselves through which
they see.[9] And without knowing the instruments of war, they
approach the visions against which they mean to war.

The second type are those who presume to be pious or are
pious fools. In their eyes no one is pure unless he, like them,
aggrandizes vanities and denigrates sciences. People of both
types have learned and set ethical standards from what they
observe among the habits of the third group who are presently
sprouting anew daily. The latter trample on everything holy
and every outstanding early scholar is subject to scorn and
derision in their eyes. They cannot refrain from spitting even in
the face of this princely man. More than that,[10] they selected
him more than many other scholars of renown as a target for
their arrows—their quivers are full of them[11]—and are open
like a grave—to constantly shoot their arrows at him. They
besieged him and persecuted him and disturbed his peace until
the gate of the dunghill.[12] And all this is only because they are
oppressed by their irascibility in viewing the shining light of this
man. There is none like him, free and mighty, and knowledge-
able in all matters[13] relating to the connection and relationship
of our religion and science.[14] And in all this there is also none
like him in his knowledge and understanding of all the details

---

[6]Literally: spots or stains.

[7]Maimonides. Allusion to Malachi 3:20.

[8]Literally: sin.

[9]Allusion to Exodus 38:8.

[10]Literally: on no account; far from it; not only this.

[11]Allusion to Psalm 127:5.

[12]Allusion to the gate in Jerusalem through which the ashes or dung were
taken out of the city (Sha'ar Ha'Ashpot). See Nehemiah 3:14.

[13]Literally: investigations.

[14]Literally: wisdom.

of the precepts and commandments of our written and orally
transmitted religion. He bends his shoulder to carry them with
love and with reverence and so, too, he commands to all those
that follow him, and he teaches[15] with intelligence and with
knowledge in his wonderful books to everyone who is called an
Israelite.

Let these two aforementioned types of people know and
understand whom they are insulting and against whom they are
raising their voices.[16] And for that very reason that he became
the target of the instigation and insult of the scorners, he has
been for the early scholars their jewel and splendor; a teacher
and an educator for all generations.

You [Moshe Steinschneider] have now published a valuable
treatise of this marvelous man which [by itself] would have
given us sufficient reason to greatly honor him. It appears[17]
that he wrote it in his old age after he wrote his beautiful book
Guide of the Perplexed that he cites in this work. Although this
work [*Ma'amar Hayichud*] contains a number of items that are
repetitious of what he wrote at the beginning of his work
Mishneh Torah, one should not see this as a redundancy[18]
because his intent was to teach in Arabic that which he had
already taught in the Hebrew language.[19] Moreover, he selected a few additional items [for inclusion in the *Ma'amar
Hayichud*] as he added to his knowledge over the many years as
can readily be seen by one who delves into it. He also added[20]
new concepts and placed them all in [a logical] order and
arrangement according to his usual precious way of learning
and convincing the reader.

May all those who admire his teachings, and they are many,[21]
rejoice in this small composition. Also, the righteous[22] will bless

---

[15]Literally: proves or admonishes.
[16]Allusion to Isaiah 37:27.
[17]Literally: if we would know.
[18]Literally: unnecessary talk.
[19]His *Mishneh Torah* was written in Mishnaic Hebrew.
[20]Literally: annexed.
[21]Literally: not few.
[22]Literally: pure-hearted.

you [for publishing this work]. Furthermore, they will thank you immensely[23] for your intelligent footnotes, for they were written with understanding even though at times your proofs are somewhat lengthier than necessary. It is for me only to record here a few additional comments because all that I wrote when I still had the manuscript is lost from me to this day.

I still think, as I did then, that this composition [*Ma'amar Hayichud*] is also known by the name *Sefer Hanimtzah*, which was bound with the work *Amarot Tehorot* by Don Abraham Chayun, published in Salonica in the year 5356[24] (*Sifsei Yeshainim*, letter *aleph*, number 157). The character of the treatise, as it now appears before us, shows that the name *Hanimtzah* is more appropriate than *Hayichud* because it deals more with "existence" than it does with "unity." It also explains [since it deals with "existence"] that the *Sifsei Yeshainim* appended to it medical subjects and matters relating to the fear of God [which would not fit in with it if it were dealing exclusively with "unity"]. Indeed, at the end of this composition, there are included some items pertaining to medicine. Perhaps that which is mentioned in *Sifsei Yeshainim* is from a different, far better copy, as far as we can best evaluate to explain the name change from *Yichud* to *Nimtzah*.

And if there is any validity to this suggestion, I am grieved at not having access to that published work because the edition before me is not adequate to satisfy all the questions[25] of the reader. A single deficiency can tell the character of the whole work. For the translator took even the scriptural verses cited by Maimonides in Arabic and translated them from Arabic into Hebrew but not into their correct Hebrew as they are in the Bible, but into his own stammering language,[26] to the point that the reader cannot recognize their source [as biblical passages]. I believe it is to this that the scribe refers when he wrote at the end of the book as follows: "translated from Arabic

---

[23] Literally: not a little.
[24] 1596.
[25] Literally: desires.
[26] See Isaiah 28:11.

and copied by the scholar Rabbi Isaac ben Nathan, the Pious. And it follows the method of the Rabbi [Maimonides] in his translation in that he translated sentences [not literally but] in a manner to retain the melody of the language." I have already told you about these for your own sake. Therefore, all those places need notes as you provided for some of them.

There are some additional places about which one should comment such as immediately at the beginning of the book. [There Maimonides states:] "And it is written in the Torah that the actions of the Creator are perfect and His attributes exist in truth; He is the faithful God; there is no imperfection in Him; He is the righteous one; He is the just one." In all this he [Maimonides] had in mind the scriptural verse (Deuteronomy 32:4): "The Rock His doing is perfect; for all His ways are judgment; a God of faithfulness and without iniquity, righteous and upright is He." All that was necessary was to add the small explanations on the phrase "for all His ways are judgment," that is to say His attributes exist in truth.

Similarly, on p. 24, "the prophet Samuel told Saul . . . go to that group of prophets who make themselves available to prophesize . . . and you will be transformed into another man," the intent is to the scriptural verses (1 Samuel 10:5–6:) "thou shalt meet a band of prophets . . . and shalt be turned into another man." Other examples [could be cited]. I have only found the name of the translator, Rabbi Isaac ben Nathan, in one other place; in Wolf's *Hebrew Bibliography*, Part 1, Number 4, it states that he translated from Arabic into Hebrew comments on certain difficult passages in the *Guide of the Perplexed* by the Arabic scholar Abdullah Abubkar. It can be found in the public library of the city of Vienna. There he is noted as Rabbi Isaac ben Nathan from Cordoba.

I also have a few comments on the main body of the composition:. . . .[27] On page 6, he states: ". . . next are *Cherubim*; next are *Ishim* . . . and the first level is *Ishim* . . . and

---

[27]Here Rapoport offers several linguistic and philological corrections to Steinschneider's Hebrew edition. These have been incorporated into my English translation.

they are called by this name because their level approximates
the level of the human intellect." All this is repeated from his
book, *The Mishneh Torah* (*Yesodei Hatorah* 2:7) where he states:
"the tenth level is the level of the form of those called *Ishim*, and
these are the angels that speak with the prophets . . . they are,
therefore, called *Ishim* because their level approximates the
intelligence of human beings." This matter is problematical[28] in
two respects. Firstly, what is his source for this assertion?
Secondly, the author of the *Zohar* has already used this treatise
of Maimonides and wrote (*Zohar Chadash*, p. 8b): "There are ten
watches of ministering angels in the heavens . . . those of the
last watch are called *Ishim*." The scholar *Yaavetz* [R. Jacob
Emden] in *Mitpachat Sepharim*, wrote: "I do not know where it is
alluded that there are angels called *Ishim*." Rabbi Moshe Cor-
dovero [*Ramak*] in *Ben Yochai* (*Ma'aneh* 110) points out the
words of Maimonides that are mentioned in his *Mishneh Torah*.

In the explanation of foreign words by Rabbi Samuel Ibn
Tibbon at the end of the *Guide of the Perplexed* (letter *samach*), I
found that he wrote the following: "And every action . . . and
it is my opinion that when Maimonides[29] in his composition
[*Mishneh Torah*] states that they are called *Ishim*. . . . I do not
know where Maimonides found that name, but I believe that he
found it in the words of the Sages, of blessed memory, in
Midrashic books or other books [of the Sages]. We could say
that the author of the *Zohar* also saw it there in homiletical
books. However, it is my opinion that Maimonides' source[30]
is the interpretation of the Sages (in *Yoma* 77a but found only in
the *Eyn Yaakov* and not in our editions of the Talmud):
"And the honor of the God of Israel ascended from the Cherub
and was taken to the man dressed in white linen . . . and
behold the man dressed in white linen . . . had not the hot
coals cooled from the hand of the Cherub to the hand of
Gabriel . . ." *Rashi* there states that "dressed in white linen"

---

[28]Literally: wondrous.
[29]Literally: the teacher or the Rabbi, of blessed memory.
[30]Literally: intention.

refers to Gabriel in the book of Daniel. Furthermore, in the *Kuzari* (Part 1:87), the active intellect is called Gabriel. So, too, the present treatise on page 14 states "The essence of the angel of *asiyah*[31] (that is to say the active intellect) that we have mentioned and which is called *Ishim* in our language." Thus, this angel called *Ish* by the Sages, of blessed memory, is Gabriel and represents the active intellect that spoke with Ezekiel and Daniel, and it is one level below the level of a Cherub.

I also found that even the original *Zohar* makes use of this treatise of Maimonides and repeats the latter's words even more. See the book *Erchey Hakinuyim* where it states as follows: "*Ishim* are angels. No group of angels can mingle with the essences of this world as can that group called *Ishim*; *Zohar* on Genesis, p. 184." I cannot find that page in my *Zohar*. However, I believe the author of the work *Erchey Hakinuyim* because he is the author of *The History* [*Seder Hadorot*]. I further found in the commentary of Rabbi Bachya on the verse "and there wrestled a man [*Ish*] with him" (Genesis 32:25) that he wrote: "And I will here write for you an explanation of this verse in the manner that one of the philosophers of our Torah-scholars explained in the Song of Songs which he wrote in Arabic,[32] (and he refers to Rabbi Yoseph ibn Aknin, disciple of Maimonides; see *Mekor Chayim* there) that Jacob broadened his imagination . . . at the level of the active intellect that Scripture termed *Ish* and refers to Gabriel."[33]

[Rapoport here adds a few linguistic and other corrections.]

With greetings and friendship and love, I am Shlomo Yehudah Leib Rapoport, the *Kohen*[34]

---

[31]See note 127 in the main text.
[32]Literally: a strange language.
[33]See note 20.
[34]Priest, that is as opposed to Levite or Israelite.

TREATISE ON THE UNITY OF GOD

These are the prophetical and intellectual principles[1] ordered by the First Being[2] who does not change at all. It, therefore, follows that His actions do not change at all from what they are. Since all existences are ordered by Him in absolute perfection and organized in positive order, one cannot conceive of any increase or diminution, and that is the intent of what is written in the Torah [Deuteronomy 32:4], that the actions of the Creator are perfect and His cognomens exist in truth.[3] He is the faithful God. There is no imperfection in Him. He is the righteous One. He is the just One.[4]

---

[1]Hebrew: *peshatim*, literally: plain meanings. Kalisch translates: abstract ideas.

[2]Literally: First; sometimes translated: First Cause; that is, God.

[3]In his *Mishneh Torah* (Laws Concerning the Basic Principles of the Torah or *Yesodei Hatorah* 1:1), Maimonides states: "the basic principle of all basic principles and the pillar of all wisdom is to realize that there exists a First Being who brought every existing being into existence. And all celestial, terrestrial, or in-between existences exist only from His true existence."

[4]Maimonides paraphrased Deuteronomy 32:4 whose exact wording is "The Rock, His work is perfect; for all His ways are judgment; a God of faithfulness and without iniquity; Just and right is He."

Concerning the actions of God, Solomon said (Ecclesiates 3:14) that there is naught to add or to take away from them.[5] Were His actions changeable, He would undoubtedly be mutable.[6] Although in the book of the Torah we find figurative expressions such as hand and foot and face and speech and their like,[7] which might bring us to think of corporeality and change [in relation to God], know that these terms are only used for the benefit[8] of the intellectually limited and for the understanding of those beings of limited creation who are limited to the sensory and who do not have the capacity to rise above the sensory to the [nonphysical] horizons of intellect.

The Sages stated (*Berachot* 31b): "The Torah speaks in the language of human beings," that is to say the Torah speaks to people according to their understanding and their intellect. For this reason [in the Torah] God uses metaphors relative to the human body and to human character using such terms [relative to God] as kindness[9] and weakness because it is impossible for all people to have an equal perception of the unity [of God] because they have a wide range of intellects. Some people's perception is perfect whereas others are lacking; some have strong perceptions whereas others have weak imaginations in their understanding of the perfection of Divine wisdom and the principles of wisdom and mercy and Lordship[10] that extend over all as it is written: "And His tender mercies are over all His works (Psalm 145:9).[11] His mercy extends over all His creations in order that no person should lack the success of perceiving

---

[5]The sentence in Ecclesiastes begins with: "whatsoever God doeth shall be forever" meaning that the conditions imposed by God upon the scheme of human life are fixed for all time and unchangeable.

[6]Literally: He would change greatly.

[7]See also Maimonides, *Yesodei Hatorah* 1:9.

[8]Literally: to straighten.

[9]Literally: having mercy with.

[10]In a footnote, Steinschneider points out that the term Lordship, *rabani* in Arabic, was incorrectly translated by many medieval translators including the famous Samuel Ibn Tibbon and that only in later times, after the dissemination of Greek knowledge among the Arabs, was the term *rabani* changed.

[11]Steinschneider's edition erroneously has Psalm 148:9.

[His unity], even the smallest of men,[12] and so that each individual should achieve according to his perceptions and believe in His truth. Therefore, God speaks in metaphors.

Therefore, we find that most of the prophets often speak to individual people according to the latter's understanding of the knowledge [of the Creator] and according to the latter's perception of this perfection by using analogies to what is beneath it.[13]

Just as the true First Being is noncorporeal, it follows that He is detached from all that is implied, or follows, from corporeality. Just as one cannot conceive of Him as a compound [consisting of separate "parts"], nor separation, nor as occupying space,[14] having neither quantity nor quality, neither height nor depth,[15] nor right and left, nor front and back, nor as standing and sitting. He is not confined by time and He has no beginning nor end. Death does not apply to Him, nor does life like our life, nor purpose or knowledge like our knowledge, nor movement or at rest, and neither anger or satisfaction, nor fear or courage, and not speech or taciturnity.[16] The Sages said that

---

[12]Literally: the last man. ? man who was created last.

[13]Literally: of what is below it. See Maimonides, *Yesodei Hatorah* 1:9 where he states: "All these [metaphorical] expressions are used according to the understanding of [most] human beings who only have a clear perception of physical bodies. And the Torah speaks in the language of human beings."

[14]Literally: whether.

[15]Literally: neither up nor down.

[16]See Maimonides, *Yesodei Hatorah* 1:11 where he states: "since it has been clarified that He is not corporeal nor human, it is clear that none of the occurrences of physical bodies can occur to Him: neither conjunction nor separation, neither space nor dimension, neither ascent nor descent, neither right nor left, neither front nor back, neither sitting nor standing. Nor does He exist in time so that He would have a beginning and an end and a fixed number of years. And He does not change for there is nothing that can effect a change in Him. And He does not die, nor does He have life like the life of a living creature. Nor does He have folly nor wisdom like the wisdom of a wise man, nor sleep nor wakefulness, nor anger nor frivolity; nor joy nor melancholy, nor silence nor speech like the speech of human beings" . . .

in Heaven there is no standing and no sitting and no front and no back and no cohesion.[17]

It is a general principle that He is totally immutable. If one were, for example, to say that sometimes He is pacified and sometimes He is angry, sometimes He speaks and sometimes He is silent, then He would be mutable and everything that changes must, of necessity, be changed by something. But The Most High, the true First Being is without any deficiency [and can never be changed]. Therefore, all such expressions mentioned in the books of the Torah and in the recorded books of the prophets are all to be understood allegorically.[18] Thus, too, did [prophet] Jeremiah of blessed memory say, "Thou, O God, dost not change."[19]

Chapter 1

And this First Being, may He be praised, commanded all understanding people to love Him and to fear Him.[20] It is written in the Torah: "and thou shalt love the Lord, thy God, (Deuteronomy 6:5 and 11:1), and it is written: "thou shalt fear

---

[17]Steinschneider points out that the talmudic text cited here by Maimonides (*Chagigah* 15a) reads: In Heaven, there is no sitting and no emulation and no division and no cohesion. Maimonides also cites this talmudic dictum in his commentary on *Chelek* (see *Maimonides' Commentary on the Mishnah. Tractate Sanhedrin*, translated by Fred Rosner. New York: Sepher-Hermon Press, 1981, p. 151). In his *Guide of the Perplexed* (Part 1, Chapter 12) and in his *Mishneh Torah* (*Yesodei Hatorah* 1:11), he states that in Heaven there is neither sitting nor standing, for standing sometimes occurs in the sense of rising. In the Talmud (*Chagigah* 15a), some texts include the phrase "no standing." Maimonides interprets the word *ippuy* to mean cohesion (as in Isaiah 11:14) whereas others, including Rashi, translate *ippuy* as weariness.

[18]See Maimonides, *Yesodei Hatorah* 1:12 where he states that all these expressions and their like, which are mentioned in the Torah and in the words of the prophets, are all metaphors and allegories.

[19]Maimonides is paraphrasing the quotation from Lamentations 5:19 whose precise words are: "Thou, O Lord, art enthroned forever, Thy throne is from generation to generation." See also Malachi 3:6.

[20]See Maimonides, *Yesodei Hatorah* 2:1.

the Lord thy God" (Deuteronomy 6:13).[21] And if you will say: "which road leads to the love of God?" know that if you delve into this wonderful existence [that is, the world], which was arranged by His infinite[22] wisdom, and if you examine the details of His actions, and consider in your mind His kingship over heaven and earth after pondering about His providential care [of the world], and how He brought you forth from nonexistence[23] into existence, and endowed you with intellect, which is the most excellent of His creations, and which is closer to Him than they are, and that He cautioned you to His service and commanded you to remember Him [at all times], and that He adorned you with infinite pleasantness and unending bliss, perfection and immortality,[24] the likes of which no eye has ever seen nor any ear ever heard, as it is stated in Isaiah: "No eye hath seen a God beside Thee" (Isaiah 64:3), that is to say, no eye has seen it[25] and nobody knows the true character thereof except God—then, having reflected considerably [on this], you will see that human intellect and thinking are too weak[26] to grasp the existence of God, His perfection and the beauty [created by Him]. And there is no doubt that you will become desirous and aroused by this existence [of God] and you will fervently love Him with an incomparable love and ardent desire,[27] as [King] David, of blessed memory, said: "My soul thirsteth for God" (Psalm 42:3).

After you delve into and ponder well in your heart[28] with humility and reverence and introspection about this important

---

[21]Steinschneider's edition erroneously has Deuteronomy 3:13.
[22]Literally: great.
[23]Literally: absence.
[24]Literally: without an end and residue.
[25]See *Berachot* 34b.
[26]Literally: short.
[27]In his *Yesodei Hatorah* 2:2, Maimonides states as follows: "When a person contemplates His great and wondrous works and creatures and from these perceives His wisdom which is incomparable and infinite, he will immediately love and praise and glorify Him and long for Him with an exceedingly strong longing to know His great name." See also *loc. cit.* 4:12.
[28]Literally: soul.

matter, and [recognize] your smallness in size and your insignificance and the lowliness of your essence,[29] and that you are
a vessel of dirt and filth and a dwelling place of uncleanliness
and repulsiveness, and that you [began as] a foul-smelling drop
and will end as a decaying carcass—and if you compare the
substance of your body to the terrestrial globe, you will note
that there is no relationship [in size] between the two. Furthermore, the earth is one one-hundred-and-seventieth[30] the size
of the sun and the sun is distinguished by it size,[31] and its size
is miniscule compared to the entire universe.[32] You will, thus,
not see any importance at all in the infinitesimally small size of
your body,[33] as stated by [King] David of blessed memory:
"When I behold Thy heavens" (Psalm 8:4). Because of all this,
you will be anxious to meet the great, mighty, powerful King
whose greatness is extreme, and, when you reflect thereon, you
will be [deeply] moved and your body will tremble because of
the greatness and majesty to which everything humbles itself.

And now that we have reached this point in the treatise it
seems appropriate that we mention some of what the wise men
have said about the construction of this universe[34] and the
works of the Creator. For it is according to your knowledge of
His works that you come closer to the knowledge of the
Creator.[35] We will mention that which will awaken the sleeper
from the sleep of his unconsciousness and arouse him from the
slumber of his ignorance. It is proper for the reader to know

---

[29]Literally: matters. See *Yesodei Hatorah* 4:12.

[30]Steinschneider points out that in his *Mishneh Torah*, Maimonides also
states that the sun is 170 times large than the earth. On the other hand, Rabbi
Judah Halevi, in his famous *Book of Kuzari* gives the figures 160 (Part 3:49)
and 166 (Part 4:3). In his *Keser Malchus*, Ibn Gabirol cites the 170 figure.

[31]Literally: sphere.

[32]Literally: the last sphere.

[33]In his *Yesodei Hatorah* 2:2, Maimonides states as follows: "and when a
person ponders about these matters, he will immediately recoil with fright
and be fearful and recognize that he is a small and lowly and obscure
creature, endowed with only slight and meager intelligence [standing] before
the One who is perfect in knowledge." See also *loc. cit.* 4:12.

[34]Literally: order of this existence.

[35]Alternate translation: a worker is recognized by his works.

that the existences[36] created[37] by the First Being, may He be praised, are divided into three categories. The first category includes beings composed of matter and form, and these are beings that perish, such as the bodies of living creatures and plants and minerals.[38]

The second category is comprised of beings also composed of matter and form but [these beings] do not change or age, nor does their form change as the first category of beings change. Rather, their form is permanent and everlasting. Their activities occur with the assistance of their Creator whose existence is immutable and whose law is unchangeable. They never undergo change except in very rare accidental occurrences such as a shift in space or in place. And their form exists in their own permanent primordiality. And these are the spheres and all the things contained within them. And their primordiality is not like the primordiality of the earthly elements, and their form is not like their form but they [spheres] are different from them; [earthly elements] in form and in matter.[39]

The third category is comprised of separate forms that are totally devoid of matter and completely incorporeal. And these are the angels and it has been established that they are absolutely not corporeal.[40] And if the prophets state that angels possess wings and that some of them consist of fire and that some of them are shaped in the form of human beings or birds or their like, these [depictions] are [to be understood] in the allegorical sense.[41] The same is also true in the depiction[42] of

---

[36]Literally: It is appropriate for you to know that the existences . . .

[37]Literally: arranged.

[38]In his *Yesodei Hatorah* 2:3, Maimonides states that the first category is comprised of: "beings composed of matter and form, and these constantly come into being and perish such as the bodies of human beings and animals and plants and minerals."

[39]See Maimonides, *Yesodei Hatorah* 2:3.

[40]*Ibid.*

[41]See Maimonides, *Yesodei Hatorah* 2:4.

[42]Steinschneider refers the reader to the end of chapter 11 of Part 2 of Maimonides' *Guide of the Perplexed* and section 13 of part 4 of Judah Halevi's *Book of Kuzari*.

the Creator in the Torah where it states that the Lord "is a devouring fire" (Deuteronomy 4:24). There is evidence for this fact in that one finds some of the prophets portraying a single angel in many different forms. It is obvious that it appears to him as if the angel for a short time has changing forms and does not have a permanent form. And if you will ask: "how can they be distinguished one from the other since they are incorporeal?" know that they are in fact recognizable by their positions and ranks. For the rank of each essential being is known and each of them takes precedence over its fellow being in rank, and all this was arranged by the First Being, may He be praised.[43] [King] Solomon hinted to this fact when he said "For one higher than the high watches over" (Ecclesiastes 5:7).

And the level or rank of angels does not at all refer to their position in space, because in the absence of corporeality they also have no [human] qualities. Rather, their various names differ according to their rank and their elevation, or rank refers to their closeness to the First Being, may He be praised. Therefore, the ones on the highest[44] level are the *Chayot Hakodesh*. These are above all the others and are closest to the true First Being, may He be praised. Adjacent to this group are the *Ophanim* which are on the second level. Adjacent to them are the *Erelim* which are on the third level. Next are *Chashmalim*. Next are *Seraphim*. Next are *Malachim*.[45] Next are *Elohim*. Next are *Bnei Elohim*. Next are *Cherubim*. Next are *Ishim*. They are called by these ten names according to their ten levels. It is decreed that each angel is called by its name according to its level. There is nothing above the highest[46] level except

---

[43]See Maimonides, *Yesodei Hatorah* 2:5 where he states: "each of them [i.e., angels] is below another in rank and each exists from his power, one above the other, and all exist from the power and goodness of the Holy One, Blessed be He."

[44]Literally: first.

[45]*Malachim* are missing in the Hebrew text but Steinschneider points out this omission in a footnote where he refers the reader to Maimonides' *Mishneh Torah* (*Yesodei Hatorah* 2:7) where *Malachim* are cited between *Seraphim* and *Elohim* to complete the list of ten varieties of angels.

[46]Literally: tenth.

God,[47] may He be praised. And [the highest level] is called
Chayot Hakodesh. Therefore, the prophets stated that these
[*Chayot Hakodesh*] are beneath the Throne of Glory.[48] And the
lowest[49] level is called *Ishim* according to the emanation of their
forms.[50] These are the angels who speak to the prophets and
they are called by this name[51] because their level approximates
the level of the human intellect.

And these ten forms[52] live and know their Creator to a
certain extent[53] according to their different types[54] and their
different levels. Even so, none know the truth of God's essence
but He Himself, although the perception of the first level [of
angels] is higher than the perception of the next level. The
perception [of God] that is the least of all is the perception of
the tenth level. Even the latter has a perception [of God] which
cannot be attained by a human being who is composed of
matter and form.

And all beings except for the First Being, from the highest
level of angels[55] to the smallest creature[56] proceeds to existence
from the very essence of the First Being. Since He, may He be
blessed, knows Himself as He really is[57] of necessity He knows
all that was arranged by Him so that nothing at all is hidden

---

[47]Literally: the truth.

[48]This sentence in the Steinschneider version occurs after the next sentence
but more properly belongs here to conform to Maimonides' *Yesodei Hatorah*
2:7.

[49]Literally: first.

[50]Meaning unclear.

[51]*Ishim*, literally: men.

[52]That is, categories of angels.

[53]In his *Yesodei Hatorah* 2:8, Maimonides states: "to an exceedingly great
extent."

[54]Literally: times. Steinschneider suggests that the word *times* may be a
copyist's error for *knowledges*.

[55]Literally: from the first form.

[56]In his *Yesodei Hatorah* 2:9, Maimonides states: "to the tiniest insect that is
in the interior of the earth."

[57]In his *Yesodei Hatorah* 2:9, Maimonides states: "and realizes His greatness,
glory and truth."

from Him.[58] [King David, may he rest in peace, said (Psalm 94:9): "He that planted the ear, shall He not hear?"[59]

But with all this, know that the Creator, may He be praised, does not have knowledge that is external to Himself as is our knowledge. For our knowledge is separate from our essence, but His essence is perfect and cannot be separated from any aspect thereof. His knowledge and His life are One in all respects. For if His knowledge were separate, there would be a plurality in Him,[60] and His essence would be lacking in that it would require [different] portrayals to know Him and there would result a great confusion.[61] Rather, He is a separate Unity. There is no plurality in Him at all. He is absolutely and completely One and He is our Unique One[62] and our Torah and our faith revolve around Him. Some do know Him. Only a fool denies Him. He is only denied by one who denies Him because of a wall[63] which prevents him from understanding the truth about His Unity.[64]

And know that all that I have mentioned here on this topic is like a drop in the ocean in regard to what the topic intrinsically requires[65] because intelligence is too short and minds and speech would tire to speak about even a small part of this topic. These profound matters are called Divine Secrets by our Sages and they warned us in the strongest possible terms not to explain any part of them to the masses or [even] to the people of highest intellect and greatest understanding.[66] Rather, they

---

[58]Literally: so that He is not devoid of knowing anything at all.

[59]Kalisch erroneously cites Psalm 99:9.

[60]In his *Yesodei Hatorah* 2:10, Maimonides adds: "namely, He Himself, His life and His knowledge."

[61]Literally: uplifting or exaltation.

[62]In his *Yesodei Hatorah* 2:10, Maimonides states: "but it is not so. He is One in every aspect, from every angle, and in all ways in which Unity is conceived."

[63]Literally: veil.

[64]In his *Yesodei Hatorah* 2:10, Maimonides states: "This matter is beyond the power of speech to express and cannot be heard by the human ear nor properly understood by the human heart."

[65]See Maimonides, *Yesodei Hatorah* 2:11.

[66]Literally: first in understanding and highest souls.

should be copied from book to book.[67] Nowadays, however, since I have observed the loss of intelligence[68] from these people [of Israel] and their lack of wise men and expounders of its knowledge because of the oppression of the ruling nations, I look with favor upon the one who is worthy to properly view some of the fundamental prophetic concepts and the true ideations handed down to us from the disciples of the prophets and the Sages, of blessed memory.[69]

Chapter 2

The spheres in that language[70] are called *Shamayim*,[71] *Rekiya*,[72] *Zebul*,[73] *Machon*,[74] *Ma'on*,[75] *Vilon*,[76] and *Arabot*.[77] Each of these

---

[67]In his *Yesodei Hatorah* 2:12, Maimonides states: "the ancient Sages commanded us not to discuss these matters [publicly] but with an individual who is wise and able to understand from his own intellect. We give him the outlines of the subject and inform him of a minute portion of the topic and he will discern the matter by himself and understand the outcome and depths of the matter. And these matters are exceedingly profound and not every intellect is able to grasp them."

[68]Literally: kindnesses, that is knowledge and understanding.

[69]Kalisch adds the following note at the end of his English translation of chapter 1: "The hypothesis which our author laid down, that there are spirits or angels of different ranks, I shall not argue; because although such ideas are mere productions of a dreaming fantasy, it is nevertheless very probable that the human spirit stands not on the top of the grand scale of beings in the whole erection of innumerable worlds. It may be that in higher regions there are in existence purer and more perfect spirits than the human who are not prohibited, by a separation of a corporeal and spiritual perfection, to unite their real internal with the external spiritual world. Nay, there may be holy spirits who need not any sensual stimulation to exist, but live spontaneously in pure self-subsistence of their spiritual power. The existence of such beings as spirits or angels, however, can not be known by experience, and therefore all opinions, conceptions and narratives about them belong merely to the poetical province."

[70]Hebrew. Steinschneider suggests that there may be a copyist's error here and Maimonides' intent may have been Arabic.

[71]Heaven.

[72]Firmament.

[73]Celestial abode.

names has deep meaning and it is a prophetic secret.[78] The closest
of all the spheres is the Lunar sphere; above it is the sphere of
Mercury, and above the latter is the sphere of Venus. After that is
the Solar sphere, above which is the sphere of Jupiter, followed by
the sphere of Saturn.[79] Next is the eighth sphere which is the one
containing the stars, and after that is the ninth sphere which is the
last substantive one and which revolves from East to West; and it
is the one which encircles all and guides all.[80]

The reason why it appears to the observing eye that all these
stars are in a single sphere[81] is because the substances of the
spheres are transparent like glass and, therefore, the stars that
are in the eighth sphere appear to be below the Lunar sphere.[82]
Among these spheres, some move[83] from East to West such as
the ninth sphere, whereas others move from West to East.

---

[74]Dwelling.

[75]Habitation.

[76]Curtain.

[77]Celestial clouds.

[78]In his *Yesodei Hatorah* 3:1, Maimonides only cites four of these seven
spheres. The Talmud (*Chagigah* 12b) cites seven but the sequence is different
from that given by Maimonides here, and the Talmud substitutes *Shechakim*
(clouds, from *shachak* meaning dust) for *Shamayim*. Steinschneider points out
that these seven heavens as well as seven earths are also cited in the Koran. He
also cites sources that discuss seven gardens of Eden. Kalisch asserts that
Maimonides is mistaken about this system being handed down to us by the
prophets, because the very name given to the sixth sphere shows clearly its
birthplace. *Velon* is not a Hebrew but a Latin word, *velum*, corresponding to
the English *veil*. Kalisch also asks if this system has been founded on tradition,
how is it possible that a dispute took place about it? (See *Chagigah* 2.)

[79]Steinschneider refers the reader to Maimonides' *Guide of the Perplexed*
(Part 2, Chapter 9) where he discusses these spheres.

[80]See Maimonides, *Yesodei Hatorah* 3:1.

[81]In his *Yesodei Hatorah* 3:1, Maimonides adds: "although in reality they are
at different altitudes."

[82]In his *Yesodei Hatorah* 3:1, he substitutes: "below the first sphere."

[83]In his *Yesodei Hatorah* 3:2, Maimonides has: "revolve."

There is no emptiness between them at all nor any substance between them.[84]

And the substances of the spheres are not heavy or light, nor do they have taste or odor or color.[85] The reason they appear blue is related to their remoteness and the effect of the air.[86] These spheres are perfectly round like a globe in the middle of which is the center, and around which the earth rotates.[87] And water encompasses most of the earth, and air also encompasses the earth and the water, and then fire encompasses all three. And the rotation of the Lunar sphere encompasses these four types of matter. And some stars have small spheres and are fixed therein; such spheres do not revolve around the earth.[88]

The number of spheres that revolve around the world is eighteen and there are eight spheres which do not revolve.[89] And from the courses of the stars, and from the amount of their declination to the north or to the south, and from their distance from the earth and their approximation to it, we can ascertain the number of these spheres. The Greek sages[90] have already written compositions on this subject.[91]

And the ninth sphere, which encompasses all, was divided by the ancients into twelve divisions; and they called each division

---

[84]In his *Yesodei Hatorah* 3:2, Maimonides omits the phrase "nor any substance between them."

[85]Literally: appearance.

[86]In his *Yesodei Hatorah* 3:3, Maimonides states as follows: "all the spheres are neither light nor heavy. They do not have a red nor black color nor any other color. That which we see them as having a blue color is only an optical phenomenon and relates to the height of the air. Similarly, they have no taste nor odor because these characteristics are only found in bodies [that exist] below them."

[87]Literally: its rotation is the earth.

[88]See Maimonides, *Yesodei Hatorah* 3:4.

[89]Steinschneider points out that Judah Halevi's *Book of Kuzari* (Part 5, end of section 21) cites 40 rotating spheres and elsewhere in the same work (Part 5, end of section 14) that "these things are still less satisfactory than the *Book of Creation*" (see Part 4, section 25). See also Maimonides' *Guide of the Perplexed* (Part 2, Chapters 11, 19, and 24).

[90]That is, astronomers.

[91]See Maimonides, *Yesodei Hatorah* 3:5. Kalisch points out that Aristotle and Tracaster, respectively, maintained there are 56 and 77 rotating spheres.

according to the stars directly opposite them in the eighth sphere which is below it.[92] These are the constellations which are called in our language[93] *teleh* [Aries], *shor* [Taurus], *te'omim* [Gemini] and so forth.[94] These twelve [stars] that are in the eighth sphere were not found opposite the twelve divisions that are in the ninth sphere until the time of the deluge, because it was at that time that it was divided. However, at present they[95] have somewhat shifted from that position, and their movement has slackened and is extremely slow, and their movement is from East to West.[96]

And among these stars there are some that are smaller than the earth and there are some that are larger. And the moon is one part of the body of the earth, and the earth is like one one-hundred-and-seventieth part of the sun. There is no star that is larger than the body of the sun and none smaller than the body of Mercury.[97]

And these stars and spheres have intelligent souls, understanding, and knowledge. And each of them knows its original beginning according to its position and rank among existing beings. And they praise their Creator and give thanks to Him

---

[92] In his *Yesodei Hatorah* 3:6, Maimonides states: "the ninth sphere which encompasses all was divided by the ancient Sages into twelve divisions. They assigned each division a name according to the form that the stars directly below the division seemed to assume."

[93] That is, Hebrew.

[94] In his *Yesodei Hatorah* 3:6, Maimonides cites the entire list of the signs of the Zodiac.

[95] These twelve stars in the eighth sphere.

[96] In his *Yesodei Hatorah* 3:7, Maimonides states: "At present, they have somewhat rotated because all the stars in the eighth sphere rotate like the sun and the moon except that they rotate with difficulty, so that a distance traversed by the sun in one day takes each of these stars approximately 70 years to traverse."

[97] In his *Yesodei Hatorah* 3:8, Maimonides states: "of the visible stars, there are some stars so small that the earth is larger than each of them, and there are some stars that are several times as large as the earth. And the earth is about 40 times larger than the moon. And the sun is about 170 times larger than the earth. Hence the sun is approximately 6800 times the size of the moon. There is no star among all the stars that is larger than the sun nor smaller than a star in the second sphere."

and extol Him with all types of praise and acknowledgment. And they perceive their essence like the angels except that their perception is below [that of angels] but above that of human beings.[98] And [King] David, of blessed memory, said (Psalm 19:2): The heavens proclaim the essence of the Creator and the sphere tells us the wonders of His works,[99] but not by discourse[100] nor by speech. He who thinks that these two expressions [the heavens proclaim the essence of the Creator and the sphere tells us the wonders of His works] were stated in a metaphorical sense is mistaken. Only the [words] proclaiming and telling [are to be understood metaphorically] but [the aforementioned expressions] are cited in the Hebrew language because of their truth and not for allegory. It is correct to state that the heavens do not discourse nor use [human] speech. Rather, this [proclaiming and telling] is an allusion to internal speech that is human perception.[101]

And the Creator created in the concavity[102] of the Lunar sphere, a simple substance that is different from the substances of other spheres, and its form differs from the forms of the other spheres. This substance has four forms. The first of these forms is the fire; it is part of this substance that touches the Lunar sphere and it is the essence of fire. The second form is

---

[98]In his *Yesodei Hatorah* 3:9, Maimonides states: "all the stars and spheres have souls and possess understanding and intelligence. And they are alive and stand and recognize Him who spoke and the world was, each according to its greatness and its rank. They praise and glorify their Creator like the angels. And just as they recognize the Holy One, blessed be He, so do they recognize themselves. And they recognize the angels that are above them. And the knowledge of the stars and the spheres is less than the knowledge of the angels but greater than the knowledge of human beings."

[99]Slight modification of Psalm 19:2 where the text reads: "The heavens declare the glory of God, and the firmament showeth His handiwork."

[100]Steinschneider here inserts a lengthy philological footnote.

[101]Kalisch translates: they (the heavens) have intuitive speaking similar to human abstract ideas.

[102]Hebrew: *katzuv*, literally: fixed or limited; but Luzzatto points out the Hebrew word should be *Ka'or* meaning concavity. See my introduction to this book.

the air;[103] it is that part of this substance that is contiguous to the essence of the fire and therefrom is the essence of the air. The third form is the water; it is the part that is contiguous to the essence of the air and therefrom is the essence of the water. And the fourth form is the earth that is part of the remainder of the primordium, and it is the essence of the earth. Thus, the Lunar sphere rotates with these four essences. However, the earth is surrounded by the water except[104] for that which was clearly ordained by Divine wisdom to have the form of living creatures; and the air surrounds water and the earth on all sides; and the fire surrounds all three. And no part of them is at all empty.[105]

And these four essences do not have souls nor knowledge.[106] Rather, they are passive causes that are conducted through the help of their Creator with the powers bestowed upon them.[107] They generally encompass [each other] and maintain their place and their activities. When they are obliged to leave their natural places, He returns them and establishes them to remain there. This is the law of the Creator in regard to these

---

[103]Hebrew: *avir*. In his *Yesodei Hatorah* 3:10, Maimonides uses the word *ruach*, literally: wind or spirit.

[104]Literally: if not.

[105]This paragraph is cited somewhat differently in *Yesodei Hatorah* 3:10 as follows: "below the Lunar sphere, God created matter unlike the matter of the spheres, and He created four forms of this matter that are not like the form of the spheres. And each form was fixed in a certain portion of this matter. The first form is fire which combined with part of this matter and from these two there was the body of the fire. The second form is air [or spirit or wind; see note 103] which combined with part of it [i.e., fire] and from these two there was the body of the air. The third form is water which combined with part of it [i.e., air] and from these two there was the body of the water. And the fourth form is the earth which combined with part of it [i.e., water], and from these two there was the body of the earth. Thus there are four separate bodies below the firmament, one above the other. Each surrounds the one below it on all sides like a sphere. The first body, which is closest to the Lunar sphere, is the body of the fire; below that is the body of the air; below that is the body of the water; below that is the body of the earth. And there is no free space between them at all without a body."

[106]Kalisch translates: consciousness.

[107]See *Yesodei Hatorah* 3:11.

elements.[108] There is no substitute for His law and no change in His existence. [King] David, of blessed memory, said in the Psalm in which God is praised by the heavens that proclaim . . . (Psalm 148:6) that the fire and the water and His other wonderful creatures, do not overstep the boundaries that were created for them, and it is a law for them and they will not trangress it nor change it.[109]

And one who is stimulated and reflects upon the prophecy of Ezekiel and upon the general matters contained therein, in the spirit of his people, concerning the enumeration of the four fundamental elements[110] and the spirit of the four spheres, and [reflects upon] the fact that their movement is controlled by one Mover, and that there is a connection between the lower world and the upper world—his intellect, analytic powers, and understanding—will agree that these matters related to existence are deep secrets and wondrous topics. We have already explained all this in the *Guide of the Perplexed* and from there the connection and the relationship between the sensual world and

---

[108]Literally: portrayals or pictures.

[109]Maimonides is paraphrasing Psalm 148:6 whose text reads: "He hath established them forever; He hath given a law which shall not be transgressed": [i.e., the laws of nature do not change]. In his *Yesodei Hatorah* 3:11, Maimonides cites Psalm 148:7–8.

[110]Kalisch here adds the following footnote: "The ancient philosophers having had a very imperfect knowledge of astronomy and not having conjectured in the slightest degree the system of gravitation, they thought and even Aristotle and all his followers were of the same opinion, that the stars, being in constant motion, must consequently be animated living beings. Some, as for instance the Chaldeans, considered them as gods and worshipped them. Some venerated them as demi-gods, and some thought that they were angels. They observed also that some stars have more influence on the earth than others, they supposed them to be of different ranks, consisting of superior and inferior gods or angels. That our ancestors considered the stars as living beings or angels, is proved by several passages in the Bible. See Judges 5:20, Job 38:7, 8, etc. It is no wonder when on a starry night innumerable spirits shone so brightly over a people with a fiery oriental imagination, that they had appearances of God and angels on every corner. Any phenomenon that happened in the atmosphere was surely nothing else than the appearance of God or an angel. Since the stars are only shining bodies of matter, the angels cease to appear any more."

the spiritual world becomes clarified. Were it not for this connection and relationship, there would not be an appropriate path leading up to Him, but one would be withheld from perceiving the holy existence (?). And this is the meaning of the ladder of ascension that our forefather Jacob, of blessed memory, saw in his dream that is mentioned in the Bible.[111] We have also explained this [matter] in the *Guide of the Perplexed* and we completely elucidated it. Let the ignorant be stimulated and let the slumberer awaken so that they can perceive the clear light that shines for the worthy.

The four essences that are in the concavity[112] of the Lunar sphere [that is fire, air, earth and water] are the fundamental elements of all beings and things that perish including minerals, plants, living creatures, and others.[113] After this point has been clarified, there is no doubt that all natural bodies, other than the four fundamental elements, are composed of substance and form and their substance is compounded from the four fundamental elements. But each of the fundamental elements is composed only of substance and form; and each is not a [physical] body at all or something that exists with [physical] activity. This primordiality is the simple object that the noblemen of the children of Israel[114] saw portrayed in prophecy. This matter is explicitly clear to one who delves into

---

[111]Genesis 28:12. Steinschneider cites numerous ancient and medieval interpretations of Jacob's ladder including those of the poet Emanuel, Aristotle, Al Gazali, and several other Arabic writers. Much of the debate centers around the argument as to whether Jacob actually saw angels descending and ascending the ladder or whether it was all a dream.

[112]See note 102.

[113]In his *Yesodei Hatorah* 4:1, Maimonides states: "these four bodies which are fire, air, earth, and water, are the fundamental elements of all created things that are beneath the firmament. The substance of all things—man, beast, bird, reptile, fish, plant, mineral, precious stones and pearls, stones for buildings, mountains, and clods of earth—is composed of these four fundamental elements."

[114]That is, elders and prophets of Israel. The expression "nobles of the children of Israel" is used in Exodus 24:11 where it refers to Moses, Aaron and his sons, and the 70 elders.

it and becomes accustomed to the liking of the heavenly bodies. This, too, we have explained in the *Guide of the Perplexed.*

The nature of the fire and its movement is to ascend from the center to the periphery and to rest there. The nature of the earth is just the opposite. Similarly, the place of the water is where it rests naturally and to which it is directed. When there goes out from it of necessity in an upward direction, it spreads over the earth. And the air is found between the water and the fire and it, too, has its own specific place.[115]

The fire is naturally hot and dry and it is the lightest of the four fundamental elements. And the air is hot and moist; and the waters are cold and moist; and the earth is cold and dry; and the latter is the heaviest of them all. Next in heaviness is the water and for this reason water surrounds it.[116]

The rapidity and strength of the movement of the sphere results in the latters' binding to two [of the fundamental elements] including some fire which is always in air;[117] and it also traverses through water until it reaches dust, after which it takes refuse to its place through the powers with which it is endowed and during the time it traversed to the hollow of the earth.[118]

---

[115]In his *Yesodei Hatorah* 4:2, Maimonides states: "the nature of fire and air is to move from below, that is, from the center of the earth upward toward the firmament. The nature of water and earth is to move from below the firmament downward toward the center, because the center of the firmament is the lowest point below which there is no lower. Their movement is not conscious nor voluntary but represents conduct that was established in them and a nature impressed upon them."

[116]In his *Yesodei Hatorah* 4:2, Maimonides states: "the nature of the fire is hot and dry and it is the lightest of all. And the air is hot and moist and the waters are cold and moist, and the earth is dry and cold and it is the heaviest of all; and the water is lighter than the earth and is therefore found above on [the surface of] the earth. And the air is lighter than the water and therefore blows on the surface of the water. And the fire is lighter than the air."

[117]Literally: the air. The meaning here is unclear.

[118]I tried to translate this sentence as literally as possible but Maimonides' meaning is unclear. Steinschneider suggests that the phrase "after which it takes refuse to its place" its a textual misprint and should be "after which it returns to its place." Even with this emendation, the meaning is unclear.

These four substances and their properties undergo mixing and blending. The first type of mixing results in [different] types of minerals and these have various forms according to their various locations and rank. On the next level, if the mixing is better and closer to an equal mixture [of the four substances] there develop [different] types of plants, which receive their identification and form from those forms. These [plants] are more complete and more perfect than the forms of minerals because the former receive nourishment and grow. After that, with an increasing equality of mixing [of the elements], there develop living creatures that have perfect form for perception, voluntary movement, and respiration.[119] The most perfect of living creatures in mixture [of elements] and the most honorable among them and the closest to an equal [mixing] is the human being. Furthermore, even the human species is subdivided one from the other in terms of a range of levels of human forms. On the highest level among them and the most honorable among them are the prophets. Next are the renowned and prominent leaders, and after them are the Sages immersed [in Torah], followed by the masses. May He be praised that there [120] is the ultimate purpose for us to correctly perceive of His wisdom.

The parts of all bodies compounded from these four fundamental elements undoubtedly dissolve but their natural substance is not immediately lost since it is transformed into many other species[121] and in the end it returns to become [transformed back into] the four fundamental elements and

---

[119]In his *Yesodei Hatorah* 4:2, Maimonides describes the fact that the substance of every body that exists beneath the firmament, including man, beast—domestic and wild—bird, fish, plant, mineral, or stone, is composed of fire, air, water, and earth. He further notes that the predominating element in animals is fire and therefore the quality of heat is particularly noticeable in them. In stones, earth is the predominant element and therefore their main feature is dryness. Varying proportions of these four elements determine the nature of the body formed therein.

[120]That is, in man?

[121]Literally: it is impossible that it not return into many species.

there the transformation stops.[122] Accordingly, it is appropriate that we see existences coming into being and perishing. The
coming into being and the perishing do not overpower each
other and nothing is added to them nor subtracted from them.
Also, whatever is removed from one is added to another, but
nature is protected according to the relationship of the
spheres.[123]

These fundamental elements are constantly changing a little
at a time up to the movement of the spheres.[124] This [change]
occurs only in some of their closest parts.[125] Know also that
there is no form without matter and no matter without
form;[126] however, they are separated. But the intellects [of
humans] are not essences. The soul of a living being is the form
that the Creator, blessed be He, gave to it through the instru-
mentality of the angel of *asiyah*,[127] which we have mentioned

---

[122]In his *Yesodei Hatorah* 4:4, Maimonides states: "not everything that
perishes, perishes immediately [and transforms] into the four fundamental
elements. Rather it perishes and changes into something else and that
something else into yet something else. At the end, however, it reverts to the
fundamentals and thus all things continually recur."

[123]The meaning of this phrase is unclear.

[124]In his *Yesodei Hatorah* 4:6, Maimonides states that this change occurs
because of the movement (rotation) of the spheres.

[125]In his *Yesodei Hatorah* 4:5, Maimonides states: "these four fundamental
elements are constantly changing into one another, every day and every hour,
but only part of them, not all of them. How so? That part of the earth that is
closest to the water changes, crumbles, and becomes water. So too, that part
of the water closest to the air changes, becomes attenuated and transforms
into air. Similarly, that part of air closest to fire changes, becomes void and
turns into fire . . . these changes occur slowly over a long time period. And
not all of an element changes so that all the water would become air or all the
air fire because it is impossible for one of the four fundamental elements to
be totally nullified. Rather, only part of the fire turns to air and part of the air
to fire and so on between each and the other. Thus, transformations occur
among the four in a perpetual cycle."

[126]See *Yesodei Hatorah* 4:7.

[127]Literally: angel of performance or angel of creation. In his *Yesodei
Hatorah* 4:6, Maimonides states: "through the tenth [Hebrew: *asiri*] angel
which is the form called *Ishim*." Perhaps *asiyah* is a copyist's error for *asiri*!
Steinschneider interprets the angel of performance to refer to man's intellect.

and which is called *Ishim* in our language. The form of man is
the soul that speaks and apprehends abstract concepts of
substances, and this occurs when the soul is completed so that
it does not need an intermediary vessel[128] for its apprehension.
So, too, this intellectual human soul is not a physical substance
according to our understanding and we abide by the Torah of
Moses our teacher, may He rest in peace.[129] And this is an extra
teaching in the Torah in that [the soul] is not a physical
substance. By this we mean to say that God, praised be He,
endowed man with a soul that has the property of the aforementioned [nonphysical] form. Solomon, of blessed memory,
in his book[130] said: "and the spirit returneth unto the Lord"
(Ecclesiates 12:7), not in physical form with structure and
image. May God be praised for that which we have [just]
explained.

This power of speech is not the soul from which emanate
eating and drinking and fantasying[131] and reproduction and
nutrition. Rather, this power of intellect is the form of the
soul.[132] And the uninformed soul, by comparison with the
changes that occur to those [physical] forms of the soul [which
disintegrate], becomes ennobled when it separates from the
physical substances.[133] He who is devoid of that form is lacking

---

[128]Steinschneider changes the textual Hebrew term *keli atzmi*, literally its
own vessel, to *keli emtza'i*, intermediary vessel.

[129]*In his Yesodei Hatorah* 4:8, Maimonides states: "the soul of all flesh is the
form that God has given it. And the superior intelligence that is found in the
soul of man is the form of the man who is perfect in intelligence. It is to this
form that the Torah refers when it says, 'let us make man in our image, after
our likeness' [Genesis 1:26]; that is to say that man should have a form which
knows and which perceives temperaments that have no physical substance
[such as angels] and which resembles them. The Torah does not speak of this
form in regard to visible physical features such as the mouth, the nose, the
cheeks and other distinguishing body parts."

[130]That is, Ecclesiastes.

[131]Steinschneider amends the textual word *hora'ah* meaning teaching to
hirhur meaning meditation or reflection or fantasying.

[132]See *Yesodei Hatorah* 4:8.

[133]This sentence is stated slightly differently by Maimonides in his *Yesodei
Hatorah* 4:9.

success and goodness as Solomon, of blessed memory, asserted—that it is not good for the soul to be without intellect. He stated "also, that the soul be without knowledge is not good" (Proverbs 19:2).[134]

And now that it is verified that this soul is not at all physical and does not require physical [substance or body for its existence], there is no doubt that when it separates [from the human body] it returns to its beginning and to its origin from which it was formed[135] and it endures for all eternity. Its endurance has no limit. However, in bodily pleasure or in Gehenna, it is lost.[136] This is the [meaning of the] statement of Daniel: "And many of them that sleep in the dust of the earth shall awake . . . some to everlasting abhorrence" (Daniel 12:2) and this is a great curse.[137] And Isaiah said: "And they shall go forth and look upon the carcasses" (Isaiah 66:24), which means that the people of spiritual bliss will go forth and look upon the carcasses of the heretics who deny My existence—their judgment shall be overturned, "for their worm shall not die" (Isaiah 66:24).[138]

And these things, which are described in this chapter[139] and

---

[134]Steinschneider and Kalisch erroneously quote Proverbs 19:4.

[135]Steinschneider cites several opinions about the separation of the soul from the body at the time of death and the return of the physical body to the fundamental elements.

[136]The meaning is unclear. I have translated the phrase literally.

[137]This scriptural phrase from Daniel is frequently quoted in relation to the resurrection of the dead. Some Sages understand the phrase literally whereas others, including Maimonides, interpret it allegorically. See *Moses Maimonides' Treatise on Resurrection* (Fred Rosner, translator. New York: Ktav, 1982). Contrary to the prevailing view which held that resurrection of the dead and the world to come are a single continuum of spiritual existence, Maimonides espoused the opinion that resurrection includes not only spiritual but also physical resurrection and that the world to come, which is separate from and will follow the resurrection, will be wholly a spiritual world with spiritual beings without corporeality.

[138]The scriptural phrase ends with the phrase: "and they shall be an abomination unto all flesh." The word abhorrence (Hebrew: *dayra'on*) occurs again only in Daniel 12:2 in a similar connection.

[139]According to Steinschneider, this chapter refers to chapter 4 of Maimonides' *Yesodei Hatorah*.

are related to this topic, are like a drop from the ocean[140] in that these matters are deep and secret and cannot be fathomed save by one who is worthy thereof. But they are not as deep as the matters that we described in an earlier chapter.[141] These matters and their like are called *Maaseh Hayad*[142] by our Sages, which is an allusion to the sensual world. The earlier chapter is called *Yediyat Metziyuth Hakedushah*[143] and is an allusion to the spiritual world. And they have already warned, in the strongest possible terms, that the rare wise men[144] who are the extraordinary and exceptional people, who rise above the vista of animals[145] and quietly attempt to find the most high, and who strive with their soul to establish the truth of the delicacy of these matters, should not teach these matters at all to any single individual from among the masses. Behold, if you obtain the will of God by delving into these distinguished matters, and raise your head to the heavens to the existences on high, and analyze these creations, from angels to spheres, to the essences

---

[140]In his *Yesodei Hatorah* 4:10, Maimonides says: "all these matters that we have discussed in this matter are like a drop in the bucket and these matters are deep . . ."

[141]Chapters 1 and 2 of *Yesodei Hatorah*.

[142]Literally: work of the hand, that is, creation. In his *Yesodei Hatorah* 4:10, Maimonides uses the more usual expression *Maaseh Bereshit*, literally, Work of Creation, that is cosmology.

[143]Literally: knowledge of the existence of holiness. In his *Yesodei Hatorah* 4:11, Maimonides used the more usual expression *Maaseh Merkabah*, literally the "Work of the Chariot" referring to the first chapter of Ezekiel. The Talmud (*Chagigah* 13a) discusses the qualifications of a man to whom the mysteries of the Torah, that is, the Work of Creation (*Maaseh Bereshit*) and the Work of the Chariot (*Maaseh Merkabah*) may be taught. In his *Yesodei Hatorah* 4:11, Maimonides states: "the topic of the Work of the Chariot may not be expounded to an individual unless he is wise and understands from his own intellect. Even then only the headings of the topics are given to him. But the topic of the Work of Creation may be taught to an individual even if he cannot understand from his own intellect. We inform him as much as he is capable of understanding about these matters. And why is this topic not taught in public? [literally: to many] Because not every one has the breadth of understanding needed to clearly grasp the explanation and meaning of all these matters."

[144]Literally: survivors, remnants.

[145]That is, the materialistic and sensual horizon.

of the stars within them, and their movements, and how the upper world connects to the lower world, and the world of coming into being and perishing, and the wisdom of the Creator, may He be blessed, which is visible in man, and how that which is not material is revealed in a material body, and how it[146] is a microcosm related to the total world, there is no doubt that your love of the Creator will increase.[147] These creations are arranged by Him according to their relationship to Him in terms of their perfection and beauty and marvelous ranking, as well as the order that followed, which is protected[148] life. How fitting is the verity and perfection of these marvelous things and activities that were arranged by Him? In truth there are no real existences except these because if you direct the eyes of your heart and your mind[149] to all these existences and what is contained therein, you will arrive at the simple conclusion that without Him it would be impossible to understand these matters lest you die.

And just as you tire of looking at the sun [indirectly] on the wall, certainly you cannot hope of seeing its essence as it is.[150]

---

[146]That is, the material body, meaning man.

[147]See *Yesodei Hatorah* 4:12.

[148]That is, human.

[149]Literally: eyes of your heart and your mind will be strengthened. Maimonides uses a similar expression in his *Yesodei Hatorah* 4:7 where he states: "and the forms that have no substance are not visible to the eye but are known in the eye of the heart just as we know the Lord of the Universe without physical vision." Steinschneider, in a lengthy footnote, discusses the terms "eye of the heart" and "eye of the mind." He cites the analogy of a candle being the eye of light just as the intellect is the eye of the soul, and the sun is the light of the world just as the soul is the light of the body. Steinschneider also speaks of the "eye of reward and punishment."

[150]Steinschneider points out that the analogy of one's inability to look directly into the sun is an old one. The Talmud (*Chullin* 59b) describes a discussion between the Emperor and Rabbi Joshua ben Chananiah in which the former said, "I wish to see your God." He replied "You cannot see Him." The Emperor insisted so he placed the Emperor facing the sun during the summer solstice and said to him, "Look up at it." He replied, "I cannot." Said Rabbi Joshua, "If at the sun which is but one of the ministers that attend the Holy One, blessed be He, you cannot look, how then can you presume to look upon the Divine presence?" See also Maimonides' *Guide of the Perplexed* 1:59

And [King] David, may he rest in peace, said [about this matter] that silence [is appropriate] when apprehending [God].[151]

And delving into these matters was called *Pardes* by the Sages.[152] You already know their famous statement[153] about the four scholars who entered the *Pardes*, only one of whom departed in peace because of their different degrees of Divine apprehension.[154]

And from these fundamental principles of the Torah you can recognize that the Creator can appoint anyone He wishes as a prophet, and that He can speak with whomever He chooses

---

where he states that philosophers assert: "we are dazzled by His beauty, and He is hidden from us because of the intensity with which He becomes manifest, just as the sun is hidden to eyes that are too weak to apprehend it." Steinschneider cites other sources where this analogy is mentioned.

[151]Steinschneider suggests that Maimonides is referring to Psalm 65:2, "Silence is praise to Thee", which is quoted in his *Guide of the Perplexed* 1:59 immediately after the analogy to the sun.

[152]Literally: paradise, garden, enclosure, preserve, park.

[153]*Chagigah* 14b: "Four men entered the *Pardes*, namely, Ben Azzai, Ben Zoma, Acher [Elisha ben Abuyah] and Rabbi Akiba. Rabbi Akiba said to them: When ye arrive at the stones of pure marble [giving the illusion of water), say not water, water [i.e., how can we proceed?]. For it is said: "He that speaketh falsehood shall not be established before mine eyes" [Psalm 101:7]. Ben Azzai cast a look and died. Of him Scripture says: "Precious in the sight of the Lord is the death of His saints" [Psalm 116:15]. Ben Zoma looked and became demented. Of him Scripture says: "Hast thou found honey? Eat so much as is sufficient for thee, lest thou be filled therewith, and vomit it" [Proverbs 25:16]. Acher mutilated the shoots [i.e., became an apostate]. Rabbi Akiba departed unhurt." Some commentators interpret this account of the entry of the four Rabbis into paradise literally. Others consider *Pardes* a figurative expression for the mystical realm of theosophy. Rashi explains that the four scholars ascended to heaven and Tosafot adds that it only appeared to them that they did so. Rabbi Chananel and others explain that the entry of the Rabbis into the *Pardes* was only a vision.

[154]Literally: because of the strengths of their measure. In his *Yesodei Hatorah* 4:13, Maimonides states: "And the topics of these four chapters which relate to these five commandments are what the earliest Sages called *Pardes* as they stated: four went into the *Pardes*. And although they were great men of Israel and great Sages, they did not all possess the capacity to know and to grasp all these subjects clearly." See also Maimonides, *Guide of the Perplexed* 1:32 and 3:51.

from among human beings.[155] However, prophecy does not fall upon one unless he is worthy of it.[156] And the Sages have stipulated that he be a great Sage,[157] honorable, apt in the conduct of his affairs, and whose intellect reigns and triumphs over his physical passions. What is an apt man? He who carries himself so that the impression of his soul becomes so strong that he raises his head to ascend to the higher beings; and he who distances himself from the physical and sensual world[158] to the eternal world and who, according to his ability, totally turns to apprehension of His Creator; and he who avoids mingling with the masses and associating himself with them. Rather, he

---

[155]See Maimonides, *Guide of the Perplexed* 2:32.

[156]In his *Yesodei Hatorah* 7:1, Maimonides states as follows: "It is among the fundamental principles of our faith to recognize that God appoints prophets from among human beings. But prophecy does not occur save to a scholar who is great in wisdom and strong in his moral characteristics. His passions do not overcome him in anything whatsoever but he always overcomes his passions through his rational faculty. He has an extremely broad and sedate mind. A person who is full of these characteristics, perfect in his body when he enters the *Pardes*, and dwells continuously on these great but abstruse matters, and has the proper intellect to understand to grasp them, and who sanctifies himself, and withdraws from the ways of the average people who walk in the darkness of the times, and who zealously trains himself and his soul not to entertain a single thought of senseless matters and the vanities of the time and its intrigues, but whose mind is always facing upwards as though bound beneath the Celestial Throne."

[157]Steinschneider suggests that the word physician is an error of the translator from Arabic into Hebrew. The Arabic word *chakim* means physician but also wise man or philosopher. Steinschneider also suggests that Maimonides is referring to the talmudic expression (*Shabbat* 92a) that prophecy only rests upon one who is wise, strong, wealthy, and tall. Elsewhere (*Nedarim* 38a) the Talmud substitutes humble for tall. The actual talmudic phrase has the phrase "Divine presence" instead of "prophecy." In quoting these talmudic expressions in his *Eight Chapters* (see edition by J. I. Gorfinkle, New York: AMS Press, 1966, p. 80), Maimonides explains that "wise" refers to mental perfection and that "wealth" refers to moral contentment. The personal traits needed for prophethood are also described by Maimonides in his *Introduction to the Commentary on the Mishnah* (see edition of Fred Rosner, New York: Feldheim, 1975, p. 50) and in his *Mishnah Commentary on Sanhedrin* (see edition of Fred Rosner, New York: Sepher-Hermon, 1981, pp. 152–155); see also his *Guide of the Perplexed* 3:54.

[158]Literally: world of causes and touching.

withdraws from that which is not Divine and purifies his soul and concentrates[159] on the contents of his heart so that it becomes bound with the Celestial Throne,[160] and immerses his character to comprehend those amazing forms.[161]

There is no doubt that the angels will flutter with their wings over such a person[162] and will cleave to him with the Holy Spirit. When he reaches such [a level] there is no doubt that he has attained the high level of the angels which are called *Ishim*.[163] The Sages have metaphorically used the expression "active intellect" to describe this state. He will then find himself to be among the celestial beings and try to raise himself even higher to a level that is too lofty for us.[164] And one may say that he has gone from darkness to light,[165] and turned to the fire that is everlasting fire and to the heaven that is everlasting heaven.[166] It is to this that Isaiah alluded when he spoke (Isaiah 66:22) of the renewal of the heaven and of the earth.[167] These matters and the ascent to these levels [of spirituality] are like death, as the prophet Samuel told Saul when they enthroned him over the children of Israel: "go to that group of prophesiers who consider themselves to be prophets; adopt their

---

[159]Literally: calls.

[160]Literally: throne of the king.

[161]That is, spiritual beings. In his *Yesodei Hatorah* 7:1, Maimonides uses the expression "pure and holy forms."

[162]Literally: soul.

[163]In his *Yesodei Hatorah* 7:1, Maimonides states: "And when the spirit rests upon him, his soul will mingle at the level of the angels called *Ishim*."

[164]In his *Yesodei Hatorah* 7:1, Maimonides states: "He will be changed into another man and will himself understand that he is not as he had been but has become exalted above other wise men."

[165]Steinschneider, citing other authors, speaks of the darkness of atheism and the light of faith.

[166]Literally: fire except fire and heaven except heaven.

[167]Steinschneider refers the reader to *Laws of Repentance* 18:8 (but there are only 10 chapters in Maimonides' *Laws of Repentance*) and the *Guide of the Perplexed* 2:29, which deals with the explanation of scriptural phrases implying the destruction of heaven and earth. Steinschneider also cites other sources (such as the Talmud, the Midrash, the *Book of Kuzari*, and several Arabic works) dealing with the renewal of the world, the world to come, and the resurrection of the dead.

beliefs and be among them and you will be converted by their influence and be transformed into another man." [1 Samuel 10:6]

And there are different levels of prophets who prophesy, just as there are different [levels] of wisdom among the Sages.[168] The form of their prophecy is not restrained, whether it was through a vision during the night[169] or during the day at a time of wakefulness after they have been overcome by a deep sleep.[170] It [171] belongs to the sensual world and is associated with trembling and quivering [of the limbs of the prophet], and diminution in physical strength and loss of one's ideas and thoughts and sensations. Only the power of speech remains, which is within the abstract intellect and is repulsed by physical substances. And he understands what he is to prophesy and the forms, such as allegories, of the matters that he is to use, and they become impressed in his soul and he grasps their meaning and what they signify to him and how they are to be interpreted.[172] Then his internal speech is transformed into his external speech and these are the qualities[173] that point to these matters.

Indeed, some prophets recite the allegory and explain it,[174] whereas others prophesy using only the allegory. Prophets do not prophesy at any time that they please; rather they must prepare their thoughts and purify their souls and set aside any bond with worldly matters and be cheerful[175] and good tempered.[176] Our

---

[168]See *Yesodei Hatorah* 7:2.

[169]That is, in a dream.

[170]Literally: rest. In *Yesodei Hatorah* 7:2, Maimonides actually uses the term *tardemah* meaning an overpowering sleep.

[171]That is, prophecy.

[172]In his *Yesodei Hatorah* 7:3, Maimonides states: "The matters that are communicated to a prophet in a prophetic vision are communicated to him in an allegorical form. Immediately he engraves in his heart the interpretation of the allegory in the prophetic vision and he understands its meaning . . ."

[173]Literally: *goodnesses* (Hebrew *tovot*); perhaps: *words* (Hebrew: *teyvot*).

[174]In his *Yesodei Hatorah* 7:3, Maimonides states: "and interpret it."

[175]Literally: encourage their souls.

[176]Literally: goodhearted. In his *Yesodei Hatorah* 7:4, Maimonides states: "All the prophets did not prophesy at any time they pleased but had to concentrate their minds and be restful and happy and cheerful and in solitude . . ."

Sages said[177] that prophecy does not rest upon prophets if they
are lazy or angry but only if they are diligent and joyful. For this
reason, the disciples of the prophets employed different types of
musical instruments and the harp and melodies when they prepared themselves to prophesy.[178] Thusly did Elisha, of blessed
memory, act when the king asked him whether he should wage
war with the enemy, and Elisha became angry when he saw the
[idolatry of the] masses of the people; and he said: "bring me a
musician" (2 Kings 3:15), and his soul became calmed and the
Divine spirit rested upon him.[179] So too did [King] David, of
blessed memory, prepare himself (2 Samuel 6:14) after he sang in
the Holy Temple[180] and he rejoiced in what he saw until he
brought himself [in the proper frame of mind] to the point that he
leaped and removed his regal clothes and set aside his princeliness.
And when this was pointed out to him, he said: "how precious and
exalted it is to appear before one's Master with abandon,"[181] and
he removed the veil[182] so that this should not be foreign on him.

---

[177]Talmud *Shabbat* 30b and *Pesachim* 66b and 117a. See also Maimonides,
Eight Chapters, Chapter 7.

[178]In his *Yesodei Hatorah* 7:4, Maimonides states: "Therefore the pupils of
prophets had before them the psaltery, the tabret, the flute and the harp, and
they seek prophecy . . ." See 1 Samuel 10:5.

[179]Steinschneider cites several sources including Saadyah Gaon who speak
of the relationship of music to prophecy and the use of music by kings.

[180]There was no Temple at the time of David; must be a mistranslation
from the Arabic.

[181]Hebrew: *pereeshut*, usually translated "self restraint" but here meaning
separating oneself from the physical world for the sake of spiritual ecstasy.

[182]In a lengthy footnote, Steinschneider cites numerous authors who speak of
the removal of the veil or the setting aside of an intervening covering or curtain
or shade. The analogy refers to the removal of impediments to the proper
recognition and understanding of the conditions needed for a prophet to
prophesy. Steinschneider points out the use of this metaphor in Eastern cultures,
especially among the Persians. The metaphor is also used in relation to Moses
(Exodus 34:34) who is said to have seen God through a clear glass (*Yebamot* 49b).
The physical body and the sensual world are coverings or impediments to the
proper spiritual serving of God. Other interpretations of this veil or covering are
physical death and the human heart. In his *Guide of the Perplexed* 3:9, Maimonides
speaks of the screen and partition that prevents him from perfectly perceiving
abstract ideas. He further states (*Yebamot* 3:51) that we should remove everything

And some of those who prepare themselves for prophecy
and who seek the work of prophethood succeed in finding it
and others do not succeed in finding it.[183] The prophecy may
be vouchsafed to a prophet, intended for him alone,[184] for God
provides him with prophecy in that He extends to him and
teaches him of His wisdom and does not send anyone else.[185]
He may be sent to a particular nation or to the inhabitants of a
certain city to make them conduct themselves properly,[186] and
to remind them what they are to do and to warn them against
doing evil. Such [action on the part of the prophet] is impossible without him having intimate Divine perception and political
power.

---

that is an obstruction and a partition between us and God. The metaphor of the
veil is also found in the *Targum* translation of Psalm 101:6. Elsewhere, Maimonides
(*Eight Chapters*, Chapter 7) devotes an entire chapter to these walls or veils which
separate.

[183]In his *Yesodei Hatorah* 7:5, Maimonides states: "Those who seek to
prophesy are called the pupils of the prophets. Although they concentrate
their minds, the Divine Presence might or might not rest upon them."

[184]Literally: and the prophecy will be in the lap of that prophet alone.

[185]Steinschneider discusses at length the differences and similarities between a prophet and a messenger of God. Although some authors posit that
a prophet foretells the future and a messenger comes to teach us Torah,
Steinschneider considers this view to be erroneous. He equates the two terms
and cites numerous biblical, talmudic, Arabic, and other ancient and medieval
works to prove his point. Moses said to the Lord: "send, I pray thee, by the
hand of him whom thou wilt send" (Exodus 4:13) in speaking of his mission
to Pharaoh. All angels are messengers of God. Steinschneider also discusses
the individuality of human beings, no two people being alike since the creation of Adam in the image of God. Also described is the meaning of the
expression "opening of the heart" in relation to a prophet. In addition, the
various names given to Moses such as the Master of all Prophets are cited. See
also Maimonides, *Guide of the Perplexed* 2:34. Finally, Steinschneider discusses
the various books of the prophets and returns to an elucidation of the terms
prophet and messenger citing Judah Halevi's *Book of Kuzari* 41:4 which states
that "a prophet is a messenger," and Maimonides' *Yesodei Hatorah* 10:1 which
speaks of "a prophet who claims that God sent him," and the *Guide of the
Perplexed* 3:29 which states "a prophet is a messenger of the moon." Maimonides is here quoting the opinion of the Sabeans.

[186]Literally: to straighten them. See *Yesodei Hatorah* 7:7. Steinschneider has
another lengthy linguistic footnote dealing with the term *to straighten*. He
points out that prophets are called straighteners or leaders.

Any human being who achieves prophethood after Moses our teacher, of blessed memory, and who states that God has sent him, does not have to [prove his] command by splitting the sea, for instance, or by changing the laws of nature.[187] Rather, he should reprimand the people,[188] and what he says should be correct, and he must possess the requisites needed for prophethood that we have mentioned.[189] And he should instruct the people to serve the Lord, may He be praised, and [to believe in] His unity and to reject Divine plurality.[190] He must, in general, command [the people to do] good, which leads to the ultimate success,[191] and warn them against doing evil, which would prevent it.[192] We are obligated to accept [such a prophet] at all times since his teachings do not contradict any of the fundamental principles of the Torah of Moses our teacher, of blessed memory, and these are the thirteen

---

[187]In his *Yesodei Hatorah* 7:7, Maimonides states that a prophet may show a sign or a token or perform a miracle to prove that God has, in truth, sent him. But not everyone who shows a sign or performs a miracle is believed to be a prophet. Only if a man whom we know is worthy of prophethood by virtue of his wisdom and deeds, whereby he stands above all his contemporaries and conducts himself in the ways of prophethood, in its sanctity and its renunciation, shows a sign or token or performs a miracle and says that God sent him—is it one's duty to listen to him.

[188]Literally: speak in the world. Prophets reprimand as exemplified by Isaiah 29:21 and Amos 5:10.

[189]See footnote 156.

[190]Literally: to distance any partners from Him.

[191]Does ultimate success refer to his mission or perhaps the world to come or to the material or spiritual success of the Jews on this world? The meaning is unclear.

[192]In a lengthy footnote, Steinschneider points out that since we have a single Torah that, we believe, is never changing, prophets after Moses can only reprimand the people and call them to return to and obey the laws of the Torah and to seek the truth and justice and righteousness and to avoid evil and falsehood and to believe in reward for the righteous and punishment for the wicked. Steinschneider then draws on Jewish and Arabic sources to discuss whether or not Abraham was a prophet and recognized God before He spoke with him, and whether there were other prophets before Moses such as Adam and Noah. Steinschneider concludes with a discussion of characteristics of prophets and the contents of their prophecies.

fundamental principles that we have mentioned.[193] Our intention is to serve God and to eliminate images of Him, and to walk in the path of righteousness.[194]

Chapter 3

There are different human intellects just as there are different [body] constitutions. There are some people who are irascible and are assuaged only with such extreme difficulty that it is nearly impossible to do. There are others who are calm and easily appeased and who hardly ever get angry. There are yet others who are very arrogant and others who are extremely humble.[195] The same is true about the other tenden-

---

[193]In his Commentary on the Mishnah, Tractate Sanhedrin, *Perek Chelek* (see English edition by Fred Rosner entitled *Moses Maimonides' Mishnah Commentary on Sanhedrin*, New York: Sepher-Hermon, 1981), pp. 151–158.

[194]Chapter 8 of Maimonides' *Yesodei Hatorah* deals with the prophecy of Moses and challenges to it by other prophets. Chapter 9 deals with prophets other than Moses and their prophecies and rules that apply toward the recognition of prophets. Chapter 10 deals with false prophets. None of these three chapters is recapitulated in the present treatise, perhaps because of his lengthy discussions of prophethood elsewhere, especially in his *Guide of the Perplexed* and his *Commentary on the Mishnah*. (See footnote 157.)

[195]See Maimonides, *Laws of Temperaments (Hilchot De'ot)* 1:1 in his *Mishneh Torah* where he states that: "every human being is endowed with many temperaments and each is different from the other and very far apart from it. There is one type of man who is quick-tempered and always angry and there is another type of man whose mind is at ease and who is not angry at all; and if he does become angry, he is only mildly vexed once in many years. And there is another type of man who is excessively arrogant; and one who is extremely humble. And there is one who is a sensualist whose soul's desire can never be satisfied; and there is one whose heart is extremely pure and does not even long for the few things that the body needs. And there is one who is so greedy that his soul would not be satisfied with all the money in the world as the matter is stated: "He that loveth silver shall not be satisfied with silver" [Ecclesiastes 5:9]. And there is one who is frugal so that he is content with even a very small amount which is insufficient for him; and he does not pursue the attainment of all his needs. And there is one who tortures himself through starvation and hoarding; he does not consume a penny's worth of his own without great anguish. And there is one who intentionally squanders all his money. The other temperaments can be similarly viewed: such as the

cies and qualities with which people are endowed. There are
some people inclined to extremes and others who have an
intermediate tendency; the latter is the best path to follow. It is
proper for someone desirous of having praiseworthy characteristics, and commendable and esteemed qualities, to remain
far from both extremes and to follow an intermediate course in
all his activities.[196]

One example of this is that a person should not [always]
refrain from anger and indignation against living creatures,
nor should he totally suppress his power of anger because he
needs it to overcome his sensual desires[197] and specific animal
instincts,[198] and to neutralize the evil at its source.[199]

A person who follows an intermediate course in all his activities
and who distances himself equally from the two extremes is called
by us a Sage.[200] And if he improves his soul and regulates it so that
he inclines it somewhat in the direction of one of the extremes, he
is called a righteous man.[201] Such is one who leans in humility
towards the extreme. There are other similar examples[202] and this

---

jovial and the melancholic, the miserly and the generous, the cruel and the
merciful, the soft-hearted and the stout-hearted, and their like."

[196]See *Hilchot De'ot* 1:2.

[197]Literally: the power of lust.

[198]Literally: soul of animals.

[199]In his *Hilchot De'ot* 1:4, Maimonides states that "one should not be an
angry person, easily enraged nor like a dead person who cannot feel. Rather,
steer the middle course. One should become irked only over something
serious over which it is proper to become angered in order that such a thing
not be done again. Similarly, one should not lust for things save those that the
body needs and without which it is impossible to live."

[200]See note 157. Here Maimonides certainly refers to a wise man as he
specifically states in his *Hilchot De'ot* 1:4 that "every man whose temperaments
are intermediate and follows the middle path is called a wise man."

[201]Steinschneider refers the reader to Maimonides' *Eight Chapters*, Chapter
5 and his *Guide* 3:23 concerning the terms pious, righteous, saintly, and so on.

[202]See *Hilchot De'ot* 1:5 where Maimonides states: "and he who is extremely
strict with himself and deviates slightly from the intermediate temperament
to one side or the other is called a righteous man. How is this done? He who
removes himself from haughtiness of an extreme degree and becomes
excessively humble is called a righteous person and this is the characteristic of
righteousness. If one only removes oneself to the intermediate degree and

is the healing of his soul and its medication.

However, He [203] also commanded us in following the middle course by conducting ourselves with the attribute of compassion.[204] Our Sages have asserted that when the Almighty, praised be He, said in the Torah (Leviticus 19:1 ff) that we should serve Him and emulate His attributes, it means that we should be merciful because He is merciful; we should be gracious because He is gracious; we should be holy because He is holy.[205] If anyone finds himself straying from the intermediate and middle path, he should try to lean towards the correct and righteous path and cure himself of such bad conduct and evil diversions.[206]

---

becomes humble, one is called a wise man and this is the characteristic of wisdom. Similarly with all the other temperaments. And the righteous men of old used to direct their temperaments from intermediate degrees towards the two extremes."

[203]The Almighty.

[204]From the biblical phrase "and thou shalt walk in His ways" (Deuteronomy 28:9) the rabbis deduce (*Shabbat* 133b) that we must emulate God by displaying His attributes of mercy, compassion, graciousness, holiness, and so on. See also Maimonides, *Guide of the Perplexed* 1:54.

[205]In his *Hilchot De'ot* 1:5, Maimonides cites Deuteronomy 28:9 rather than Leviticus 19:1—"And we are commanded to follow these intermediate paths and these are the good and the proper paths as it is written: "And thou shalt walk in His ways" (Deuteronomy 28:9).

The Sages taught the following explanation for this commandment: "Just as He is called Gracious, so you too should be gracious; just as He is called Merciful, so you too should be merciful; just as He is called Holy, so you too should be holy." And in this manner did the prophets call the Almighty with all those attributes: Long-suffering, Abundant in kindness, Righteous and Just, Perfect, Strong and Powerful and their like in order to tell us that these are good and just paths, and a person is obligated to conduct himself by them and to emulate Him as much as one can."

[206]In his *Hilchot De'ot* 1:7, Maimonides gives advice on how to prevent such evil digressions or deviations. He states: "How should a person accustom himself to these temperaments so that they become ingrained in him? Let him practice again and again the actions that he performs according to these intermediate temperaments and repeat them constantly until these acts become easy for him and until they are no longer a burden on him. And then these temperaments will become ingrained in his soul." See also Maimonides, *Commentary on Tractate Abot* 3:19.

And the soul has health and sickness just like the physical
body. The method that clearly reveals its condition as to
whether it is healthy or sick is to examine it. If one observes it[207]
to be absorbed in a beneficial activity, deriving pleasure therefrom and being happy thereby, and if it would be grieved if an
undesirable activity would result therefrom and it would be
pained thereby, and it strives for that [beneficial] activity, then
it is apparent that it is completely perfect and that great
goodness has been prepared for it. But if one observes it
deriving pleasure from an evil activity from which there
develop afflictions to the welfare[208] of another and even to the
welfare of his enemy, and if the result thereof gives it great
pleasure as long as it itself is not pained thereby, and if it
considers it bad to see good in the welfare of another and finds
it difficult to remove this from the soul even when isolated,[209]
if it [210] has such a characteristic, it is undoubtedly walled off
from the truth[211] and cannot reach it. The above has been
verified by intellect, analysis, and explanation[212] as I will
mention; that is to say, it is well known that nothing can receive
anything unless the latter resembles it and is appropriate for it.
Now that we have established that it is impossible for each soul
not to stand before the True One, may He be praised,[213] to
receive recompense for what it[214] has done, there is no doubt
that it will not transgress, since truth is the only thing that

---

[207]That is, the soul.

[208]Literally: veracity or truth.

[209]Meaning unclear.

[210]The evil soul.

[211]Literally: has a veil from the truth. See note 182.

[212]In his *Hilchot De'ot* 2:1 Maimonides states that "people whose souls are
sick lust for and love bad temperaments and despise the proper path and are
lazy to walk therein and it is extremely burdensome on them according to the
severity of their ailment." See also Maimonides, *Eight Chapters*, Chapter 3.
Maimonides also describes the cure for people with sick souls; see *Hilchot De'ot*
2:1–2.

[213]Steinschneider points out that this phrase, as applied to the term truth,
is derived from the talmudic assertion (*Shabbat* 55a) that the seal of the Holy
One is truth.

[214]The soul.

stands by the soul of a person. For the truth is good and does not accept disgrace. It is a complete good, and one who is steeped in evil will not dwell in His holy dwelling.

Therefore, a person is admonished to know his soul and to purify it from evil activity and adorn it with excellent attributes. The lowliest qualities are haughtiness, insolence, and constant lowly physical lusts.[215] Excellent attributes[216] are humility, the performance of [217] good for one's enemy and certainly for one's friend [because a man does not deserve praise for loving his friend], and contentment and restraint with that which lies within one's view.

In the matter of Divine Providence, His will is directed toward and bestowed upon those whom He desires and these are the prophets and the leaders. And the known [future] prosperity of the righteous is the ultimate life,[218] and that is life in which there is no death; it is good and there is no bad mixed in; it is pure and there is no turbidity blended therein. And that is what is written in the Torah: "and that thy days may be prolonged" (Deuteronomy 6:2), that is to say that it may be well with you in the world that is all good and long[219] and has no end nor limit.

And the reward and the recompense of the righteous from

---

[215]Literally: physical toils.

[216]In a lengthy footnote, Steinschneider indicates that Maimonides is here listing the lowly qualities that disqualify a person for prophecy and the admirable qualities that are a necessary requisite for prophethood. Steinschneider also feels that Maimonides is here alluding to Mohammed and that the latter could not have been chosen by God for prophethood because he did not possess the qualities of wisdom, strength of spirit, and humility. Mohammed himself, in the Koran, admits that he was an unlearned man, and that he had a lust for coitus.

[217]Literally: acceptance of.

[218]Literally: the last life.

[219]In his *Commentary on Chelek*, Maimonides cites Deuteronomy 22:7 that states "that it may be well with thee, and that thou mayest prolong thy days." Rabbis (*Kiddushin* 39b and *Chullin* 142a) interpret the first half of this Scriptural sentence to refer to "the world which is all good" and the second half to "the world which is infinitely long." See also Maimonides, *Guide of the Perplexed* 3:28.

God is that they will attain these pleasantnesses and will live this [eternal] life and will prosper in that prosperity. Similarly, the death of heretics separates them from all these pleasant-nesses[220] and they remain with suffering that no man can portray.

And the Sages who know the Torah have stated that in the ultimate world there are no physical bodies at all.[221] The souls of the righteous, which are hidden, see but do not eat[222] but are like angels that feast on the abundant and splendid and great light. There is no higher light than this truth. Since they lose their physical substance [in the eternal world], they also lose their need and striving for eating and drinking and sexual intercourse. These attributes[223] become sanctified and purified and elevated from the deficiencies, and these are the attributes of angels. He who cannot see sweetness and cannot see enjoy-ments other than in eating and drinking and sexual intercourse and their like—as he portrays [to himself] certain enjoyments in the Garden of Eden—says to this implicitly deprived person: "perhaps the life of angels is sweeter and more pleasant than the enjoyments of eating and drinking." These souls that are

---

[220]Steinschneider refers the reader to Maimonides' *Eight Chapters*, Chapter 7 and his *Guide of the Perplexed* 3:51.

[221]For Maimonides' concept of eternal life, the world to come, the Messianic Age, and the resurrection of the dead, see his *Treatise on Resurrec-tion* (Fred Rosner, translator, New York: Ktav, 1982) and his *Commentary on Chelek*. Briefly, Maimonides makes a rigid demarcation between the Messianic Age in which events retain their physical context, and the world to come where existence is spiritual only. Denial of miracles is heresy, continues Maimonides. Intellectuals attempt to explain miracles as supernatural events whereas rabbinic sages try to explain them as natural phenomena. Mai-monides points out that the biblical phrases that pertain to resurrection are allegorical and not to be understood literally. The immortality of the soul is a natural phenomenon whereas the resurrection of the dead is a miracle. Maimonides repeats that he firmly believed in resurrection and that he regarded it as one of the cardinal principles of Judaism.

[222]See *Berachot* 17a where it states that "in the future world, there is no eating nor drinking nor procreation nor business nor jealousy nor hatred nor competition, but the righteous sit with their crowns on their heads feasting on the brightness of the Divine Presence."

[223]Literally: matters.

dependent on[224] sprouting and nourishment are not vital.[225] Rather, it is the activity[226] of the soul that speaks. The activity is the intellect and such a soul, which is perfected by such an activity, has, according to its ability, traversed and reached the existence of its Creator, and has reached the holy and separate forms. There is no doubt that it will reach the highest exis- tence and will live an everlasting life.[227] And this is the splendid recompense and the great and good reward that the intellect cannot fathom. There is no pleasanter [reward].

And since we have already discussed some aspects of the health of the soul, we will add[228] some general principles and regulations, as appropriate, concerning the preservation of one's physical health. The latter is a precondition for the health of the soul and the orderly discharge of its activities.[229]

It is appropriate for a person to avoid those things that are injurious and detrimental to the body. He should consume simple and nutritious foods[230] that will keep him in tranquility and preserve his health.[231] Among these [rules] it is appropri- ate that he not eat except when he is hungry, and not drink except when he is thirsty. And he should examine himself at all times in regard to the excretion of superfluities and should not carry that burden at all whenever he feels the need [to eliminate his wastes], and this is very important.[232]

---

[224]Literally: from which are arranged.

[225]That is, physical.

[226]Literally: form.

[227]Literally: a life with no end.

[228]Literally: compose or write.

[229]Maimonides' concept of a healthy mind in a healthy body is one of the earliest descriptions of psychosomatic medicine. See *Moses Maimonides' Two Treatises on the Regimen of Health* (A. Bar Sela, H. E. Hoff and E. Faris, Philadelphia: American Philosophical Society, 1964).

[230]Literally: equal and honorable foods.

[231]In his *Hilchot De'ot* 4:1, Maimonides asserts that "since when the body is healthy and sound one treads in the ways of the Lord, it being impossible to understand or know anything of the knowledge of the Creator when one is sick, it is obligatory upon man to avoid things that are detrimental to the body and acclimatize himself to things that heal and fortify it."

[232]In his *Hilchot De'ot* 4:1, Maimonides continues, "These are as follows: A

It is proper not to fill one's abdomen to satiation but one
should diminish one's intake so that one remains one-fourth
short of satiation.[233] And one should drink very little water
when one consumes food. Before eating, one should perform
some exercises and eliminate superfluities. Washing after the
exercises is appropriate and after that one can eat.[234] After
eating it is appropriate to rest. Movement during eating or
[immediately] thereafter gives rise to many sicknesses.[235]

person should never eat except when he is hungry nor drink unless he is
thirsty. He should not postpone his eliminations for even a single moment;
rather, every time that micturition or defecation become necessary, he should
respond thereto immediately." See also *Berachot* 62b and *Makkot* 16b where it
states that withholding one's bodily functions comes under the heading of
"You shall not make yourselves abominable" (Leviticus 11:43). Besides, it
gives rise to bad diseases and endangers life (*Hilchot Maachalot Assurot* 17:31).
Also (*Shabbat* 33a): More people die from intestinal disorders than from
hunger.

[233]In his *Hilchot De'ot* 4:2, Maimonides recommends that "a person should
not eat until his stomach is replete but should diminish his intake by
approximately one-fourth of satiation. One should not drink water during
meals save a little and mixed with wine. When the food commences to be
digested in the intestines, one may drink as much water as one finds
necessary. However, even after the food has been digested, he should not
imbibe the water excessively." See also *Gittin* 70a, *Berachot* 42b, and *Niddah*
24b.

[234]See *Hilchot De'ot* 4:2 where Maimonides states that "one should not eat
until one has examined oneself carefully lest it be necessary to excrete wastes.
A person should not eat until he has walked prior to the meal so that his body
begins to become warmed, or he should perform a physical task or tire
himself by some other form of exertion. The rule in this matter is that one
should exert one's body and fatigue it every day in the morning until one's
body begins to warm. Then one rests a little until one's soul has settled and
then one may eat. If one washes with warm water after the exercise, so much
the better. After this, one should wait a little and then eat." See also the
Talmud: Anybody who takes in more drink than food undermines his health
(*Niddah* 24b). He who requires easing himself and still goes on eating is like a
furnace stoked on top of its ashes—which is the beginning of a bad odor
(*Shabbat* 82a). There are three kinds of perspiration that do the body good,
among them that which comes from work (*Avot deRabi Nathan* 41). Work is
valuable, because a man gets warmed up by it (*Gittin* 16b).

[235]See *Hilchot De'ot* 4:3 where Maimonides asserts: "When a person eats, he
should always be sitting in his place or reclining on the left side. He should
not walk nor ride nor exercise nor agitate his body, nor should he promenade

The number of hours in the day and the night is twenty-four and it is sufficient for a person to sleep for one-third of them.[236] He should not sleep on his face nor on his back but lying on his left side at the beginning of the night and then on his right side at its end. And he should not go to sleep immediately after a meal but about four hours later.[237] Before eating it is proper to consume laxative[238] foods such as grapes and figs and the heart of gourds but one should not consume them with the meal but somewhat before it. After the meal one should consume constipating[239] items such as pomegranates and apples.[240]

And if a person has before him fowl and beef, he should give precedence to fowl over other meats. And he should give precedence to eggs over fowl. And the general rule is that he should give precedence to the lighter [food] over the

---

until the food is digested in his intestines. Any one who promenades immediately after his meal or who fatigues himself brings upon himself serious and grave illnesses." See also *Gittin* 70a, *Berachot* 46b, *Pesachim* 108a, *Shabbat* 129b, and *Taanit* 10b.

[236]In his *Hilchot De'ot* 4:4, Maimonides states that "The day and night consist of 24 hours. It is sufficient for a person to sleep one-third thereof which is eight hours. These should be at the end of the night so that from the beginning of his sleep until the rising of the sun will be eight hours. Thus, he will arise from his bed before the sun rises."

[237]See *Hilchot De'ot* 4:5 where Maimonides states that "A person should not sleep on his face nor on his back but on his side; at the beginning of the night on the left side, and at the end of the night on the right side. Further, he should not go to sleep shortly after eating but should wait approximately three or four hours after a meal. One should not sleep during the day." See also *Berachot* 13b and *Niddah* 14a. King David is reported to have taken short naps during the day, some sixty respirations in all (*Sukkah* 26b).

[238]Literally: composite.

[239]Literally: binding.

[240]In his *Hilchot De'ot* 4:6, Maimonides states that "Things that purge the intestines such as grapes, figs, mulberries, pears, melons, various types of cucumbers, and types of gourds should be eaten before the meal. One should not mix them with the food but should wait until they have passed out of the upper abdomen and then one may eat one's meal. Things that bind the intestines [i.e., constipate] such as pomegranates, quinces, apples, and small pears should be consumed immediately after the meal, but one should not eat excessively thereof." See also *Ketubot* 10b.

heavier.[241] During the summer one should prepare cooling foods and avoid an excess of seasoning and during the winter one should do the reverse. One should also follow this [directive] in hot and in cold climates.[242]

There are some foods that are extremely injurious, and it is proper to totally avoid them such as large salted fish and salted cheese and truffles and mushrooms and salted meat that is older . . . and fresh [unfermented] wine and any food whose odor has changed and putrefied fruit because these are nearly [as harmful] as deadly poisons.[243] There are other foods that are somewhat less injurious than the above, but one should consume very little of them such as large fish, cheese that is nearly fat,[244] sour milk, meat of large oxen, large goats, beans, lentils, barley bread, cabbage, onions, garlic, mustard, and

---

[241]In his *Hilchot De'ot* 4:7, Maimonides states that "if a person wishes to eat fowl meat and cattle meat together, he should first consume the poultry meat. Likewise, if he desires eggs and poultry meat, he should eat the eggs first. If he lusts for the meat of small cattle [e.g., lambs] as well as large cattle [e.g., cows], he should first consume the meat of the small. A person should always begin with something light and then proceed to the heavier food."

[242]In *Hilchot De'ot* 4:8, Maimonides states that "In the warm [summer] months, one should eat cooling foods, not use seasoning to excess, and consume vinegar. In the rainy [winter] months, one should eat warming foods, abundantly spice the food and eat a little mustard and asafetida. In this manner, one should prepare food in cold climates and warm climates, in each and every place that which is best suited thereto." See also *Shabbat* 111b, *Erubin* 56a, and *Berachot* 40a.

[243]In his *Hilchot De'ot* 4:9, Maimonides asserts that "There are some foods that are extremely detrimental and it is proper for man never to eat them, such as old large salted fish, old salted cheese, truffles, mushrooms, old salted meat, unfermented wine, and a cooked dish that has been kept until it acquires a foul odor; likewise, any food whose odor is bad or excessively bitter; all these are like a fatal poison unto the body." See also *Baba Batra* 74b and *Eduyot* 6a.

[244]Steinschneider points out that in his *Regimen of Health* (p. 19; see note 229), Maimonides states that cheese is a very bad and heavy nutrient, excepting the cheese that is fresh, white in color, sweet in taste, and light in fat. In his *Medical Aphorisms* 20:45 (see Fred Rosner and S. Muntner, *The Medical Aphorisms of Moses Maimonides*, New York: Bloch, 1973, Vol. 2 p. 71). Maimonides, quoting Galen, asserts that the best type of fresh cheese is one made from milk whose fat has been removed.

radishes. All these are not suitable foods and are injurious. Indeed, he who totally avoids beans, lentils, and onions and does not consume them is doing the proper thing.[245]

And there are foods that are less injurious than the afore-mentioned and these are water fowl, small young pigeons, *alma*,[246] dates, and bread toasted in olive oil.[247] And one should avoid the excessive consumption of fruits and certainly before their ripening is completed, or if they are ripe but putrefied because these are poison or nearly so. However, grapes, figs, and almonds are suitable [for eating] whether fresh or dried.[248]

---

[245]In his *Hilchot De'ot* 4:9, Maimonides states that "there are other foods that are also detrimental but are not injurious as the aforementioned ones. Therefore, of these, one should eat only a little and only after intervals of many days. One should not accustom oneself to make a meal of them or to eat them regularly with his meals. Examples of this type of food are large fish, cheese, and milk that is kept for 24 hours after milking. The meat of large oxen and large he goats, beans, lentils, peas, barley bread, unleavened bread, cabbage, leeks, onions, garlic, mustard, and radishes—all these are detrimental foods. A person should not partake of these except a very small amount and only during the rainy [winter] season. However, during the warm [summer] months, one should not eat thereof at all. Beans and lentils alone should not be eaten either in the warm months or in the rainy season. Cucumbers may be consumed during the warm season." See also *Pesachim* 42a, *Avodah Zarah* 29a, *Kiddushin* 62a, and *Nedarim* 49a.

[246]This word is not found in *Hilchot De'ot* and its meaning is unknown.

[247]In his *Hilchot De'ot* 4:10, Maimonides asserts that "there are other foods that are also detrimental but not as much as the aforementioned ones. They are water fowl, small young pigeons, dates, bread toasted in oil or bread that was kneaded with oil, fine meal that was completely sifted so that not a trace of bran remains, gravy, and brine of salted fish. One should not consume these foods excessively. A person that is wise and can control his inclinations and does not yield to his appetite, and does not eat any of the aforementioned [detrimental foods] unless he needs them as a medicine, is indeed a strong man." See also *Pesachim* 2:7 and *Nedarim* 51b.

[248]In his *Hilchot De'ot* 4:11, Maimonides states that "A person should always abstain from fruits of trees and not consume them excessively even when they are dried, and needless to say when they are fresh. Indeed, before they are completely ripe they are like swords to the body. Likewise, carob-pods [locust beans] are always injurious. All sour fruits are detrimental, and one should not eat therefrom save a little and only in the warm season and in warm climates. Figs, grapes, and almonds, however, are always good whether

Honey and wine are injurious to the body but are beneficial for
the elderly, especially in the winter season.[249]

And it is appropriate for a person to always have soft bowel
movements[250] for he will thereby be spared from many sicknesses. This is a fundamental principle in the preservation of
one's health.[251] And he who performs exercises and eats to less
than satiation[252] and has soft bowel movements will nearly
never become ill. Rather, his strength will increase even if he
consumes unsuitable foods.[253] He who follows the opposite of
this regimen will suffer from many disorders, illnesses will
develop, his strength will wane and he will inherit new
diseases.[254]

---

fresh or dried, and a person may eat therefrom as much as he requires. One
should not eat them constantly even though they are better than all other
fruits of trees." *Midrash Kohelet* 5:10 states that the fig is good for consumption, nice to look at, and beneficial to the intellect.

[249]In his *Hilchot De'ot* 4:12, Maimonides states that "Honey and wine are
bad for children but salutary for the elderly especially in the rainy season. A
person should eat in the warm months two-thirds of what he eats in the rainy
months."

[250]Literally: soften his nature.

[251]In his *Hilchot De'ot* 4:13, Maimonides asserts that "Man should always
strive to have his intestines relaxed all the days of his life and his bowel
function should approximate diarrhea. This is a fundamental principle in
medicine, namely whenever the stool is withheld or is extruded with difficulty, grave illnesses result. How can a person heal his intestines if they are
slightly constipated? If he is a young boy, he should eat salty foods, cooked
and spiced with olive oil, fish brine, and salt without bread, every morning; or
he should drink the liquid of boiled spinach or cabbage in olive oil and fish
brine and salt. If he is an old man, he should drink honey mixed with warm
water in the morning and wait approximately four hours, and then he should
eat his meal. He should do this for one day or three or four days, if it is
necessary, until his intestines soften [and move freely]." See also *Ketubot* 10b.

[252]Literally: a little satiation.

[253]In his *Hilchot De'ot* 4:14, Maimonides affirms that "Another major
principle of bodily health, physicians state, is that as long as a person labors
and becomes greatly fatigued and does not satiate himself and keeps his
bowels soft, no illness will befall him and his strength becomes fortified even
if he eats detrimental foods."

[254]In his *Hilchot De'ot* 4:15, Maimonides state that "Anyone who lives a
sedentary life and does not exercise or he who postpones his excretions or he

And because of natural body constipation, it is appropriate to cleanse oneself[255] every seven days. And one should not enter the bath[256] hungry nor full but after the first digestion. And he should pour[257] tepid water over the body and hot water over the head according to the tolerance of his body. Then he should wash with water more tepid than the first and then in water that is even more tepid. But he should not pour any tepid water at all over his head nor on his back except after he has completed his perspiration. And one should not prolong one's stay in the bath nor enter it except after the cleansing of the body.[258] And

---

whose intestines are constipated, even if he eats good foods and takes care of himself according to proper medical principles—all his days will be painful ones and his strength will wane. Excessive eating is like a deadly poison to the body of any man and it is a principal cause of all illnesses. Most diseases that man is afflicted with are due to bad foods or because he fills his abdomen and eats excessively, even of good [i.e., wholesome] foods. This is what Solomon in his wisdom stated: 'Whoso keepeth his mouth and his tongue keepeth his soul from trouble' [Proverbs 21:23]; that is to say, he who guards his mouth from consuming deterimental food or satiation, and his tongue from speaking except where necessary [will remain healthy]." See also *Berachot* 32a where it says that he who stuffs himself with food is sure to contract many diseases.

[255]Literally: to perform cleansing.

[256]Literally: bathhouse.

[257]Literally: place.

[258]In his *Hilchot De'ot* 4:16, Maimonides asserts that "the correct manner of bathing is for a person to enter the bathhouse and bathe every seven days. One should not enter the bath immediately after eating nor when one is hungry but when the food begins to be digested. He should wash his entire body with hot water that does not scald the body and the head alone may be washed with water hot enough to scald the body. Then he should wash his body with lukewarm water and then with tepid water and so on until he washes with cold water. Over his head he should not pour either lukewarm or cold water. In the rainy season, one should not bathe in cold water. One should not bathe until one perspires and one's entire body becomes supple, nor should one remain too long in the bath; rather as soon as one perspires and the body becomes supple, one should rinse the body and leave the bath.

One should examine oneself prior to entering the bath and after leaving it, lest excretion of wastes be necessary. Similarly, a person should always examine himself before meals and after meals, before sexual intercourse and after sexual intercourse, before and after he exercises and exerts himself, and before and after he goes to sleep. The total number of circumstances is thus

he should remove his clothes in the outer chamber[259] and cover his head and rest a little. If he desires, he should sleep a little and after that eat but not drink cold water when he leaves [the bath] and certainly not when he is in it. If he has need [of water] he should mix it [with wine or honey].[260]

And it is appropriate not to let blood except at a time of exceptionally great need. If he wishes, he should do so in the spring. One must rest at the time of bloodletting. However, a person over fifty years of age should not be bled at all.[261]

And the semen is the strength of the body and its vitality and the

ten." The Talmud (*Shabbat* 41a) states that a man taking a hot bath and not following it up with cold water is like iron that has been kept in the fire without being immersed in cold water afterwards which—Rashi explains—makes for much stronger iron.

[259]Literally: the cold house.

[260]In his *Hilchot De'ot* 4:17, Maimonides asserts that "When a person leaves the bath, he should put his clothes on and cover his head in the outer chamber so that he should not be caught in a cold draft. Even in the summer one must be careful in this regard. After he leaves, he should wait until his soul has settled, his body has rested, and the warmth [from the bath] dissipated and then he may eat. If he should sleep a little after leaving the bath before eating, this is excellent. He should not drink cold water upon leaving the bath and certainly not while in the bath. If he is thirsty upon leaving the bath and cannot restrain himself from drinking, he should mix water in wine or in honey and then drink it. If, in the winter, he anoints himself with oil in the bath after the rinsing, this is beneficial." The Talmud (*Shabbat* 140a) speaks of the mixture of water in wine or in honey. The Talmud (*Shabbat* 41a) also states that a warm drink is advisable in that a man taking a hot bath and refraining from having a warm drink is like a furnace that has been stoked from without, not from within, and is therefore of no use.

[261]In his *Hilchot De'ot* 4:18, Maimonides states that "a person should not accustom himself to constant bloodletting. He should not phlebotomize himself except if there is extraordinary need. One should not let blood either in the sunny [summer] months nor in the rainy [winter] season; rather a little in the month of Nissan [approximately April, or Spring] and a little in the month of Tishri [approximately October or autumn]. After 50 years of age, he should not be phlebotomized at all. A person should not be bled and take a bath the same day nor be bled and then undertake a journey nor be bled on the day he returns from a journey. On the day of phlebotomy, he should eat and drink less than he is accusomted to, and he should rest on the day of phlebotomy and not fatigue or exert himself or promenade." The Talmud (*Gittin* 70a) states that bloodletting is among the eight things our Sages advised should be applied with moderation. See also *Shabbat* 129a and 129b.

light of one's vision. He who emits it excessively destroys his body, his strength will decrease, and his vision will become weak. King Solomon, may he rest in peace, said: "Give not thy strength unto women" (Proverbs 31:3),[262] meaning: do not give the essence of your strength and your vitality to those who corrupt[263] the intelligent. And if one engages in sexual intercourse rapidly, with all his strength, his body will rapidly be destroyed, his eyes will weaken, a repulsive odor will emanate from his mouth, the hair of his head will fall out, and his teeth will fall out, and his afflictions will be many. He who wishes to live a good life and be spared of serious illnesses and difficult maladies should minimize his sexual intercourse. The general rule is that excessive sexual intercourse shortens one's life.[264] And it is appropriate for one not to engage in sexual intercourse at a time when one is hungry or satiated. One should not engage in sexual intercourse while standing nor while lying on one's side or one's back, nor in the bathhouse ever, nor on the day he enters therein [to take a bath], nor on the day of bloodletting, nor on the day one sets out on a journey, nor on the day of one's return.[265]

Completed[266] is the Treatise on the Unity.

---

[262]Kalisch erroneously cites Proverbs 6:3.

[263]Literally: cause the loss of.

[264]Literally: shortens the time.

[265]In his *Hilchot De'ot* 4:19, Maimonides states that "Effusion of semen represents the strength of the body and its life, and the light of the eyes. Whenever semen is emitted to excess, the body becomes consumed, its strength terminates, and its life perishes. This is what Solomon in his wisdom states: "Give not thy strength unto women" (Proverbs 31:3). He who immerses himself in sexual intercourse will be assailed by premature aging. His strength will wane, his eyes will weaken, and a bad odor will emit from his mouth and his armpits. The hair of his head, his eyebrows, and eyelashes will fall out, and the hair of his beard and armpits and the hair of his legs will increase excessively. His teeth will fall out and many maladies other than these will afflict him. The wise physicians have stated that one in a thousand dies from other illnesses and the remaining nine hundred and ninety-nine in a thousand from excessive sexual intercourse. Therefore, a man must be cautious in this matter if he wishes to live wholesomely. He should not cohabit unless his body is healthy and very strong and he experiences many involuntary erections, and when he diverts his thoughts to another thing, the erection persists, and when he senses a heaviness from the loins and inferiorly

as if the testicular cords are being tightened and his flesh is warm. Such a person requires coitus and it is therapeutic for him to have sexual intercourse.

A person should not cohabit when he is satiated nor when he is hungry but after the food is digested in his intestines. He should examine whether need for excretion [of urine or feces] exists before coitus and after coitus. One should not have sexual intercourse standing or sitting and not in a bathhouse nor on the day when he takes a bath nor on the day of phlebotomy nor on the day when setting out on a journey or returning from a journey nor on the previous or following days of such occurrences." See also *Gittin* 70a, *Nedarim* 20b, and *Shabbat* 152a. See also Maimonides, *Treatise on Sexual Intercourse* (Fred Rosner, *Sex Ethics in the Writings of Moses Maimonides*, New York: Bloch, 1974).

[266]Although the *Treatise on the Unity* ends here, chapter 4 of *Hilchot De'ot* concludes with the following four paragraphs:

"I guarantee anyone who conducts himself according to the directions we have laid down that he will not be afflicted with illness all the days of his life until he ages greatly and expires. He will not require a physician, and his body will be complete and remain healthy all his life, unless his body was defective from the beginning of his creation, or unless he became accustomed to one of the bad habits from the onset of his youth, or unless the plague of pestilence or the plague of drought comes onto the world.

"All these helpful rules that we have presented should be followed only by a healthy individual. However, an ill person or someone who has ailing organs or someone who has accustomed himself to a bad habit for many years—for each of these there are different directions and rules to follow according to the nature of his illness, as is expounded in the book on medicines: 'A change in one's living habits is the beginning of illness.'

"In any place where there is no physician, both the healthy and the sick should not deviate from the rules that we have prescribed in this chapter, because each and every one of them [if observed correctly], will produce a salutary outcome.

"No disciple of a Sage should reside in a city that does not possess the ten following things, and these are: a physician, a surgeon, a bathhouse, a lavatory, a water supply such as a river or well, a synagogue, a school teacher, a scribe, a charity treasurer, and a court of law with authority to punish with lashes and imprisonment." See also *Ketubot* 110b, *Baba Batra* 152a, and *Sanhedrin* 17b.

Additional Chapter from the Words of Maimonides, May His Memory Be Blessed, to One of His Friends. It Represents the Completion of the Treatise.

Listen to what will benefit you in this [world] and the next one. Know that men of religion and exactness can be subdivided into two categories. One comprises the intellectuals who are perfect in their intellect as they are perfect in their religion. The other includes lunatics who have no understanding.[267] A man in the latter category harms others and, even more so, himself.[268] Such a person is called a pious fool by our Sages, of blessed memory, and they consider him among those who destroy existence and who make people perish. They said: "a naked[269] wicked man, a licentious woman and a pious fool[270] are among the destroyers of the world" (*Sotah* 21b).

And I will explain to you the conduct of a man in the first category and the conduct of the man in the second category. Indeed, [a man in] the first does not occupy himself except with that which pertains to him in terms of his Torah and his world. He sets [other] people to one side and does not mingle with them. He does not listen to their stories. In this manner he does not have to ignore those who should be ignored, nor hate those who should be hated. And he does not need theological speculation. And he rids himself of the too heavy burden which he cannot carry in terms of [his lack of fiscal] profit because of

---

[267]Hebrew: *da'at*. Alternate translation: knowledge.

[268]Literally: his soul.

[269]Naked of religion and good deeds; a man who neglects everything else and is therefore destitute.

[270]Kalisch falsely equates these foolish pietists with pious orthodox Jews in this country. He then proceeds to maliciously accuse them of "breaking the holy law and profaning the festivals . . ." His lengthy diatribe also calls them "blind hypocrites" and "the greatest enemies that Judaism ever had." Such a shocking and extremely emotional outburst seems totally unworthy of Kalisch.

his [engagement in] knowledge and religion and intellect. And his intent is to fulfill all the commandments[271] between himself and his Creator, and he performs them in secret.[272] And he appears as one who is undoubtedly deprecated [by others]. And it is written:[273] "and walk humbly with thy God" (Micah 6:8). And one who is thus is desired by the Creator and beloved above all people. And he will not be harmed by any rebellion or disobedience, nor will he have to pay for extortion by an oppressor because he associates with no one.

On the other hand, the conduct of [a man in] the second category is such that he occupies himself with that which does not pertain to him and becomes involved with the opinions of others and with authorizations and negativism and authority. He mingles with others and listens to their stories and listens to that which he should safeguard and carries perverted judgment and dogmatic prejudices. He cannot stay away from constant rebellion and from contact with other people. And he cannot stay away from quarrels, and it is impossible for him not to be angry and cry out. And he asserts that which is inappropriate and acts in an inappropriate manner. And he loses his religion, because he thinks that he is a zealot. And he destroys his world because of his association with people who will end up hating him.

And because the great Sages knew this, they chose seclusion and asceticism and the avoidance of sitting in judgments. And they devoted themselves to the study of Torah and nothing else. And may Almighty God lead us together to success in both worlds.

And now my master, consider carefully this commandment and what is the most appropriate therein and that which a man should always place before his eyes. And may Almighty God assist us in putting into practice that which has been decreed therein.[274]

---

[271]Literally: servitudes, Divine services.
[272]That is, privately, modestly.
[273]Kalisch erroneously cites Micah 8.
[274]That is, in the Torah.

Completed is this chapter and herewith is completed the *Treatise on the Unity* with perfection and praise to the Lord.

(In the Vatican manuscript No. 170, at the end of the treatise, the following words appear: translated from Arabic and copied by the scholar Rabbi Isaac ben Nathan the Pious. And it follows the method of the Rabbi [Maimonides] in his translation in that he translated sentences in a manner to retain the rhythm of the language.)[275]

---

[275] In his letter to Steinschneider, Rapoport explains this note of the scribe as follows: the translator, Rabbi Isaac ben Nathan the pious, followed Maimonides' own practice in his Arabic writings of citing scriptural verses not in their literal translation but in melodious terms. However, Rapoport is critical of the translator Rabbi Isaac for taking such liberties to the point that the source of some scriptural citations is no longer apparent to the reader.

BIBLIOGRAPHY

by Jacob I. Dienstag

מאמר הייחוד להרמב"ם
ביבליוגראפיה של הוצאות, תרגומים ומחקרים

א. מאמר הייחוד, מקור ותרגום

1] מאמר הייחוד להרמב"ם. העתיקו מלשון ערבי... יצחק בר נתן החסיד. יצא
ראשונה לאור עם הערות... ונלוה אליו מכתב מאת ... ש"י ראפאפורט... אל המוצא
לאור משה שטיינשניידער... ברלין, בהוצאות צבי הירש קאלוואריא, תר"ו. י', 40,
XIV עמ'.

שער לועזי:

Maamar Ha-Jichud. (Abhandlung uber die Einheit). Aus dem Arabischen
des R. Moses B. Maimon. Hebraisch von R. Isaack B. Natan. Zum ersten Mal
herausgegeben, nebst sachlichen und sprachlichen Erlauterungen und einer
deutschen Inhaltsubersicht von M. Steinschneider. Nebst einem Sendschreiben
an den Herausgeber von...Rabb. S.L. Rapoport...Berlin: Friedlandersche
Buchdrucker, 1846.

Review by Z. Frankel, *Zeitschrift fuer die Religiosen Interessen des
Judenthums*, 3 (1846), 465-466.

2] ...שני המאורות. כולל... מאמר הייחוד להרמ"בם ז"ל. העתיקו מלשון ערבי... יצחק
בר נתן החסיד עם הערות בביאור המלות והענינים. נלוה אליו מכתב מאת... ש"י
ראפאפורט... ושלש שאלות נשאלו לרב... אברהם בן עזרא ותשובותיו יצאו מוגהות
מתחת יד... שד"ל... שניהם נדפסו... ע"י משה שטיינשניידער... בערלין,
פרידלענדערשע בוכדרוקקערייא, תר"ז. [4] דף י', 40, ... XIV עמ'.

שער לועזי:

89

Schene Ha-Meoroth enthalt Maamar Ha-Jichud (Abhandlung uber die Einheit). Aus den Arabischen des R. Moses B. Maimon. Hebraisch von R. Isaack B. Natan. ...herausgegeben nebst...Erlauterungen und einer deutschen Inhaltsubersicht von M. Steinschneider...Nebst einem Sendschreiben an den Herausgeber von... Rabb. S.L. Rapoport und drei astronomische Bemerkungen...von R. Abr. Ibn Esra. Berlin: Friedlandersche Buchdruckerei, 1847.

3] Maimonides' "Maamar Hayichud" Treatise on the Unity of God. In: Isidor Kalisch, *Studies in Ancient and Modern Judaism;* selected writings. New York: George Dobsavage, 1928, pp. 135-163. Reprinted from the 'Israelite, [1863] ix, Nos. 49, 50, 51, x. Nos. 1,2,3,7,11. Nos. 1-3, 6-7, 11 [1863].

ב. ליקוטים ממאמר הייחוד

4] פרק ממאמרי הרמב"ם ז"ל. **אוצר נחמד** ב' (תרי"ז 1857), 101-100. יצא לאור ע"י אברהם גייגר שהעתיק אותו מכתב יד פאריז; נדפס שוב **בקבוצת מאמרים** מאת אברהם גייגר, ורשה, תר"ע, 1910, עמ' 130-129.

ונעלם מגייגר שזהו פרק שבסוף **מאמר הייחוד** שהוציא שטיינשניידר. ראה ש. זק"ש, **ישרון**, שנה ג' (תרי"ט), עמ' ס"ס"א.

5] פרק ממאמרי הרמב"ם ז"ל. בס' **דברי משה**... הרמב"ם... יצא לאור על ידי יעקב מהרש"ק. ורשה:ח. קעלטער, תרמ"ו 1886, עמ' 41. כנ"ל.

ג. מאמרים ומחקרים

6] בכר, בנימין זאב, 1913-1850
הרמב"ם פרשן המקרא. תל-אביב, תרצ"ב, עמ' 9.
"אפשר שהוא באמת של הרמב"ם, ובכל אופן הוא מתאים לשיטתו." ראה גם במדור הלועזי.

7] גריץ, צבי, 1891-1817.
דברי ימי ישראל, מתורגם... מאת שאול פנחס ראבינוביץ, חלק ד', ווארשא, תרנ"ה 1894 (הדפסות: תרס"ח 1908; תרע"א 1911), עמ' 459.
גריץ, יריבו של שטיינשניידר, שולל לגמרי את יחוסו של ה"מאמר הייחוד" להרמב"ם. וכשהוא מזכירו הוא משתמט מלהזכיר את שמו של רמש"ש כמוציאו לאור. הוא מציין רק מקום ותאריך: ברלין 1846. ולא עוד, אלא שגריץ מגנה את מבואו של רמש"ש, שהוא לפי דעתו "רב המלין ומעט הענין." על היחסים שבין גריץ ושטיינשניידר עי' S.W. Baron, *History and Jewish Historians* (Philadelphia, 1964, pp. 293, 302-303, 461-469).

8] דינסטאג, ישראל יעקב
משה שטיינשניידר כחוקר הרמב"ם. **סיני**, כרך 66 (אדר א'-ב', תש"ל), שמח-שנ. הערות ביבליוגרפיות.

9] זקש, שניאור, 1815־1892

הערה על מחקרו של גיגר ("פרק מדברי הרמב"ם," **באוצר נחמד**, ב', תרי"ז, עמ'
100־101). **ישרון**, שנה ג' (תרי"ט), ס־סא. שהפרק ההוא אשר העתיק גיגר מכ"י פריז
הוא פרק שבסוף **מאמר היחוד** והמובא בבית האוצר הוא רק תרגום שני ממגלת
מאמר הייחוד.

10] לוצטו, שמואל דוד, 1800־1865

אגרת מיום כ"ו כסלו תר"ז, למשה שטיינשניידר. **באגרות שד"ל**, חלק ז', קראקא,
תרנ"א, עמ' 1007־1008.
תיקונים והערות **למאמר הייחוד.**

11] רבינוביץ, מרדכי דב, 1877־1959

הערות **לספר המאור**, כרך ראשון: אוצר ההקדמות: **הקדמה למסכת אבות**
("שמונה פרקים"). תל־אביב: הוצאת "ראשונים," תש"ח עמ' קצב; נדפס שוב
בהקדמות לפירוש המשנה, ירושלים: מוסד הרב קוק, תשט"ו (הרבה הדפסות), עמ'
קצו, הערה ט'.
על הדיבור הציורי "מאחרי מחיצה", מסך, פרגוד שהרמב"ם משתמש בהם
בשמונה פרקים, פרק ז' ובמורה נבוכים, ח"ג, ט, נא **ובמאמר הייחוד.**

12] רייפמן, יעקב, 1818־1894

לקוטי תולדות חכמים: רמב"ם. **בית תלמוד** ד (תרמ"ה), 299־302. "זה רבות
בשנים בררתי במ"ע המליץ, כי תחת: היחוד צ"ל: היסוד, וכי הוא אך קצור מהלכות
יסודי התורה אשר בספר המדע להרמב"ם" (עמ' 301).

13] רפופורט, שלמה יהודה, 1790־1867

מכתב מיום ה' אלול, תר"ו, למשה שטיינשניידר. **במאמר הייחוד** להרמב"ם...
המוציא לאור משה שטיינשניידר, ברלין, תר"ו, עמ' ז־י: נדפס שוב **בשני המאורות.**
כולל **מאמר הייחוד...** ברלין, תר"ז, עמ' ז־י.
הערות ותיקונים **למאמר הייחוד.**

14] Altmann, Alexander, 1906-1987

The Ladder of Ascension. *Studies in Mysticism and Religion Presented to
G.G. Scholem.* Jerusalem, 1967, p. 11, note 39; reprinted in his *Studies in
Religious Philosophy and Mysticism.* Ithaca, N.Y.: Cornell Univ., 1969, p. 51,
note 39. Questions the authenticity of the *Treatise* as a work of Maimonides.

15] Bacher, Wilhelm, 1850-1913.

Die Bibelexegese Moses Maimun's. Strassburg: K.J.: Trubner, 1897, p.
XV. Affirms its authenticity as a work of Maimonides. See Hebrew edition.

16] Baron, Salo Wittmayer, 1895-1989

A Social and Religious History of the Jews. 2nd edition, revised and
enlarged. Vol. VIII. New York and London: Columbia University Press;
Philadelphia: Jewish Publication Society of America, 1958 (3rd printing:
1971), p. 308. Does not contest its authencity.

17] Cohen, Boaz, 1899-1968
    The classification of the Law in the Mishneh Torah. *Jewish Quarterly Review*, n.s. XXV, no. 4 (April 1935), p. 531. In affirming its authenticity, Cohen quotes Prof. Louis Ginzberg, who "is of the opinion that the *Treatise on Unity* is an early work of Maimonides, for it betrays symptoms of immaturity, and lacks the finish Maimonides was wont to give to his later writings. The reference to the *Moreh (Guide for the Perplexed)* is a later interpolation."

18] Frankel, Zacharias, 1801-1875
    (Review of) the *Mamar ha-Yiḥud. Zeitschrift fuer die Religiosen Interessen des Judenthums* 3 (1846), 465-466. Believes that the original title was not *Mamar ha-Yiḥud.*

Ginzberg, Louis, 1873-1953
    See Cohen, Boaz.

19] Graetz, Heinrich, 1817-1891
    Geschichte der Juden. 3te Auflage. Band 6, Leipzig, 1894, p. 389.
    "...mit einer nichtssagenden Einleitung." See my note on the Hebrew edition.

20] Kaufmann, David, 1852-1899
    Geschichte der Attributenlehre in der judischen Religionsphilosophie Gotha: F.A. Perthes, 1877, p. 378, note 25.
    Doubts Maimonides' authorship of the Treatise.

21] Scholem, Gershon G., 1897-1982
    Ursprung und Anfange der Kabbala. Berlin: Walter de Gruyter, 1962, p. 287, note 235. Questions it authenticity.

22] Scholem, Gershon G., 1897-1982
    Les Origines de la Kabbala. Traduit de L'allemand par Jean Loewenson. Paris: Aubier-Montaigne (c. 1966), p. 343, note 235.

23] Steinschneider, Moritz, 1816-1907
    Lesarten zu Maimonides, מאמד הייחוד (Berlin 1847), nach Ms. Munchen 150 u. and. *Magazin f. die Wissenschaft des Judenthum*, 19 (1892), 86-88.

24] Steinschneider, Moritz, 1816-1907
    Catalogus librorum hebraeorum in Bibliotheca Bodeleiana. Berelini, 1852-1860, col. 1916-17.

25] Steinschneider, Moritz, 1816-1907
    Die hebraeischen Uebersetzungen des Mittelalters, Berlin, 1893, pp. 436-437.

26] Steinschneider, Moritz, 1816-1907
Die arabische Literatur der Juden. Frankfurt a. M.: J. Kauffmann, 1902,
pp. 208-209.

27] Vajda, Georges, 1908-1981
L'amour de Dieu dans la theologie Juive du Moyen Age. Paris: J. Vrin,
1957, p. 126, note 3. Questions its authenticity.

28] Weiss, Adolf, 1849-1924
Mose ben Maimons Leben und Werke. In: *Mose ben Maimon, Fuehrer
der Unschlussigen.* Ins Deutsche uebertragen...von A. Weiss. I. Buch. Leipzig:
F. Meiner, 1923, p. CLX-CLXII.

ד. ציונים ביבליוגרפיים לכתבי-יד של מאמר הייחוד

29] שטיינשניידר, משה, 1816־1907.
דברים עתיקים. **הכרמל** שבועון 6 (תרכ"ו), 320.
כתב יד פוקוק 280B

30] Adler, Elkan Nathan, 1861-1946
Catalogue of the Hebrew Manuscripts in the collection of Elkan Nathan
Adler. Cambridge Univ. Press, 1921, p. 72, no. 666.

31] Assemani, Stephanus Evodius, 1707-1782
Bibliothecae Apostolicae Vaticanae Codicum Manuscriptorum Catalogus.
Vol. I: (Codices Ebraicos). Romae, 1756 (photograf. ed. Paris, 1926), no. CLXX
(3).

32] Freimann, Aron, 1871-1948
Union Catalogue of Hebrew Manuscripts and their Location, vol. 2. New
York: American Academy for Jewish Research, 1964, no. 4606.

33] Mortara, Marco, 1815-1894
Die Gemeindebibliothek zu Manua. *Hebraeische Bibliographie 4* (1861),
p. 48 (no. e).

34] Neubauer, Adolf, 1832-1907 and Cowley, Arthur Ernst, 1861-1931
Catalogue of the Hebrew Manuscripts in the Bodleian Library and in the
College Libraries of Oxford, including mss. in other languages written with
Hebrew characters or relating to the Hebrew language, or literature, and a few
Samaritan mss... Oxford, 1886-1906, no. 1317 (2).

35] Rodriguez de Castro, Jose, 1730-1799
Bibliotheca Espanola. Tomo primero, que contiene la noticia de los
escritores rabinos espanoles desde la epoca conocida de su literatura hasta el
presente. Madrid, 1781, p. 62.

36] Steinschneider, Moritz, 1816-1907
Catalog der hebraischen Handschriften in der Stadtbibliothek zu
Hamburg... Hamburg, 1878, no. 256 (1).

37] Steinschneider, Moritz, 1816-1907
Die hebraeischen Handschriften der K. Hof-und Staatsbibliothek in
Muenchen. Muenchen, 1875 (2. Auflage, 1895), no. 150 (1).

Book II

SEFER HANIMTZAH
TREATISE ON THE ONE WHO EXISTS

INTRODUCTION

S*efer Hanimtzah* is a small and somewhat obscure medical–
moral work attributed to Moses Maimonides, first published in
1596 and appended to two other works (see bibliography). The
work begins with an introductory plea in very flowery language
for moral conduct, not at all typical of Maimonidean writings.
The work itself starts with praises to God the Creator who "is
everything and bears everything and everything is dependent
upon Him." Galen and Plato are cited. The physical and
spiritual parts of the human body are described and analogies
are made between the sun and the planets of the "large world"
and the heart and other major organs of the "small world." The
spirit and the soul, the powers of imagination, thought, and
memory, the four fundamental elements: fire, air, water, and
earth, and the medieval concept of body humors as the
modulators of health and disease are cited. The heavenly
constellations, signs of the Zodiac, and seasons of the year are
all briefly discussed.

The second half of *Sefer Hanimtzah* is devoted to medical
rules and regulations for the preservation of health. Large
sections of these rules seem to be taken verbatim or only
slightly modified from chapter 4 of the laws of temperaments

(Hilchot De'ot) in Maimonides' *Mishneh Torah.* Some quotations cited exactly from *Hilchot De'ot* are commented upon, sometimes at length. Others are just paraphrased or modified or cited without comment. The last third of Chapter 4 of *Hilchot De'ot* is not quoted at all, nor paraphrased in *Sefer Hanimtzah.* No reason is apparent for this omission.

Whether or not Maimonides actually wrote *Sefer Hanimtzah* is not clear, nor is the reason for its composition. The original publisher, Abraham Akara, as well as the subsequent editors, Gabriel Polak and Judah Leib Maimon (see bibliography), consider Maimonides as the author. This view is also supported by other scholars such as Shlomo Rapoport. On the other hand, the renowned Hebrew bibliographer Moritz Steinschneider, as well as other scholars such as Zaks and Zabara, consider *Sefer Hanimtzah* to be spurious and falsely attributed to Maimonides.

The supposition of Rapoport and others that *Sefer Hanimtzah* is identical with Maimonides' *Ma'amar Hayichud* is rejected by Steinschneider who asks: "if it is identical with *Sefer Hanimtzah,* why did the translator render the original Arabic into *Ma'amar Hayichud?*" One must assume that Isaac ben Nathan faithfully translated the title. Furthermore, the word *Sefer* or book (Arabic: *kitab*) is less appropriate for such a small work than is *Ma'amar* or treatise. Finally, the published versions of the *Sefer Hanimtzah* do not resemble the *Ma'amar Hayichud* at all except for the last section dealing with the regimen of health, which is found paraphrased from Chapter four of *Hilchot De'ot* of the *Mishneh Torah* in both *Ma'amar Hayichud* and *Sefer Hanimtzah.* Although there is considerable debate about the authorship of *Sefer Hanimtzah,* there seems to be no challenge to the authenticity of *Ma'amar Hayichud* as a Maimonidean writing.

The words, *Sefer Hanimtzah,* are difficult to translate and many suggestions have been put forth. The Hebrew word *nimtzah* means *found* and, therefore, some writers (see bibliography) translate *Sefer Hanimtzah* as *The Found Book* or *The Discovered Book.* The original publisher, in his introduction to the work, says that it is called *Sefer Hanimtzah* "because in it one finds a good thing, sweet to the soul and healing to the body." In the work itself, the author says he wrote it "so that the reader

can find in it his need and his desire, and find each medical
therapy. . . . Therefore, it is called *Sefer Hanimtzah.*"

Another suggestion is that the Hebrew word *nimtzah* means
exist and, therefore, the work should be translated as *The Book
of That Which Exists.* Alternatively the term *nimtzah* could refer
to God as found in the *Yigdal* prayer recited daily at the
beginning of the morning service. Thus, *Sefer Hanimtzah* can be
translated as *The Book of He Who Exists* or *The Book of the One Who
Exists.* This interpretation is consonant with the phrase used
several times in the book "regarding the Book of the One Who
Exists With Wisdom and With Understanding."

Still another interpretation of *Sefer Hanimtzah* is that the book
has no specific name at all. This suggestion is based on the fact
that the word *Sefer* in the original version is printed in larger
letters and on a different line than the word *Nimtzah.* The latter
is printed on the same line as the words "Luminary of the Exile,
Moses Maimonides, of blessed memory." Thus, one might
translate the entire title line as "This is the book that was found
(or discovered, written by) the Luminary of the Exile, Moses
Maimonides." Perhaps this suggestion coincides more closely
with the aforementioned names *The Found Book* or *The Discovered Book.*

Although there is considerable controversy among scholars
as to the authenticity of *Sefer Hanimtzah* as a Maimonidean
work, some confusion about the meaning of the word *nimtzah,*
and even the erroneous suggestion that *Sefer Hanimtzah* is
identical with Maimonides' *Ma'amar Hayichud,* because of considerable similarities in both works, I considered it important
and worthwhile to translate the former into English and to
present it together with a translation and analysis of Maimonides' *Ma'amar Hayichud.*

Literature Survey

Sefer Hanimtzah was first published in 1596 (5356 in the
Hebrew calendar) in Salonika (Thessaloniki) by Rabbi Abraham ben Solomon Akara and printed at the end of the work

Amarot Tehorot by Rabbi Abraham Chayun, appended to the commentary on Lamentations by Rabbi Samuel ben Chabib Di Vidash. Akara wrote his own introduction to *Sefer Hanimtzah*[1] which he attributes to Moses Maimonides whom he refers to as the "Luminary of the Exile," "the great Rabbi," and "the soaring eagle."[2] Akara considers the work to be a medical–moral essay in which Maimonides recommends that a person must strive not only for the health of his soul but also for the health of his body because God created both, and in order to serve God properly one must have a sound body and soul. Akara asserts that the work

> is called *Sefer Hanimtzah* because in it one finds a good thing, sweet to the soul and healing to the body. It is a beneficial moistener that moistens appropriately and is wet enough to moisten something else.[3] One should pay attention to all its contents and not deflect one's attention therefrom. Because of its great benefit to sick people, whether internally or externally, I saw fit to publish this work.

The author of *Sefer Hanimtzah*,[4] in the work itself, writes that he wrote this book

> in a short form so that the reader can run through it [read it swiftly] and find in it his need and his desire, and find each medical therapy by itself so that he not become weak nor tired while he is searching for something. Therefore it is called *Sefer Hanimtzah*.

In 1845, a lengthy article on the medical writings of Maimonides[5] by Moritz Steinschneider describes the *Sefer Hanimtzah*. He states that it is called *liber inventi* by Wolf and Wüstenfeld, *The*

---

[1] Translated into English in its entirety at the beginning of *Sefer Hanimtzah* (see following).

[2] Titles frequently used in reference to Maimonides.

[3] Talmudic expression found in *Berachot* 25b and elsewhere.

[4] The true authorship is in some doubt although most writers attribute it to Moses Maimonides as discussed in my introduction.

[5] M. Steinschneider, "Medizinische schriften von Maimonides," *Oesterreiche Blätter fur Literatur und Kunst,* (Vienna, Jan. 28, 1845), Vol. 2, No. 12 ff. pp. 89–92, 109–112, 118–119, 123–126, 442–446, 452–455.

Found Book by Beer, and not translated by Rossi. He further states that he could not find this extremely rare work in Prague and that the Hebrew word *nimtzah* is to be understood in the philosophical sense (corresponding to the Arabic *maudschud*) and, therefore, should be translated as *The Book of That Which Exists.*[6]

Steinschneider also asserts that his learned friend, Judah Leib Dukes, provided him with a copy of a Maimonidean work entitled *Ma'amar Hayichud (Treatise on the Unity of God)* in Hebrew translation by Isak ben Nathan. Steinschneider showed this work to Rabbi Shlomo Yehudah Leib Rapoport who told him that he believed that Maimonides' *Ma'amar Hayichud* is identical to the *Sefer Hanimtzah,* which he (Rapoport) remembers having seen many years earlier.

Since copies of *Sefer Hanimtzah* were extremely rare and Steinschneider had not personally seen it, he accepted Rapoport's opinion.

In 1846, Steinschneider published a Hebrew edition of Maimonides' *Ma'amar Hayichud* with Hebrew and German forewords and a German summary.[7] In the German foreword to that work, Steinschneider writes:

> I am especially sorry because of the following: elsewhere,[8] I wrote about the orally-expressed opinion of a renowned literary historian that our work [*the Ma'amar Hayichud*] is identical with the *Sefer Hanimtzah.* I, therefore, all the more deeply regret not to have more precise proof because even that path to the elucidation of this question failed. Wolf (Vol. 1, p. 864) and Azulai (*Vaad*, Vol. 1:5, 1) assert that this alleged medical-ascetic work was printed together with the (rare) book *Amarot Tehorot* by Abraham Chayun in Thessaloniki [Salonica] in 1596. (Azulai also adds thereto the commentary to the lamentation of Samuel de Vidas.) I did not find this work of Maimonides [*Sefer*

---

[6]Steinschneider's German text has "Buch des Existirenden" which means "Book of Those Who Exist" or "Book of Existences" that is, creations, or perhaps can be loosely translated as "Book of Facts."

[7]*Sefer Shnay Hame'orot, Ma'amar Hayichud le ha Rambam* (Berlin: Friedlander Printers, 1846). (Reprinted in 1847.)

[8]See note 5.

Hanimtzah] in the printed catalogue of the Oppenheim Library
but did find it among the manuscripts in the possession of Dr.
Zun. On the other hand, in response to an inquiry from the
latter to the current owner of the famous library of the late H.
Michael in Hamburg, it was reported that the *Sefer Hanimtzah*
was not present in their copy of the *Amarot Tehorot.*

In his 1846 Hebrew edition of Maimonides' *Ma'amar Hayichud,*
Steinschneider published a letter he received from Shlomo Y. L.
Rapoport in which the latter asserts:

> I still think that this composition [*Ma'amar Hayichud*] is also
> known by the name *Sefer Hanimtzah,* which was bound with the
> work *Amarot Tehorot* by Don Abraham Chayun, which was
> published in Salonica in the year 5356 [*Sifsei Yeshanim,* letter,
> *aleph,* number 157]. The character of the treatise, as it now
> appears to us, indicates that the name *Hanimtzah* is more
> appropriate than *Hayichud* because in *Hayichud* he [Maimonides]
> speaks more of the total existence [of the world] than he does of
> the unity. One should also append to this work some of what is
> added there in the *Sifsei Yeshanim,* which includes medical
> subjects and matters relating to the fear of God. Indeed, at the
> end of this composition [*Ma'amar Hayichud*], there are included
> some items pertaining to medicine. Perhaps that which is
> mentioned in *Sifsei Yeshanim* is from a different, far better copy,
> as far as we can best evaluate to explain the name change from
> *Yichud* to *Nimtzah.* And if there is any validity to this suggestion,
> I am grieved at not having access to that published work because
> the edition before me is not adequate to satisfy all the questions
> of the reader. A single deficiency can tell the character of the
> whole work. For the translator took even the scriptural verses
> cited by Maimonides in Arabic and translated them from Arabic
> into Hebrew, but not into their literal Hebrew texts as found in
> the Bible, but into derisive stammering lips and a strange
> tongue, to the point that the reader cannot recognize their
> source.

Apparently, even Rapoport was not totally convinced that
Ma'amar Hayichud and *Sefer Hanimtzah* are one and the same
work. At the end of his German foreword in his Hebrew edition

of Maimonides' *Ma'amar Hayichud,* Steinschneider adds the
following note:

> This foreword was already in press when the awaited writing
> from Rabbi Rapoport arrived. According to his wish, I transmit-
> ted it to the printer unchanged. The conjecture enunciated
> therein that *Nimtzah* is another translation for [*Ma'amar*] *Hayi-*
> *chud* raises a variety of difficulties in regard to the title, since our
> translator probably faithfully also translated the title, and even if
> we assume that the other translator had before him, in the
> original Arabic, the reading *Mogod* for *Tochid,* the word *Sefer*
> (Arabic: *kitab*) is less appropriate for such a small treatise than
> *Ma'amar.* Accordingly, *Sefer Hanimtzah* should be rendered "Dis-
> covered Book" contrary to my earlier opinion in *Oesterreiche*
> *Blätter.*[9]

In his great bibliographical works[10-12] published nearly a
half-century later, Steinschneider lists *Sefer Hanimtzah* among
the spurious works falsely attributed to Moses Maimonides.

In 1849, in a German periodical devoted to Jewish history
and literature, the Dutch scholar Gabriel Polak[13] published in
Hebrew a little more than half of *Sefer Hanimtzah* together with
the introduction by the original publisher, Akara, from the
1596 Salonica edition. Polak added introductory comments of
his own in German in which he indicated that important
writings of famous Jewish scholars are sometimes overlooked
or lost. Some are in manuscript form only. Some were originally
written in the local vernacular and then translated into Hebrew,

---

[9]*Ibid.*

[10]*Die Hebraeischen Uebersetzungen des Mittelalters und die Juden als Dolmetscher*
(Berlin, 1893), pp. 274–275 and footnotes 1196–1197.

[11]*Die Arabische Literatur der Juden* (Frankfurt A.M.: J. Kauffmann, 1902), p.
218.

[12]*Catalogus Librorum Hebraeorum in Bibliotheca Bodleiana Jussu Curatorum*
Digessit Et Notis Instruxit M. Steinschneider (Berolini: A.D. Friedlander, 1852–
1860), pp. 1933–1934.

[13]"Notiz ueber das Sefer ha-Nimza von Mose b. Maimum," *Literaturblatt des*
Orients (Leipzig), No. 18, May 5, 1849, pp. 273–279 and No. 19, May 12, 1848,
pp. 293–298.

but the Hebrew translator gave the book a title different from
that given by the original author, or the translator used the title
given by the original author to another work. Thereby, much
confusion and many errors arose in bibliographic and literary
analysis. Thus we are obliged to seek the truth. Polak states that
this was the case with Maimonides' *Sefer Hanimtzah* and continues as follows:

> Although published, copies of this work are rare . . . probably
> because it was printed together with two other works. As a
> result, some scholars such as Azulai (*Va'ad*, Alef 5), Wolf (I, 964),
> and *Sifsei Yeshanim* (Alef 157) consider it identical to Mai-
> monides' *Ma'amar Hayichud*, which Steinschneider first edited
> and published in Berlin in 1846. Rapoport, in a letter to
> Steinschneider, also believes that *Sefer Hanimtzah* is identical with
> *Ma'amar Hayichud*.

Polak could not find *Sefer Hanimtzah* in numerous libraries
and catalogues but did locate a copy in the Etz Chayim
synagogue. This copy, written in small octavo—not in quarto as
stated by *Sifsei Yeshanim* [for *Ma'amar Hayichud*]—was comprised of three works: the commentary on Lamentations by
Samuel ben Chabib Di Vidash, *Amarot Tehorot* by Abraham ben
Don Nissin Chayun, and the *Sefer Hanimtzah* of Maimonides.
All three, continues Polak, were published together by the
learned Abraham ben Don Salomon Akara. Polak briefly
describes the three works and states that the first forty-three
pages are devoted to the commentary on Lamentations and the
next fifteen pages to *Amarot Tehorot*. *Sefer Hanimtzah* begins on
page 59 with Akara's introduction and ends on page 70. The
last few pages of Polak's copy of *Sefer Hanimtzah* were torn or
missing and, therefore, Polak's 1849 Hebrew edition of this
work is incomplete.

Two years later, Polak published the complete *Sefer Hanimtzah* in
his collection *Ben Geroni*.[14] His introductory remarks in German

---

[14]Sefer Hanimtzah in *Sefer Ben Geroni* (Amsterdam, 1851 [5611]), pp.
I–XVII.

preceding his 1849 Hebrew edition were published in Hebrew preceding his 1851 Amsterdam edition in a lengthy "note to the reader." Toward the end of this "note" Polak states that he had already published these introductory remarks two years earlier in the *Literaturblatt des Orients*.[15] He then praises God for having allowed him to now publish the complete *Sefer Hanimtzah* through information provided by his learned friend Judah Leib Dukes, who told him that he was able to locate a copy in the Oxford University library, and with assistance from his good friend Joseph Zedner, who was one of the librarians in the British Museum in London, and the kindness of Zvi Hirsh Edelman, who copied the missing pages of *Sefer Hanimtzah* from the Oxford copy and transmitted them to Polak. Finally, Polak thanks Edelman for having answered the following question that Polak posed to him: why are the words "Commentary of Maimonides" found at the top of each page of *Sefer Hanimtzah*? Edelman answers that this work contains statements of Maimonides quoted from his other writings and these statements are commented upon in *Sefer Hanimtzah*. Edelman ends by asserting that he draws no conclusion as to the authenticity of *Sefer Hanimtzah* as a Maimonidean work. He admits that Dukes feels certain that Maimonides wrote it, but he (Edelman) cannot hastily decide this matter and leaves the question open. The Polak 1851 Amsterdam version of *Sefer Hanimtzah* was reprinted in Jerusalem in 1971.[16]

After reading the 1849 Polak edition of *Sefer Hanimtzah*, Shneyor Zaks immediately concluded[17] that it was not written by Maimonides for the following reasons: Firstly, he finds it impossible to believe that Maimonides used flowery language such as "the beverage of benefit and of trust" and "take the roots of praise and of thanks and the roots of rejoicing and of trust . . ." Secondly, statements such as "it is known and clear that the Lord is everything and bears everything and every-

---

[15]See note 13.

[16]Sefer Hanimtzah in *Sefer Ben Geroni* (Amsterdam, 1851 [5611]), reprinted Jerusalem: Kedem, 1971.

[17]"Al Devar Sefer Hanimtzah Hameyuchas Le Ha Rambam Zal," *Kerem Chemed* (Berlin, 5614 [1854]), Vol. 8, pp. 22–34.

thing is dependent upon Him" is more in keeping with the writings of Abraham Ibn Ezra and not Maimonides. Thirdly, Maimonides would never assert that "the Creator placed the heart in the middle of the body just as He placed the sun in the middle of the spheres . . . and the heart in the body which is the small world." Fourthly, other expressions and terms throughout *Sefer Hanimtzah* are contrary to the usual Maimonidean writing. Zaks concludes by saying that he did not cite even half his reasons for believing that *Sefer Hanimtzah* has been wrongly attributed to Maimonides.

In 1925, the author of the preface of a work called *Sefer Sha'ashu'im*[18] comments that *Sefer Hanimtzah* has been erroneously attributed to Maimonides. In the first appendix to *Sefer Sha'ashu'im* is a song entitled *Batei Nefesh* composed by the author, Joseph Zabara. The song deals with human anatomy and physiology. Parallel passages from *Sefer Hanimtzah* and *Batei Nefesh* are placed in parallel columns in the appendix. Many words, phrases, and sequences are nearly identical in the two works so that the author of the preface suggests that the author of *Sefer Hanimtzah* made use of Zabara's *Batei Nefesh*.

The *Sefer Hanimtzah* was twice published in Hebrew by Judah Leib Maimon in 1955, in an Israeli periodical[19] and in Maimon's collection *HaRam Bamzal*.[20] Both Maimon printings omit the Akara introduction, which is published in the original 1596 edition and in all three Polak editions.[21] Maimon adds his own introductory remarks beginning with the statement that he is publishing the *Sefer Hanimtzah* of Moses Maimonides to commemorate the seven-hundred-and-fiftieth year since the death of Maimonides whom he calls the *Rosh Medabrim Bechol*

---

[18]J. Zabara, *Sefer Sha'ashu'im* (Berlin, 5685 [1925]), pp. 70–71 (preface) and 155–168 (Appendix 1).

[19]"Sefer Hanimtzah Le Ha Rambam," *Sinai* (Jerusalem: Mossad Harav Kook), Year 18, No. 36, Vol. 4, Tevet 5715 (1955), pp. 201–211.

[20]Sefer Hanimtzah in *HaRam Bamzal* (Jerusalem: Mossad Harav Kook, 1955), pp. 7–17.

[21]The 1849 version in *Literaturblatt des Orients*, the 1851 Amsterdam version, and the 1971 Jerusalem reprinting.

Makom.[22] Maimon states that the *Sefer Hanimtzah* was first cited in the book *Sifsei Yeshanim* in 1596 under the Hebrew letter *aleph:* "*Amarot Tehorot* of Don Abraham Chayun deals with matters of repentance and reverence and the *Sefer Hanimtzah* of Maimonides deals with medical matters and reverence." It is also mentioned in *Shem HaGedolim* of Rabbi Chayim Yosef David Azulai, known as *Chidah,* (*Ma'arechet Sefarim,* letter *hey,* section 77) as follows:

> The *Sefer Hanimtzah* of Maimonides consists of ethics and natural science and medicine and the composition of man and the like. It was published in Salonika in 5356 [1596] together with the *Amarot Tehorot* of Rabbi Abraham Chiyun and a commentary on Lamentations by Rabbi Samuel Vidash.

Maimon further points out that the work *Otzar Hasefarim* of Ben Yakov (letter *aleph,* number 786) states as follows:

> *Amarot Tehorot* of Don Abraham Nissim Chayun deals with matters of repentance and reverence and ethical teachings. *Chamud,*[23] Constantinople 5276–8 [1516–1518] and others, and [bound] together with it is the *Sefer Hanimtzah* attributed to Maimonides, printed at the end of the commentary on Lamentations by Rabbi Samuel Di Vidash, Salonika, 5356 [1596].

In addition, Rabbi Chayim Michal, in his book *Or HaChayim,* in the section on Maimonides, lists among the books of Maimonides:

> *Sefer Hanimtzah,* at the end of the work *Amarot Tehorot* of Rabbi Abraham Chayun, is a medical book dealing with spiritual and physical ailments. It was published in Salonika in 5356 [1596]. However, the book *Amarot Tehorot* to which is appended the *Sefer Hanimtzah* is nearly impossible to find and is extremely rare.

---

[22]Literally: main speaker in every place. The first letters of the four Hebrew words spell the acronym *Rambam* which is the popular name for Maimonides and is derived from his name *Rabbi Moses ben Maimon.* Maimonides is the Greek name for *Rambam* and means son of Maimon.

[23]Abbreviation probably representing the name of the Hebrew publisher.

Indeed, continues Maimon, the book *Amarot Tehorot* of Rabbi
Abraham Chayun was later reprinted twice in Jerusalem, in
1876 and 1903. The reprinters did not sense that it would have
been extremely important to append the *Sefer Hanimtzah* to this
book. But the scholar Gabriel Polak did publish it in his
collection *Ben Geroni* in 5611 (1851). He added to this book his
own introduction entitled "Message[24] to the Reader," as well as
the introduction of the original publisher, Rabbi Abraham
Akara. In this introduction, the publisher gives the reason why
this book is called by the name *Hanimtzah* "because in it one
finds[25] a good thing, sweet to the soul and healing to the body."
However, concludes Maimon, it seems nearly certain that it
is called *Sefer Hanimtzah* because it begins with the word
Hanimtzah, just as *Psalms Rabbah* is called *Schochar Tov* because it
begins with the words *Schochar Tov.* So, too, *Esther Rabbah* is
called *Midrash* of Aba Gurion because it begins with the name
Aba Gurion. There are many other similar examples. In
addition, Maimon reminds us that within *Sefer Hanimtzah*
another specific reason is cited in that the author states:

> I prepared and arranged this Book Concerning the One Who
> Exists with Wisdom and with Intellect[26] in a short form so that
> the reader can run through it and find in it his need and his
> desire, and find each medical therapy by itself so that he not

---

[24]Literally Hebrew: *davar;* matter, thing, news, that is, foreword.

[25]The Hebrew word *nimtzah* literally means found, discovered, existing,
available.

[26]God is said to have the attributes of wisdom and intellect and created the
world therewith. Although He is incorporeal and immutable and all concepts
of dimension, time, space, and their like do not apply to Him, He is spoken
of in human terms only metaphorically because of the limited understanding
of man. See Maimonides, *Treatise on the Unity of God (Ma'amar Hayichud),* his
Mishnah Commentary on Sanhedrin (Fred Rosner, translator, New York: Sepher
Hermon, 1981, pp. 151–152); his *Guide of the Perplexed* (S. Pines, translator,
Chicago: U. of Chicago Press, 1963, Part 1, Chapters 46, 47, 55, 56); and his
Mishneh Torah, Hilchot Yesodei Hatorah, Chapter 1 (M. Hyamson, translator,
Jerusalem: Boys Town, 1962, p. 34 ff). In his *Guide (loc. cit.),* p. 130,
Maimonides states that "He is existent, living, possessing power, knowing, and
willing, but essential attributes that are predicated of the Creator should not
be ascribed to Him and to us in the same sense."

become weak nor tired while he is searching for something [in the book]. Therefore, it is called *Sefer Hanimtzah.*[27]

Finally, Maimon asserts that it is probable that this book by Maimonides was written in Arabic and we do not know who translated it into Hebrew. However, the author's introduction, Maimon believes, was written by Maimonides himself in Hebrew and is similar to the beginning of his *Commentary on the Mishnah* where he wrote an introduction in pure Hebrew.

Although *Sefer Hanimtzah* is a rather obscure and little known work, brief bibliographic surveys of this work are found in a 1979 listing of books in print[28] and in a 1980 medical historical journal.[29]

---

[27]On the basis of the first part of this quote, *Sefer Hanimtzah* should be translated "Book Concerning He Who Exists" or "Book Concerning the One Who Exists." According to the latter part of the quote, an alternate translation would be "Book of Existence" or "Book of That Which Exists" or "Book of Findings."

[28]M. Kasher, editor *Sarey Ha'eleph,* Listing of Books in Print (Jerusalem: Beth Torah Sheleymah, 5739 [1979]), Vol. 2, pp. 490–491.

[29]S. Ashkenazi, Sefer Hanimtzah—Sekira Bibliographit, *Koroth* (Jerusalem, 1980 [5740]), Vol. 7. Nos. 11–12, p. 844.

TREATISE ON THE ONE WHO EXISTS

INTRODUCTION:[1] This is the Sefer Hanimtzah of the Luminary of the Exile,[2] Moses Maimonides

Thus states Abraham, the son of Don Solomon Akara, of blessed memory. With the help of God, I was assisted and was worthy of being among those who are deserving to bestow benefit to the public by the publication of these two books of two great luminaries such as Rabbi Samuel Di Vidash, may he be remembered forever, and Rabbi Don Abraham Chayun, may he be remembered forever. All their words are truthful and righteous. The first of these, his "Commentary on Lamentations,"[3] humbles the heart [of people], concludes with

---

[1] This first introduction is that of Akara and precedes the main work in the original 1596 edition.

[2] Title frequently used in reference to Maimonides and occasionally for other giants of Judaism such as Rabbenu Gershom.

[3] Literally: the scroll of elegies.

111

consolations, and turns the hearts of fathers and their children[4]
to the One who dwells in Heaven. From the place where he
leaves off, the other begins in his work *Amarot Tehorot* to return
the hearts of Israelites to their Father in Heaven through the
words of repentance with all its conditions, generalities, and
specifics. It is from these words of this rabbi, may he be
remembered forever, about the conditions of repentance that I
learned a wonderful lesson, just as our Sages of blessed
memory stated in the Midrash, *Leviticus Rabbah:*[5] "Ask wisdom,
what is the punishment for a sinner? . . . let him repent and
he will be forgiven."

My intent here is not to explain this statement that has
already been explained by the great scholars of the world. In
my humble opinion, I wrote only that which was shown to me
by Heaven. Thus, I asked about the end of the statement: what
is the meaning of the phrase "let him repent"; it should have
said "let him do penitence" for this is the customary expression,
that is to say "or let him do penitence." The answer is that
the conditions of doing penitence are those of the letters in the
word penitence.[6] Five conditions are required for the penitence
to be complete[7] and they are: prayer, sackcloth, confession,
shedding tears, and humbleness. He who does penitence thusly
will be forgiven. A person needs to fulfill all these things. If
otherwise, the penitence is not complete. In this manner a
person can heal his soul from its ailments and its stains and
return unto its father's house as in its youth.[8] For someone
whose soul is ailing is obligated to elucidate the words of this
rabbi, may he be remembered forever, and this will greatly
benefit his ailment and he will be rewarded and find tranquility
for his soul.

---

[4]Allusion to Malachi 3:24.
[5]Leviticus *Rabbah* 15:4.
[6]The Hebrew word for penitence is *teshuvah* and has five Hebrew letters,
each of which is the beginning of the Hebrew word for each condition
required to do proper penitence. These conditions are prayer *(tefilah)*,
sackcloth *(sak)*, confession *(viduy)*, shedding tears *(bechiyah)* and humbleness
(hachna'ah).
[7]Literally: superior, prominent, excellent, fine.
[8]Allusion to Leviticus 22:13.

Just as a person must strive for the health of his soul, he must also strive for the health of his body because God created one opposite the other.[9] It is good for a person to hold on to the one without relinquishing the other[10] as long as his intent is to serve the name of God [even] in his eating and his drinking and in everything else. This is what Maimonides, may he be remembered forever, said in the third chapter of *Hilchot De'ot*[11] and his *Eight Chapters*.[12] For the soul cannot show its activities except by means of a strong body as the wise man[13] said: there is not lacking any mingling,[14] referring to the mingling of the fundamental elements for the health of the body.

Since this is the truth, God delivered into my hands[15] this book, small in size but great in quality, of the great rabbi, the soaring eagle, Moses Maimonides, may he be remembered forever. It is called *Sefer Hanimtzah* because in it one finds a good thing, sweet to the soul and healing to the body. It[16] is a beneficial moistener that moistens appropriately and is wet enough to moisten something else.[17] One should pay attention to all its contents and not deflect one's attention therefrom. Because of its great benefit to sick people, whether internally or externally, I saw fit to publish this work. Let the healer of all mankind be recognized in the eyes of all people. And I ask the assistance of the true Helper, may He be praised, "in Whose hand are the depths of the earth.[18] My help cometh from the Lord, who made heaven and earth."[19]

---

[9]Allusion to Ecclesiastes 7:14.

[10]Allusion to Ecclesiastes 7:18.

[11]See Fred Rosner, *Medicine in the Mishneh Torah of Maimonides* (New York: Ktav, 1984), pp. 79–81.

[12]See J. I. Gorfinkle, *The Eight Chapters of Maimonides on Ethics* (New York: AMS Press, 1966), p. 104 (English) and p. 55 (Hebrew).

[13]King Solomon.

[14]Allusion to Song of Songs 7:3.

[15]Allusion to Exodus 21:13.

[16]*Sefer Hanimtzah.*

[17]Talmudic expression found in *Berachot* 25b and elsewhere.

[18]Psalm 95:4.

[19]Psalm 121:2.

Introduction of the author, may he be remembered forever[20]

The beverage of benefit and trust [is prepared as follows]: take the roots of the Sabbath, the roots of praise and of thanks, and the roots of rejoicing and of trust. Remove from them the seeds of sadness and of worry. Take the blossom of the pomegranate of knowledge and of understanding, and the roots of restraint and of contentment. Pound all this in the mortar of baseness and cook all this in the pot of humility and bind them together with eloquence[21] and mix all this in the waters of grace and of benevolence. Give two ya'im[22] of this beverage every morning and every evening to a patient suffering from the illness of despair, together with three ya'im of the waters of logic and moderation. Purify all this from the refuse of anger and of irascibility and mix all this in the essence of patience for the will of God, the Master of praise and of thanks. Give the patient drink in the vessel of praise of the Lord, may He be blessed by all, and the patient's [illness] becomes quiescent and tranquil.

Behold, I have introduced this work with these three beverages, which are all valuable and important virtues to fulfill the commandments of God[23] who assists and supports. He who conducts himself with these virtues improves himself and heals his soul and is successful in all his paths and all his deeds. He considers this world as nothing in relation to belief [in the world to come], and he finds sufficient that small amount which the Lord, may He be praised, allocated to him, as it is written: "Better is a little that the righteous hath, than the abundance of many wicked,"[24] and it is written: "Better is a handful of quietness, than both the hands full of labor and striving after

---

[20]Moses Maimonides.
[21]Literally: sweetness of the lips.
[22]Liquid measure.
[23]Literally: Heavenly wishes.
[24]Psalm 37:16.

wind,"[25] and it is written: "The teaching of Thy mouth is better unto me, than thousands of gold and silver."[26] I thus spoke of remedies for the soul, whether it is small or large. Let a wise man rejoice and increase his learning and let a discerning man acquire wise counsel.[27]

Maimonides' Commentary

[Regarding] *The Book of That Which Exists with Wisdom and with Intellect*, it is known and clear that the Lord, may He be blessed and exalted, is everything and bears everything and everything is dependent upon Him, including the existence of the atmosphere and the existence of all creatures in the atmosphere. The atmosphere was created from the power of God, may He be blessed and is proven by the fact that we can separate [some air] from the atmosphere for a short while by inflating a goatskin bottle, and anything that can be separated cannot survive. Every living creature[28] who is deprived of air[29] dies immediately, even fish and even fire.

Galen said that the scholar Plato observed people quarrying in search of silver. They were digging into the depths of the earth and were following the veins of the silver, which they discovered, until they reached a dark place. And everyone who inserted his head into that hole died. They came and inquired about this of Plato. He told them: go to that place and dig a hole above it so that the air can penetrate that place; and take a candle and insert it there. If it is extinguished, let no one enter there for he will die immediately. But if the candle is not extinguished, you may enter without fear. And do similarly for

---

[25]Ecclesiastes 4:6.
[26]Psalm 119:72.
[27]Proverbs 1:5.
[28]Literally: every creature possessing a soul.
[29]Literally: to whose soul air does not reach.

all deep places in which you dig. When the people left, his
disciples asked him about this matter and he told them: those
people died because they entered a place where the air could
not reach them and anyone whose soul is deprived of air[30] dies
immediately. They said to him: how about the air of fire? How
about the air of fish? He said to them: air enters fish through
their gills.[31]

Since the existence of the soul is dependent upon air, it is
necessary to know what the soul is. It is necessary to know
whether the soul is disseminated through the body or whether
it has a known place in the body and whether it is air or a
separate being.[32]

Galen said: the heaven and earth, the angels and human
beings [33] and all living creatures[34] move in the atmosphere just
like the yolk of an egg moves within the eggwhite, and it is
necessary to know whether the soul is disseminated throughout
the body or whether it has a known place in the body.

Galen said: if it were disseminated throughout the body and
bound to the flesh and the bone and the blood and the skin, it
would be impossible to cut away any part of the body without
also diminishing part of the soul. The latter will then be missing
in the same amount as that missing from the body, whether it is
a small or large amount of blood or hair or limbs. Rather, the
soul has a known site in the body but its power disseminates
throughout the body, just like the sun that is in a recognized
place but whose light and whose heat spreads throughout the
world. The sun is a created body and it has heat and light, and
the light of the sun is separate from its heat and its heat is
separate from its light. Just as the sun is a body and light and
heat, so, too, the soul is a pure creation and it has light and heat.

And the body has three important organs and they are

[30]*Ibid.*
[31]Literally: ears. Maimon entitles this paragraph "The Advice of Plato."
[32]Literally: creation.
[33]Literally: the upper and the lower, i.e., heavenly creatures and terrestrial beings.
[34]Literally: souls.

the brain, the heart, and the liver. Within them are the three powers that contain the vitality of man and they have three names: living soul,[35] spirit,[36] and soul.[37] The soul is the growing force that is within the liver. Every living being and plant uses this force. And this soul is an essence and it lusts for food and it is found in every wild and domesticated animal and in all living beings and in everything that grows. The spirit is within the heart and therein is the life of man in that it beats[38] and is found[39] in man, animals, and birds. The essence of the spirit resembles air and when the spirit leaves a person, that person dies. This spirit predominates and it is irascible and within it are the commands and the powers of God [?]. The living soul is the most exalted and its power is in the brain. It is the intellect[40] and it seeks knowledge and intelligence and does not participate with the others in coitus and in food intake. But the soul desires the pleasures of the bodies and its savorings for its own benefit. The spirit is in between in that it participates with the living soul in intellect and with the soul in seeking benefit to the body and its aggrandizement.

It is because the brain needs the liver and the heart, and the liver and the heart need the brain, and these are interconnected, that these opposites are called living soul, spirit, and soul because they are all connected to the body. For if a person were to eat foods that warm the blood, anger would ensue.[41] Behold, also, the condition of the body is in the spirit: if the condition of the body is appropriately blended and if a person is angry at another person because of his words or his actions, the power of the spirit predominates in the heart and heat is produced in the body. Then the heart changes because of the spirit.

The Creator, may He be blessed, placed the heart in the

---

[35]Hebrew: *neshamah.*
[36]Hebrew: *ruach.*
[37]Hebrew: *nefesh.*
[38]Literally: moves.
[39]Literally: included.
[40]Literally: soul of the intellect.
[41]Literally: increase.

middle of the body just as He placed the sun in the middle of
the spheres and placed the sphere [constellation] in the middle
of the large world.[42] Similarly, He placed the soul in the heart
and the heart in the body which is the small world. The flesh
and the bones are the vessels of the soul, and it needs its vessels just like a scribe needs the inkstand, the ink, and the
document, and just like the blacksmith needs the tongs, the
hammer, the anvil, and the utensils, for the blacksmith cannot
perform any work without the utensils. Just as the utensils[43]
need the craftsman, so, too, it is said that the soul needs its
utensils.

Within the brain there are three powers and they are in three
chambers. These [powers] are the following: imagination,
thought, and memory. Imagination means that one sees something which is not visible before him, such as if one sees
something before him in form and in shape. It is when one does
not see it with one's eyes but perceives it in one's imagination
through the power given to the soul to perceive that which is
not visible, and one recognizes it as if he sees it with his eyes.
This is the power of the imagination. The power of thought is
in the second part of the brain; it is when one perceives
something in one's mind which one becomes desirous of doing
as if it is already done, yet nothing has yet been done. Similarly,
one recognizes God following a lot of thought and understands
His works and deeds and thinks about them all the time. The
power of memory is in the third part [of the brain] facing the
nape. There is the seat of the intellect for he remembers
forgotten things with the power given to the living soul.
Therefore, if a person forgets and wishes to remember, he
lowers his head downward and the natural humor[44] descends
from the memory [part of the] brain to the thought [part of the]
brain and from the thought to the imaginative and he remem-

---

[42]That is, universe.

[43]The Hebrew text has *poor (dalim)* followed by *utensils (kelim)* in parentheses, apparently a copyist's correction to make the phrase intelligible.

[44]Literally: liquid.

bers that which he forgot. Memory functions when the channels between the various parts of the brain[45] are patent and the
humor descends rapidly from one to the other and he remembers quickly that which he forgot. However, if the humor is
decayed with putrefaction, and the channels are sealed from
the force of the sticky putrefied humor, forgetfulness occurs
immediately and, after forgetfulness, *badalatiko*.[46]

Many illnesses occur secondary to the humors of the brain if
they are sticky and do not flow. Therefore, I recommend that
you always accustom yourself to therapies that cleanse the head,
lest the patient go mad and lose his mind. Afterwards, the task
is very hard and difficult to dissolve the sticky rotten humors
that seal the channels [between the chambers of the brain]. And
the patient loses his mind and his speech and his [sensation of]
touch and ability to walk and [sensation of] smell; and he loses
his sensations because the humor is not dissolved at all and
becomes hard like glass.

The general rule in regard to the four fundamental elements: I have already stated that I prepared and arranged this
Book of That Which Exists with Wisdom and with Intellect in a short
form so that the reader can run through it[47] and find in it his
need and his desire, and find each medical therapy by itself so
that he not become weak nor tired while he is searching for
something. Therefore, it is called *Sefer Hanimtzah*.[48]

All creations in the world are [made] of four fundamental
elements. The substances of human beings, domesticated animals, wild animals, birds, fish, plants, metals, and precious
stones are composed of fire and air[49] and water and earth. All
four are combined together and each one is changed in the

---

[45]Literally: between brain and brain.

[46]Foreign word; meaning unclear; ? folly or madness.

[47]Allusion to Habakkuk 2:2, that is, can read it swiftly.

[48]See my introduction to this work.

[49]Hebrew: *ruach*; literally: spirit or wind. In describing the four fundamental elements in his *Mishneh Torah (Hilchot Yesodei Hatorah* 3:10), Maimonides
also uses the term *ruach*, whereas in his *Ma'amar Hayichud* he uses the term
avir, literally: air or atmosphere.

mixture until the composite is a mixture of all four.[50] The mixture does not resemble any one of them when the latter is alone nor does any single part [of the mixture] resemble fire by itself or air by itself or earth by itself or water by itself. When they are mixed, they change and resemble that form which God commanded to be made and they become a single being. In every being that is composed of these four elements there exist coldness, warmth, dryness, and moistness, together. However, there are some beings in which there exists an excess of one of the four elements such as a living creature in which warmth is found in excess over fire, and such as stones in which one observes an excess of earth; for that reason they are hard and dry. In a similar manner, one finds one being warmer than another warm being, and one being drier than another dry being. So, too, one finds beings in which only coldness is observed and beings in which only moistness is observed, and beings in which equal quantities of coldness and moistness are observed or equal quantities of coldness and dryness. It is according to the abundance of an element in the essential mixing [of the four elements] that the action of that element and its nature in the mixed being are noticed.

The nature of fire is hot and dry and it is the lightest of all of them. Air is hot and moist. Water is cold and moist and earth is hard and dry.[51]

These four fundamental elements transform into each other every day and every hour—part of them but not all of their

---

[50]In his *Hilchot Yesodei Hatorah* 4:1, Maimonides states: "these four bodies, which are fire, air, earth, and water, are the fundamental elements of all created things that are beneath the firmament. The substance of all things— man, beast, bird, reptile, fish, plant, mineral, precious stones and pearls, stones for buildings, mountains, and clods of earth—is composed of these four fundamental elements."

[51]A similar statement is made by Maimonides in his *Ma'amar Haychud*. Also, in his *Hilchot Yesodei Hatorah* 4:2, Maimonides states: "the nature of fire is hot and dry and it is the lightest of all. And air is hot and moist, and water is cold and moist, and earth is dry and cold and it is the heaviest of all; and water is lighter than the earth and is, therefore, found above on [the surface of] the earth. And air is lighter than water and therefore blows on the surface of water. And fire is lighter than air."

essence.[52] How so? The element earth, which is closest to water, changes and crumbles and becomes water. Similarly, some water adjacent to the air transforms and evaporates[53] and goes back and forth and becomes air. So, too, some of the air which is adjacent to fire changes, transforms, and becomes fire. Similarly, fire which is close to the earth transforms and becomes earth. This transformation occurs a little at a time over a prolonged period.[54] No fundamental element is completely transformed until all the water has become air or all the air has become fire because it is impossible for any of the four fundamental elements to be totally abolished. Rather, only a little fire changes to air and a little air to fire and a little water to earth and a little earth to water. This is the way these four transform in a continuing cycle. When these mixtures occur in equal proportions, the body is in good order and healthy. But if any of these turnings leans toward coldness or hotness or dryness or moistness, the body deteriorates and changes and the person is harmed.

Corresponding[55] to these fundamental elements are the four natures [of man] known in Arabic as *al tzafra*, *abalgam*, *alsoda*, and *aldam*. Corresponding to them are red bile and blood and white humor and black bile.[56] Red bile corresponds to the fundamental element fire in that it is hot and dry. Blood corresponds to the fundamental element air, which is hot and moist. White humor corresponds to the fundamental element water in that it is cold and moist. Black bile corresponds to the fundamental element earth, which is cold and dry.

---

[52]In his *Ma'amar Hayichud*, Maimonides states that these four substances and their properties undergo mixing and blending rather than changing into each other.

[53]Literally: dissolves, melts, thaws.

[54]Literally: according to the length of the days.

[55]Literally: opposite to.

[56]Maimonides here cites the medieval concept of body health being the result of the mixing in appropriate proportions of the four body humors: black bile (melancholy), red bile (blood), white humor (mucus or phlegm) and yellow bile. Disequilibrium of these humors results in disease. See F. Rosner and S. Muntner, translators, *Moses Maimonides' Medical Aphorisms* (New York: Bloch for Yeshiva Univ. Press, 1973), Vol. 1, pp. 168–169.

Also corresponding to them are the twelve constellations:[57]
the ram,[58] the lion, and the archer contain heat and dryness.
The twins, the balance, and the water bearer[59] contain heat and
moistness. The ox, the virgin, and the goat contain coldness
and dryness. The crab, the scorpion, and the fishes contain
coldness and moistness.[60] Seven planets make use of the twelve

---

[57]Twelve signs of the zodiac are Aries the Ram, Taurus the Bull, Gemini
the Twins, Cancer the Crab, Leo the Lion, Virgo the Virgin, Libra the
Balance, Scorpio the Scorpion, Sagittarius the Archer, Capricorn the Goat,
Aquarius the Water Bearer, and Pisces the Fishes.

[58]Literally: lamb.

[59]Literally: bucket, pail.

[60]It is surprising to see Maimonides cite the signs of the zodiac in view of
his strong opposition to astrology. The generally prevalent belief in astrology
during the Middle Ages was fully shared by the Jews, many of whom were
convinced of the fundamental truth of the power of celestial bodies to
influence human destiny. Maimonides was one of the few who not only dared
raise his voice against this almost universally held belief, but even branded it
as a superstition akin to idolatry. He unequivocally prohibited anyone to
influence his actions by astrology, as an offense punishable by disciplinary
flogging. In his treatise on "Idolatry and Heathen Ordinances" in his *Mishneh
Torah*, he categorically rejects astrology and other superstitious practices and
belief (Idolatry 11:16).

In his famous *Letter to Yemen* (See A. S. Halkin, *Moses Maimonides' Epistle to
Yemen* [New York: American Academy of Jewish Research, 1952], p. 111)
Maimonides denounces astrology as a fallacy and delusion:

I note that you are inclined to believe in astrology and in the influence of
the past and future conjunctions of the planets upon human affairs. You
should dismiss such notions from your thoughts. Cleanse your mind as one
cleanses dirty clothes. Accomplished scholars, whether they are religious
or not, refuse to believe in the truth of this science. Its postulates can be
refuted by real proofs on rational grounds.

In his pyschological and ethical treatise entitled *The Eight Chapters (She-
monah Perakim)*, see J. L. Garfinkle, *The Eight Chapters of Maimonides on Ethics*
(New York: AMS Press, 1966), XII and p. 104 (English), p. 55 (Hebrew),
Maimonides again sharply inveighs against astrology, denouncing it as a
deception that is subversive to the faith and teachings of Judaism: "I have
entered into this subject so thou mayest not believe the absurd ideas of
astrologers, who falsely assert that the constellation at the time of one's birth
determines whether one is to be virtuous or vicious."

In his *Letter on Astrology*, in answer to an inquiry from Jewish scholars of

constellations. The moon has the crab. The sun has the lion. Mars has the ram and the scorpion. Mercury has the virgin and the twins. Jupiter has the archer and the fishes. Venus has the ox and the balance; and He created *Teli*[61] with its head and tail. Saturn has the goat and the water bearer.[62]

The sphere of the sun is hot and dry and the sphere of the moon is hot and moist. The sphere of Mars is hot and dry. The head of *Teli* is hotter and drier than the nature of Jupiter and its tail is cold and dry and moist in relation to the nature of the sun and the moon. The sphere of Venus is colder and moister than the nature of the waters.

The day and the night are comprised of twenty-four hours, which are attracted to the twelve constellations and seven planets, which serve the seven days of the week. For on the first day and during the fifth night the sun rules. On the second day and during the sixth night the moon rules. Mars rules on the third day and during the seventh night. Mercury rules on the fourth day and during the first night. Jupiter rules on the fifth day and during the second night; Venus[63] on the seventh day and during the fourth night.

Corresponding to the twelve months of the year are[64] the twelve constellations: ram, ox, twins, crab, lion, virgin, balance,

---

southern France, Maimonides exposes the foibles and fallacies of astrology. Noteworthy here is the oft-quoted comment that the Second Temple was destroyed and national independence forfeited because the Jews had been occupied with astrology. Maimonides told his correspondents that he did not take the matter lightly, but had studied it thoroughly and came to the conclusion that astrology was an irrational illusion of fools who mistake vanity for wisdom and superstition for knowledge. See A. Marx, "The Correspondence between the Rabbis of Southern France and Maimonides about Astrology" (*Hebrew Union College Annual*), 3(1926):311–358, 4(1927): 493–494.

[61]Name of a constellation or planet?

[62]See Maimonides' discussion on the planets in his *Ma'amar Hayichud*, his *Mishneh Torah (Hilchot Yesodei Hatorah* 3: 1 ff) and his *Guide of the Perplexed* (Part 2, Chapter 9).

[63]The Hebrew text has *Teleh* or lamb instead of *Nogah* for Venus. ?? translator's or copyist's error.

[64]Literally: He gave, that is, God.

scorpion, archer, goat, water carrier, fishes, one for each
month. Corresponding to the four fundamental elements He
created the winds of the world. The eastern wind is hot and
moist, the western wind is cold and moist, the northern wind is
cold and dry, and the southern wind is hot and dry.

Corresponding to them are the four seasons of the year: in
the season of Nissan[65] it is hot and moist and in it the blood
prevails on account of the air. In the season of Tammuz[66] heat
and dryness prevail on account of the fire; in this season the red
bile prevails. In the season of Tishri[67] cold and dryness occur
on account of the earth; in this season the black bile prevails.
In the season of Tevet[68] cold and moistness occur on account of
the waters; in this season the white humor prevails. Similarly,
the months are divided into four parts: the first seven days are
hot and moist on account of the fundamental element blood
and every illness that occurs therein is caused by the blood. The
second seven days are hot and dry and any illness that occurs
therein is caused by the red bile. The third seven days are cold
and dry on account of the black bile and any illness that occurs
therein is caused by the black bile. The fourth seven days are
cold and moist on account of the waters and any illness that
occurs therein is caused by the white humor.[69]

If any illness occurs at the beginning of the Nissan season, the
illness becomes intensified because the blood becomes stronger
at the beginning of that season. Similarly, at the beginning of
the Tammuz season, the red bile intensifies with extreme heat
and with dryness. Similarly, at the beginning of the Tishri
season, the black bile intensifies in blackness and great
sorrow.[70] So, too, at the beginning of the Tevet season the white

---

[65]Approximately spring.

[66]Approximately summer.

[67]Approximately fall.

[68]Approximately winter.

[69]For a fuller discussion of the four humors and the illnesses related to or
caused by them, see *Moses Maimonides' Medical Aphorisms* (F. Rosner and S.
Muntner, trans.), Vol. 1 pp. 48–55, 80, 98, 103–105, 131, 181.

[70]Melancholy was thought to be caused by an excess of black bile.

humor prevails and intensifies into a strong and powerful humor.

Similarly, the twenty-four hours of the day are divided into four parts: during the first six hours, the blood prevails; during the second [six hours] the red [bile] prevails; during the third [six hours] the black bile prevails, during the fourth [six hours], the white humor prevails. They are established on account of the four fundamental elements.

The following pertains to the four fundamental substances: blood is black and red, its aroma is malodorous, its taste is sweet and it is smooth. Black bile has a black and yellow appearance like blades of grass; its aroma is pleasant and its taste is sour. The aroma of [white] humor is neutral[71] and thick consistency is mixed therein and its appearance is white and its taste is sweet and pleasant.

Five senses were created in man: taste, touch, smell, vision, and hearing. The bones in the body of a human being[72] are divided into four groups: in the head there are forty-two bones; in the arms and hands there are eighty-two bones; in the body and joints there are forty; and in the legs and feet there are eighty-four. The sum total is two hundred and forty-eight.[73]

Similarly, there are two hundred and eighty-four blood vessels in the body of a human being: one hundred in the head, one hundred in the hands and arms to strengthen the sinews that support the body, and seventy in the body and fourteen in the thighs in the upper abdomen that refers to the stomach in which all food and beverage is digested[74] to nourish the body.

---

[71]Literally: average or moderate; that is, not good nor bad.

[72]Literally: man.

[73]The 248 bones are enumerated in the Talmud (Oholot 1:8) and discussed at length in Nedarim 32b and Moed Katan 17a. These 248 bones or limbs correspond to the days of the lunar year and the 365 sinews correspond to the days of the solar year (Makkot 23b). For a fuller discussion of the numbers of bones, limbs and sinews as found in ancient Jewish and other sources, see the English version of Julius Preuss's classic book Biblical and Talmudic Medicine, Fred Rosner, translator (New York: Hebrew Publishing Co., 1978), pp. 60–67.

[74]Literally: cooked.

It is appropriate that a physician know this matter well as
follows: as soon as food that a person eats properly enters the
stomach, the stomach immediately tries to grind it with the
power of the heat of the liver, which is hot like fire. It sits in
the stomach like the hearth under the kettle and digests[75] the
food in the stomach until the end of six hours after it entered
there. When the food is digested it becomes like cooked barley
soup when it is thick. The food that has been transformed in
this matter exits from the stomach and enters into the intestines, which have twelve fingers.[76] Immediately a single tube is
formed in the liver, which the wise physicians call the gate of
the liver. This tube becomes filled until it resembles a large
blood vessel without blood, and other blood vessels coming
from it become revealed like branches, and they separate into
eight divisions. In the medical textbooks, these divisions are
called *masrik*. These divisions also subdivide into yet other
divisions, and blood vessels come out from all of them, and they

---

[75]Literally: cooks.

[76]In his *Medical Aphorisms (opus cit.* pp. 42–43), Maimonides quotes Galen
who states:

One can consider the assimiliation of nutriments to occur conceptually in
three stages. The first stage is digestion in the stomach that receives the
digestate [literally: cooked food] and adds it to the stomach substance until
it is full. Simultaneously, a portion thereof rises to the liver. The second
stage is the transition to the intestines where it adds to the skin [? omenta]
and the liver substance. At this time, a small portion is distributed
throughout the body. Consider at this time that the material that was
added to the substance of the stomach in the first stage has already become
absorbed into and inseparable from its substance. The third stage is from
the time one can consider the stomach to be nourished and that its
substance has already assimilated that which is absorbed in the second
stage. Meanwhile, the intestines and the liver digest and dilute that which
was already added to their substance.

The remainder passes to the other organs of the body and settles there.
The digestion that occurs in the stomach is one type of alteration.
Similarly, also, is the metabolism of the liver and the metabolism that
occurs in every one of the organs. After this third metabolic phase, there
is an additional metabolic phase, a fourth that is called assimilation. The
name assimilation is nothing more than another name for alimentation.

resemble large branches. These vessels, which subdivide in the liver, are called *kamusha*.

In addition, some of these vessels pull and exit somewhat from the liver and extend to below the stomach and become immersed in the stomach and in the intestines of twelve fingers. From there they draw into the liver from all the power of the food which is in the stomach and the intestines through the power of sucking and drinking, just as the vessels in the roots of a tree draw their nourishment from the moistness and wetness of the earth. In this manner, the tree becomes renewed and moist and its roots become thick. The vessels of the liver do the same thing until they have imbibed all the power of the food from the stomach and the digestate[77] which is in the intestines of twelve fingers, into the vessels which are within the liver. Everything within the liver becomes filled from the moisture of these vessels and all the food and humors become digested in the vessels and in the liver. Because of the strength of that digestion, the entire liver becomes filled with blood from that digestion and from that blood two types of foam are formed: one is thin and pure and that is the red bile that draws the bile, which is near the liver, into its sac.[78] The second type is thick and black and is called *asuda* in Arabic; and the spleen draws it into itself.

The pure and clean blood that is in the liver is imbibed by the heart which is nourished therefrom. The brain drinks from this pure and clean blood that is in the heart, and the remainder is sent to all the [blood] vessels in the body. From the thick black blood there develops the black bile, which is cold and dry in relation to the nature of the earth, and from the clear and pure part of that black bile, laughter is produced. Therefore, one finds that "he who laughs a lot is mad"[79] because of the nature of the black bile.

The water that develops from the blood and which is found in the [blood] vessels is drawn into the kidneys, which receive it

---

[77]Literally: thickness.
[78]That is, the gallbladder.
[79]Allusion to Ecclesiastes 2:2.?

from the tubes that lie on the loins and traverse within the spine from top to bottom[80] from the right and from the left. From above they are attached and from below they are separated. The water that develops from the blood of the liver and from the vessels enters those vessels and urine is generated there. The kidneys receive the urine and send it to the bladder, which is the vesicle known as *visaga*. This vesicle has no opening except one through the sex organ. When the urine exits from the kidneys it falls onto the side of the bladder where the vesicle is located. The vesicle perspires profusely internally and with strength a little exits and increases until all the urine comes into the bladder and there it is appropriately gathered and remains there until it exits through the sex organ of man. For this reason, physicians instruct one to examine[81] the urine for in it one can recognize the well being of the body or the opposite.[82]

The Holy One, blessed be He, gave the tongue nine tastes: bitter, sweet, unsalted, salted, sour, pungent, sharp, constipating, and oily. The nine tastes are of nine types. Attached to it[83] are sinews, which move it for all its needs to dissolve the food and to move during speech. He created[84] the lung to breathe for the heart so that the body not burn up because of the great heat of the heart which is a consuming fire.[85]

The trachea is there to bring in the air and the humors to the body and to give forth the voice, and He gave the esophagus the power to allow all food and beverages to pass through it. At the mouth of the trachea, to protect it from danger, there is a covering which is known as *chaviliya*. The stomach is connected to the esophagus by sinews, which assist with the natural power with which the stomach is endowed. And the natural spirit that comes from it consists of four forces; and these are *aldacha*,

---

[80]Literally: above to below.

[81]Literally: take.

[82]Early description of urinalysis and its value in assessing health or disease. See also Fred Rosner, "Moses Maimonides' Aphorisms Regarding Analysis of Urine" in the *Annals of Internal Medicine*, Vol. 71, July 1969, pp. 217–220.

[83]The tongue.

[84]Literally: gave.

[85]Allusion to Deuteronomy 4:24 and 9:3.

almascha, altzamah, and *aldafea* in Arabic. In Hebrew, they are
the drawing, the holding, the grinding, and the dispatching
[forces]. The drawing force is to draw the entering food into
the stomach. The holding force is to hold the food in the
stomach. The grinding force is to grind all the food in the
stomach, and the dispatching force is to dispatch all the food
that is in the stomach after it has been detained there for six
hours.[86] The dispatching force rapidly empties into the intestine of the twelve fingers. This intestine is serpentine so that the
food should not rapidly exit from it until the liver has extracted
from it all that it needs and the essence thereof[87] is drawn into
it[88] with a strong force, just as a magnet draws iron to it. The
heat of the liver forcefully cooks it[89] until it is converted into
blood and, from the boilings in the blood, gives rise to three
cold humors to cool off the power of the red bile, which burns
like fire. Natural humor is cold and moist and is found in the
head and chest and lung. Its nature is cold and moist and it
disseminates throughout the entire body and nourishes it and

---

[86]Quoting Galen, Maimonides, in his famous *Medical Aphorisms (opus cit.* p.
46), describes other "forces" in the body:

> The force in semen that can be found in material within blood is capable
> of making bones. It is material capable of making nerves and similar to
> other materials which make flat-appearing organs. This is called the
> *procreating force* since it gives birth to and generates material not previously
> present. It is also called the *developmental force.* The force that gives shape
> and quality to that material until the bone has reached a certain size and a
> certain form as other flat–appearing organs is called the *structure–forming
> force.* It is the one that has a different origin, namely, intellectual, in
> addition to its natural origin. The force that causes growth of that small
> bone and enables the small nerve to grow and mature is called the *growth
> force.* The force that nourishes a limb until it grows and is able to eliminate
> superfluities is called the *nutritive force.* It has four powers: attraction,
> retention, expulsion of [wastes], and alteration [of form]. The power of
> alteration is also called the *digestive force.* It does not complete its function
> save through its powers of retention and assimilation.

[87]That is, the food digestate.
[88]That is, the liver.
[89]That is, the food digestate.

becomes united with the bones and the flesh[90] and all the
channels of the body, from bone to bone and from flesh to
flesh. The remainder is dispatched to the kidneys, which
extract it until it resembles red water, after which it is dispatched to the bladder. In the bladder, there are two wide
vessels called *berabin* in Arabic, and these [waste liquids] remain
there until they become clear like water and these waters are
called urine. The latter indicates sickness of man or his well-
being. The food excess that is within the intestines becomes
feces. The red bile rapidly dissolves that which is in the
intestines and dispatches it from intestine to intestine, and
there are six intestines established to expel the feces.

The Lord, may He be praised, placed the liver on the right
side of the stomach, just like the hearth under the kettle, to
cook the food. He placed the spleen on the left side to cool off
the heat of the humors and the predominance of the (?)
therein. He made a sac for the testicles with stretched sinews to
draw into them the essence of all the dissolved [foods] and to
thereby produce procreative seed. Both in man and in all other
living creatures, the offspring resemble the parents.

He created the heart of man with two chambers. In one
resides the spirit, which is the spirit of life. The second is full of
blood, and it is the pure blood that is in the liver. It is that blood
which nourishes the heart and the brain. Within the heart are
the [person's] will, anger, harshness, compassion, strength,
softheartedness, anxiety, joy, insolence, baseness, and humility.
In it is the perverting inclination and, from the latter, the
pulsating vessels are stimulated, and from them the sign of
death and life can be seen.

After this strong [body] structure has been built, it is
important[91] that the structure not be destroyed or damaged. It
is necessary that a person avoid things that destroy the body
and damage it, and accustom oneself to those things that

---

[90]Hebrew: *basar*, sometimes translated: muscle.
[91]Literally: necessary.

maintain one's health,[92] and they are the following: a person should not eat unless he is hungry nor drink unless he is thirsty. He should not postpone his eliminations[93] for even a single moment; rather every time that micturition or defecation become necessary, he should respond thereto immediately.[94]

A person should not eat until his stomach is replete. Rather, he should diminish his intake by one-fourth of satiation. One should not drink water during meals save a little and mixed with wine. When the food begins to be digested in the intestines, one may drink as much as one needs.[95] One should not eat until one has examined oneself carefully lest it be necessary to excrete wastes. A person should not eat until he has walked prior to eating so that his body begins to become warmed, or he should perform any [type of] physical task or tire himself by any form of exertion. The rule in this matter is that one should exert one's body every day until it begins to warm, after which one rests a little until one becomes settled[96] and then one may eat. If one washes with warm water or exercises[97] it is beneficial. After this he should wait awhile and then eat.[98]

When a person eats he should always be sitting in his place

---

[92]Maimonides makes a nearly identical statement in his *Mishneh Torah* (*Hilchot De'ot* 4:1).

[93]Literally: withhold his openings.

[94]See *Hilchot De'ot* 4:1. See also *Berachot* 62b and *Makkot* 16b where it states that withholding one's bodily functions comes under the heading of "You shall not make yourselves abominable" (Leviticus 11:43). Besides, it gives rise to bad diseases and endangers life (see Maimonides; *Hilchot Maacholot Assurot* 17:31). Also: more people die from intestinal disorders than from hunger (*Shabbat* 33a).

[95]In *Hilchot De'ot* 4:2, Maimonides adds: "however, even when the food has been digested one should not drink water excessively." See also *Gittin* 70a, *Berachot* 42b, and *Niddah* 24b.

[96]In *Hilchot De'ot* 4:2, Maimonides has: "until one's soul has settled."

[97]In *Hilchot De'ot* 4:2, Maimonides has: "after the exercise."

[98]See also the Talmud: Anybody who takes in more drink than food undermines his health (*Niddah* 24b). He who requires easing himself and still goes on eating is like a furnace stoked on top of its ashes—which is the beginning of a bad odor (*Shabbat* 82a). There are three kinds of perspiration that do the body good, among them that which comes from work (*Avot deRabi Natan* 41). Work is valuable, because a man is warmed up by it (*Gittin* 16b).

and recline on the left side and rest.[99] He should not walk nor ride[100] nor agitate his body nor promenade until the food is digested in his intestines. Anyone who indulges in sexual intercourse [immediately] after the meal brings upon himself serious and grave illnesses.[101]

The day and night consist of twenty-four hours. It is sufficient for a person to sleep one-third thereof which is eight hours. He should arise at the end of the night[102] so that from the beginning of his sleep until the sun comes out there should be eight hours. Thus, he will arise from his bed before the sun rises.

A person should not sleep on his face nor on his back nor on his right side at the beginning of the night, but on his left side,[103] so that the entrails and the stomach are full with food and beverages and they are on the left side.[104] It is necessary for them to remain in their place until the food is digested [and assimilated] so that they not turn over and fall on the liver when they are full, so that they not heat it and force the red bile out from it because the body would burn and *dek alcacad* would result therefrom. For if the liver becomes heated from the trouble in the entrails and the stomach, which are full, the liver immediately swells and the gallbladder becomes heated, and

---

[99]In his *Hilchot De'ot* 4:3, Maimonides states: "or recline on the left side."

[100]In his *Hilchot De'ot* 4:3, Maimonides here adds: "nor exercise."

[101]In his *Hilchot De'ot* 4:3, Maimonides has: "anyone who promenades immediately after his meal or who fatigues himself brings upon himself serious and grave illnesses." See also *Gittin* 70a, *Berachot* 46b, *Pesachim* 108a, *Shabbat* 129b, and *Taanit* 10b.

[102]In his *Hilchot De'ot* 4:4, Maimonides states: "and these should be at the end of the night."

[103]In his *Hilchot De'ot* 4:5, Maimonides states: "a person should not sleep on his face nor on his back but on his side; at the beginning of the night on the left, and at the end of the night on the right side. Further, he should not go to sleep shortly after eating but should wait approximately three or four hours after a meal. One should not sleep during the day." See also *Berachot* 13b and *Niddah* 14a. King David is reported to have taken short naps during the day, some sixty respirations in all *(Sukkah* 26b).

[104]In the *Sefer Hanimtzah* there is now a lengthy digression on digestion and assimilation of food which has no parallel in Maimonides' *Hilchot De'ot*.

the gallbladder pours out jaundice and fever and burns the body and mixes it with yellow bitterness which assists the body. However, if he lies quietly on his left side until the food has been digested and the intestines and stomach have cooled a little and the air goes through them until half the night, and the air also goes on the liver until half the night, and the liver becomes tranquil, and the intestines and the stomach also become tranquil and begin to cool—then it is good to sleep on the right side. When they are tranquil near the liver, the liver and the gall [bladder] receive some of the coolness and it is beneficial to them, and the entrails and the stomach receive some of the heat from the liver and it is beneficial to them. Each benefits from the other.[105]

The stomach is in the upper abdomen and food and drink are digested[106] there to nourish the body. The site of the blood and its opening is the brain, the eyes, and the liver because the blood is digested in the latter. The liver is hot and moist and the red bile is in it; and it is situated to the right of the stomach and it attracts[107] the food that nourishes and is hot and moist. With the power of heat, the liver transforms [the food] to blood and colors it and then dispatches it to the heart and to the brain according to the attribute[108] with which it was endowed as will be explained.

The site of the red bile is in the gallbladder and its openings,[109] the ears, and the stomach. The gallbladder receives from the liver the hot, dry, and pure food, and there is some like its nature. And the food becomes natural and is transformed to the appearance of the red bile after which it is dispatched to the vessels and is converted to blood.

The site of the black bile is in the spleen and its openings, the nostrils, the spleen,[110] and the kidneys. The spleen is cold and

---

[105]That is, the liver from the intestines and stomach and the stomach and intestines from the liver.

[106]Literally: cooked.

[107]Literally: sucks.

[108]Literally: custom.

[109]The biliary ducts.

[110]It is unclear why "the spleen" is repeated.

dry because of the black bile and is situated[111] on the left side and it cools the intestines and the abdomen because of the dryness when the entrails are boiling because of the large amount of warming food. The blood and the liver and the red bile and the kidneys are hot and dry and are situated on the right side and on the left side. Each of them exerts its power in the lower abdomen to strengthen it and to preserve it with its heat to expel the feces and the urine from the body. The spleen receives the purest part of the food from the black bile and dispatches it to the vessels, and it mixes with the blood and with the red bile.

The site of the white humor is in the lung and its openings, the trachea and the mouth. The lung is moist on account of this humor and is situated above the stomach, receives the ground part of the food which is cold and moist, converts it to humor, dispatches it to the vessels where it mixes with the black and the red biles and with blood and there turns into blood. And the entrails and the intestines receive the remainder of the food and beverage that is in the stomach. And the lower abdomen, which is called *sani debay*[112] *onvaligo*, receives the food and the beverages from the intestines. The sinews of the kidneys, which are like two pipes, receive the urine and the superfluous waters extracted from the food that is within the intestines. The sinews of the membrum,[113] which are called *vasiga*, receive the water from the pipes and dispatch it to the membrum. In the membrum, the water gathers and is metabolized[114] there until it pours forth through the opening of the membrum.[115]

The *sharshur*[116] is the intestine called concealed; it is the intestine concealed in the anus[117] to receive the wastes and the feces and the excrements which are in the lower abdomen.

---

[111]Literally: serves.
[112]Literally: disliked by wolves; a popular name for the inner rumen. See *Chullin* 50b and 58b.
[113]The penis.
[114]Literally: cooked.
[115]The urethra.
[116]Literally: the chain or link.
[117]Literally: mouth of the ring.

The red bile expels them to excrete them rapidly with the power that the Lord, may He be blessed, endowed it. God created[118] four powers in the body to accustom the body to tranquility and security with repose and peace,[119] and they are the attracting, the retaining, the grinding, and the dispatching [forces].[120] They attract the food with Divine power, and the food is composed of the four fundamental elements. From the food there develop[121] the mixtures[122] and from their resemblances there develop vessels that are organs whereby each of these vessels is an organ with its own specific purpose. And the structure of the whole body is composed of these vessels that are organs, and the body would fall apart if they were destroyed.[123]

A general rule in eating is that if a person eats a lot or eats hard and bad foods, the stomach swells and pours them into the liver and the spleen and the gallbladder. These [organs] cannot tolerate these [foods] and pour them into the heart and the brain; and the brain and the heart pour them into the vessels throughout the body. The [food] juices and the heaviness of the blood weigh heavily on the liver. The blood immediately becomes mixed with the red bile and their heats are mixed and the food in the stomach is burned; and the body is damaged and acute fever and consumption develops therefrom, which involves[124] the entire body because of the heaviness. It enlarges the brain and ascends to the membrane. Between these two there is produced blood from which acute fever develops, which drives a person out of his mind. One should expel[125] blood from the nostrils and it will cease producing wounds. There are therapies in which one covers the head—these will be

---

[118]Literally: placed.

[119]Allusion to Isaiah 30:15.

[120]See note 76.

[121]Literally: are compounded.

[122]Meaning unclear.

[123]Meaning unclear.

[124]Literally: surround.

[125]Literally: vomit.

explained in due course[126]—by which the wounds become soothed and the distress is removed and the person becomes tranquil. There are many [therapeutic] maneuvers for each fever as will be explained, in due course, with God's help.

The stomach dissolves bad and hard foods and pours them out and disseminates them throughout the body and the body is harmed thereby and damaged. There develops therefrom tertian or quotidian[127] fever[128] according to the excess con-

---

[126]Literally: in their place.

[127]Literally: permanent.

[128]An entire chapter of Maimonides' *Medical Aphorisms (opus cit.* pp. 203–223) is devoted to fevers. In it, he discusses acute and chronic fevers including quotidian, tertian, and quartan fevers, their causes and their treatment. For example, in quoting Galen, Maimonides states:

If the cooking of foods is incomplete in the stomach or liver, then fevers will be prolonged and become sharper. Therefore, in all types of fever, it is important to pay particular attention to proper digestion of food and to the strengthening of the stomach and liver with astringent medications.

If a person is suffering from a fever and his body contains an excess of raw superfluities and his stomach is already weak from nausea, then his whole body appears swollen. The facial appearance of some of these patients becomes pale or cyanotic or ashen and their pulse becomes small and irregular. Such patients should not be phlebotomized under any circumstances, nor can they tolerate purgation although they are in need of emptying. . . .

Intermittent fevers that cease during specific intervals are of three types and these are: (a) tertian fever, (b) that which comes daily called permanent or quotidian, and (c) quartan fever. Tertian fever occurs from red bile which putrefies. Quotidian fever is produced from biles that begin to decay and are of the white type. Quartan fever develops as a result of the deterioration of black bile. If the liquid that is producing the fever becomes distributed throughout the entire body, then these three types of fever and their specific intervals will be clearly manifest. The signs of a pure tertian fever that are immediately evident when one visits and examines the patient at the beginning of the episode are eleven in number as follows: (1) severe shaking chills where one has the sensation of needle pricks; (2) thirst and burning heat that is not of long duration; (3) regularity in all respects; (4) the episode would end as quickly as possible; (5) equal distribution of the heat throughout the entire body; (6) increase in fever and its aggravation when one first places one's hand on the body, and then defervescence of the fever after prolonged placement of the hand [on the body]; (7) the movement of warm vapors from the openings after drinking wine and water; (8) the emesis of biles or excretion of biles

sumption of the hard or bad food. If the heaviness is produced from an excess of good food to which the stomach is not accustomed and it pours into the body, there will be heaviness in the body and sweetness develops in the mouth and he is benefited by immediate bloodletting. But if one does not hurry to let blood according to the excessive satiation and heaviness that is in the stomach, he develops acute consumption in the head and great heat in the stomach and the juices in the stomach will burn. And if he eats meat or something [similar] or drinks wine or does not watch himself properly, it harms the body and transforms into quartan fever.[129]

---

through the feces or urine depending upon which contains the most bilious elements, or sometimes all three occur simultaneously; (9) an evenly-distributed perspiration over the entire body; (10) the defervescence of fever and its complete disappearance; (11) the maximum fever episode terminating in twelve hours and no less than six.

When many causes for fever occur simultaneously, one should begin with bleeding by phlebotomy after which one should commence to improve and dilute the liquids and then one should soften that which is hard and shrunken and eliminate this from the skin.

Tertian fever, at its inception, begins with severe shaking chills. On the other hand, I do not recall having seen severe chills in quartan fever. However, chills do increase in intensity therein with the passing of time. In most instances, other remaining fevers become associated with it producing what is called a "complex fever."

[129]In his *Medical Aphorisms (opus cit.* p. 213) quoting Galen, Maimonides asserts:

The signs of pure quartan fever that are specific for this fever are four: (1) the lack of signs of true tertian fever, although most of the signs also occur in quartan fevers, but in the opposite form when they occur in true tertian fever; (2) quartan fever rarely occurs as a primary event but mostly develops after a fever of a different kind; (3) the pulse of such patients at the beginning of the episode feels like the pulse of an old man whose strength has waned, whereas the pulse of patients with other types of fever is not so; (4) it begins with mild chills and then becomes stronger with each episode. With every shaking chill, the patient feels extremely cold according to the severity of the chills until, at its maximum, he feels that sneezing makes him as cold as snow does.

A person should be careful and drink beverages that cool the body such as *sarav banfasig*. The same applies to all cooling vegetables such as *friyairsh, siragsh, poplinish, kuchila*, and their like. Also beneficial to him are emetics, which slowly stimulate the red bile and the black bile and the sticky humors; and loosen [his bowels] gently with juice[130] of *banfasig, cinnabar*, and Indian dates; and cool the lips and the mouth of the stomach with the juice of *spargal* seed and with *bazraktuna* and their like. [These beneficial effects occur] according to the strength of the red bile and according to the dryness that is in all the types of dry heat that were produced in the person's body from the red bile which is attached to the liver on the right. If heat is found therein, it is from the blood of the liver because the blood is hot and moist and bile is dry and hot. If the fevers are from the blood of the liver, there will not be that much, and there will not be bitterness in his mouth but there will be heat and moistness. If the fever is produced by the red bile, there develops heat and dryness and bitterness in his mouth, and the white of his eyes becomes jaundiced, and [the patient suffers from] distress together with the fever during movement of mixtures that comes from the fever.

All types of dry cold arise from black bile and from the spleen. And if moistness occurs there it stems from the humor itself. It is known that the site of the black bile is the spleen and it is situated on the left side and it gives rise to all types of mania. Bad thoughts come to man because of the strength of the black bile and from the latter there develops the illness called *palig*, also known as *phrenetico*,[131] as explained above, and

---

[130]Literally: water.

[131]Phrenesia or mania. In his *Medical Aphorisms (opus cit.* p. 106) Maimonides, citing Galen, states that the signs of phrenesia are sixteen and these are: insomnia or lack of sleep, confusion of the mind, acute fever with insidious onset that never ceases, amnesia for recent events, lack of thirst, search for conflict with neighbors, accelerated deep breathing, smallness and hardness of the pulse, collecting threads from clothes or straw from walls, licking of the tongue, occipital headaches, dryness of the eyes and their secretions, hot tears from one eye without involvement of the other eye, drops of blood from the nose, acoustic hallucinations, loss of sensation (from

uncontrolled fear and trembling that pours anger into the mouth, and quartan fever and distortion of the mouth.[132] He who has epileptic seizures[133] at known times in all places and whose eyes are unable to see and are blind because melancholy and *palig* have settled in him has an illness that literally afflicts half of his body and who feels it in half his body. The coldness ascends to the brain and cools two portions within the moistness of the head: the portion relating to memory and that of ideation.[134] The humor predominates and becomes thick and obstructs the tubes[135] between the memory and ideation and imagination [portions of the brain]. The natural humor is damaged and this person would immediately be harmed. He can be benefited by all types of hot oils if one anoints the head therewith and warms it so as to dissolve the natural humor and the detrimental humors that have gathered there, as well as the powders in the nostrils. One should cleanse the brain at all times and guard it against the cold. When the black bile becomes stimulated, all the organs in the body are damaged because it is the fundamental element of the body and the organs because it resembles the earth. Just as the earth, when it becomes aroused, arouses all that is within it, so, too, the black bile, which is of the nature of the earth, when it becomes

---

one part of the body) compared with the rest of the body or the like. Since the patient prostrates himself, he will only react to stimuli slugglishly. These symptoms can all occur simultaneously or, occasionally, only a majority thereof occur.

[132]? Bell's palsy or a stroke.

[133]Literally: those who fall. See the numerous references to epilepsy in Maimonides' *Medical Aphorisms (opus cit.)*.

[134]? Retentive and imaginative powers of man. See Maimonides' *Eight Chapters*, I. Gorfinkle, translator (Columbia Univ. Press, 1912), pp. 37–53, where he speaks of the five faculties of the soul: nutritive, sensitive, imaginative, appetitive, and rational. The nutritive faculty consists of the power of attracting nourishment to the body, the retention of the same, its digestion (assimilation), the repulsion of superfluities, growth, procreation, and differentiation of the nutritive juices that are necessary for sustenance from those to be expelled. See also Maimonides' *Guide of the Perplexed* (many editions), Section 1:72, where he discusses the powers of the nutritive faculty.

[135]? The cerebral ventricular system.

aroused, arouses all the organs in the body and harms them.[136]

Caution should be used by healthy people[137] in regard to the following things that are purgative in their action.[138] Grapes, figs, nuts,[139] melons, gourd juice, and cucumber juice should be consumed before the meal. One should not mix them with the food but wait a little until they have passed out of the upper abdomen and then one may eat one's meal. Things that bind the intestines[140] such as pomegranates, quinces,[141] and small pears should be consumed immediately after the meal, and one should not eat excessively thereof.[142]

If a person wishes to eat fowl meat and cattle meat,[143] he should first consume the poultry meat. Some people say that *kalom*, which are poultry eggs, if cooked lightly with salt and water—they are also known as *iskalpadosh*—are good.[144]

If one desires meat of small cattle[145] as well as the meat of large cattle,[146] he should first consume the meat of the small cattle. A person should always begin with something light and then proceed to the heavier food. In the warm months[147] one should eat cooling foods and not use spices to excess, but one should consume vinegar. In the rainy season[148] one should eat

---

[136]Here ends the lengthy digression by Maimonides that described digestion, assimilation of food, the four body humors, and illnesses caused by the disequilibrium in the body of the usual proportions of these humors. Especially emphasized are melancholy, madness, epilepsy, and other neuropsychiatric disease resulting from an excess of black bile. Maimonides now returns to paraphrasing chapter 4 of his *Hilchot De'ot* from his *Mishneh Torah*.

[137]Literally: the natural ones.

[138]Literally: which cause diarrhea from the intestines.

[139]Hebrew: *egozim* meaning nuts. In *Hilchot De'ot* 4:6, Maimonides has *agasim* meaning pears.

[140]That is, which constipate.

[141]In his *Hilchot De'ot* 4:6, Maimonides here adds: "and apples."

[142]See the talmudic discussion on this subject in *Ketubot* 10b.

[143]In *Hilchot De'ot* 4:7, Maimonides here adds: "together."

[144]This sentence is not found in *Hilchot De'ot*.

[145]Such as lambs.

[146]Such as cows.

[147]Literally: days of the sun (summer).

[148]Literally: days of the rains (winter).

warming foods, use spices abundantly and consume a little mustard and asafetida. In this manner, one should prepare foods in cold climates and in hot climates, in each and every place that which is best suited for it.[149]

There are some foods that are extremely detrimental and it is proper for man never to eat them, such as large salted aged fish, aged salted cheese, truffles, mushrooms, aged salted meat, wine must, and a cooked dish that was kept until it acquired a foul odor; similarly, any food whose odor is bad or excessively bitter—all of these are like a fatal poison unto the body.[150]

There are other foods that are also detrimental but not as injurious as the aforementioned ones. Therefore, of these, one should eat only a little and only after intervals of many days. One should not accustom oneself to make a meal of them or to eat them regularly with meals. Examples of this type of food are large fish, cheese, milk that is kept for twenty-four hours after milking, the meat of large oxen and large hegoats, beans, lentils, peas, barley bread, and unleavened bread, cabbage, leeks, onions, garlic, mustard, and radishes—all these are detrimental foods. A person should not partake of these except a very small amount and only during the rainy season. However, during the warm season[151] one should not eat thereof at all. Beans and lentils alone should not be eaten either in the warm months or in the rainy season. Cucumbers may be consumed[152] during the warm season.

There are other foods that are also detrimental but not as

---

[149]Nearly exact quotation from *Hilchot De'ot* 4:8. See also *Shabbat* 11b, *Erubin* 56a, and *Berachot* 40a.

[150]Exact quotation from *Hilchot De'ot* 4:9. See also *Baba Batra* 74b and *Eduyot* 6a. In his *Regimen of Health (Moses Maimonides' Two Treatises on the Regimen of Health)*, A. Bar Sela, H. E. Hoff, and E. Faris (Philadelphia: American Philosophical Society, 1964), p. 19, Maimonides states that cheese is a very bad and heavy nutrient, excepting the cheese that is fresh, white in color, sweet in taste and light in fat. In his *Medical Aphorisms* 20:45, see F. Rosner and S. Muntner, *The Medical Aphorisms of Moses Maimonides* (New York: Bloch, 1973), Vol. 2, p. 71. Maimonides, quoting Galen, asserts that the best type of fresh cheese is one made from milk whose fat has been removed.

[151]In *Hilchot De'ot* 4:9, Maimonides has: "but not in the rainy season."

[152]In *Hilchot De'ot* 4:9, Maimonides here adds: "a little."

much as the aforementioned ones.[153] They are water fowl,
small young pigeons, dates, bread toasted in oil or that was
kneaded with oil, fine meal that was completely sifted so that
not a trace of bran remains, and gravy and brine of salted fish.
One should not consume these foods excessively. A person that
is wise and can control his inclinations, does not yield to his
appetite, and does not eat any of the aforementioned unless he
needs them as a medicine, is indeed a strong man.[154]

A person should always abstain from fruits of the trees and
not consume them excessively even when they are dried, and
needless to say when they are fresh.[155] Indeed, before they are
completely ripe[156] they are like swords to the body. Likewise,
carob pods are always injurious. All sour fruits are detrimental
and one should not eat therefrom save a little and only in the
warm season and in warm climates.[157] Figs, grapes, almonds,
and pomegranates[158] are always good whether fresh or dried,
and a person may eat therefrom as much as he requires. One
should not eat them constantly even though they are better
than all other fruits of trees.[159]

Honey and wine are bad for children but salutary for the
elderly, especially in the rainy season.[160] A person should
always strive to have his intestines relaxed all the days of his life
and his bowel function should approximate diarrhea. This is a
fundamental principle in medicine; namely, whenever the stool
is withheld or is extruded with difficulty, grave illnesses result.
How can a person heal his intestines if they are slightly

---

[153]See also *Pesachim* 42a, *Abodah Zarah* 29a, *Kiddushin* 62a, and *Nedarim* 49a.
[154]Exact quotation from *Hilchot De'ot* 4:10. See also *Pesachim* 2:7 and
Nedarim 51b.
[155]Literally: wet or moist.
[156]Literally: cooked.
[157]Literally: warm places.
[158]Pomegranates are not mentioned in *Hilchot De'ot* 4:1.
[159]Nearly exact quotation from *Hilchot De'ot* 4:11. *Midrash Kohelet* 5:10
states that the fig is good for eating, nice to look at, and beneficial to the
intellect.
[160]In *Hilchot De'ot* 4:12 Maimonides continues: "a person should eat in the
warm months two-thirds of what he eats in the rainy months."

constipated? A young boy should eat salty foods, cooked and spiced with olive oil, fish brine, and salt without bread every morning; or he should drink the liquid of boiled spinach or cabbage in olive oil and fish brine and salt. An old man should drink honey mixed with warm water in the morning and wait approximately four hours; then he should eat his meal. He should do this for one day or three or four days, if it is necessary, until his intestines soften [and move freely].[161]

Physicians state another major principle in regard to bodily health, namely as long as a person toils and exerts himself greatly, does not satiate himself, and keeps his bowels soft, no illness befalls him and his strength increases even if he eats detrimental foods.[162] Anyone who lives a sedentary life and does not exercise or he who postpones his excretions or is constipated—even if he eats good foods and takes care of himself according to proper medical principles—all his days will be painful ones[163] and his strength wanes. Excessive eating is like a deadly poison to the body of any man and is a principal cause of all illnesses. Most diseases that afflict man are due to bad foods or because he fills his abdomen and eats excessively, even of good foods. This is what Solomon in his wisdom stated: "Whoso keepeth his mouth and his tongue keepeth his soul from trouble,"[164]that is to say, he who guards his mouth from consuming detrimental food or from satiation, and his tongue from speaking except where necessary, [remains] healthy.[165]

As to bathing, a person should enter the bathhouse every seven days. He should not enter immediately after eating nor when he is hungry, but when the food begins to be digested in his intestines. He should wash his entire body with hot water

---

[161]Exact quotation from *Hilchot De'ot* 4:13. See also *Ketubot* 10b.

[162]Exact quotation from *Hilchot De'ot* 4:14.

[163]Ecclesiates 2:23.

[164]Proverbs 21:23.

[165]Exact quotation from *Hilchot De'ot* 4:15. See also *Berachot* 32a where it says that he who stuffs himself with food is sure to contract many diseases.

that does not scald the body and afterwards wash his body with
lukewarm water and after that with cold water.[166]

There are four important organs: the brain, the liver, the
testicles, and the heart. Therefore, if a perforation occurs in the
liver or the heart or the brain, the body immediately perishes.
But the testicles are connected to them through a different

---

[166]The language is somewhat different in *Hilchot De'ot* 4:16 where Maimonides
asserts that:

> The correct manner of bathing is for a person to enter the bathhouse and
> bathe every seven days. One should not enter the bath immediately after eating
> nor when one is hungry but when the food begins to be digested. He should
> wash his entire body with hot water that does not scald the body and the head
> alone may be washed with water hot enough to scald the body. Then he should
> wash his body with lukewarm water and then with tepid water and so on until
> he washes with cold water. Over his head he should not pour either lukewarm
> or cold water. In the rainy season, one should not bathe in cold water. One
> should not bathe until one perspires and one's entire body becomes supple, nor
> should one remain too long in the bath; rather, as soon as one perspires and
> the body becomes supple, one should rinse the body and leave the bath. One
> should examine oneself prior to entering the bath and after leaving it, lest
> excretions of wastes be necessary. Similarly, a person should always examine
> himself before meals and after meals, before sexual intercourse and after
> sexual intercourse, before and after he exercises and exerts himself, and
> before and after he goes to sleep. The total number of circumstances is thus
> ten.

> The Talmud (*Shabbat* 41a) states that a man taking a hot bath and not
> following it up with cold water is like iron that has been kept in the fire without
> being immersed in cold water afterwards which—Rashi explains—makes for
> much stronger iron.

The next section in *Hilchot De'ot* deals with how a person should conduct himself
when leaving the bath. *Hilchot De'ot* 4:18 deals with bloodletting and 4:19 is
concerned with sexual intercourse. The final four sections deal with general
statements on healthy living and the necessity to abide by the rules and regulations
described in chapter four of *Hilchot De'ot* to preserve one's health. Maimonides
concludes the chapter with the famous statement that "no disciple of a Sage should
reside in a city that does not possess the ten following things, and these are: a
physician, a surgeon, a bathhouse, a lavatory, a water supply such as a river or well,
a synagogue, a school teacher, a scribe, a charity treasurer, and a court of law with
authority to punish with lashes and imprisonment." See also *Ketubot* 110b, *Baba
Batra* 152a, and *Sanhedrin* 17b.

The last third of this fourth chapter of *Hilchot De'ot* is not quoted at all nor
paraphrased in the *Sefer Hanimtzah*. No reason is apparent for this omission.

power. They are connected to the heart and the brain to sustain the semen and to make hair grow on the beard and to tolerate physical blows and pains more than women. If you doubt this fact,[167] just look at eunuchs whose strength is feeble and whose beard's moistness dries up and whose voice is weak like that of women and whose conduct is also like the conduct of women without strength and without aggressiveness. The spirit weakens within him until it participates with the sensations of sexual desire and valor [both of which] have already been lost. If you say that there are women who are strong in aggressiveness and heroic like men and there is seen in them strength and courage—true, the matter is so because there are some women who develop the sensation of heroism over the strength of their ovaries[168] and who grow beards, but less than men.

All the organs created in men were also created in women as it is written in the *Book of Creation*:[169] the male [was created] with *emesh*[170] and the female with *asham*;[171] but his front was reversed posteriorly and transformed into a woman.[172] The male sex organ is external and the female sex organ is internalized[173] and her ovaries are internal near the site that is called the vestibule to the uterus, and through them a woman conceives. Concerning this it is said: the male [was created] in *emesh* and the female in *asham* but his front was reversed

---

[167]Literally: but if not.

[168]Literally: eggs. The same Hebrew word is used for testicles.

[169]Hebrew: *Sefer Yetzirah*, an eighth-century compact discourse on cosmology and cosmogony. See G. Scholem's article in *Encyclopedia Judaica* (Jerusalem: Keter, 1971), Vol. 16, pp. 782–788 and his critical edition of this work.

[170]*Emesh* is an acronym or acrostic for *aleph*, *mem* and *shin* for the first, thirteenth and twenty-first letters, respectively, of the Hebrew alphabet.

[171]*Asham* is an acronym or acrostic for *aleph*, *shin* and *mem*, the first, twenty-first and thirteenth letters, respectively, of the Hebrew alphabet. In the female the *shin* and *mem* are thus in reverse chronological order.

[172]Literally: reversed internally.

[173]Maimonides seems to be alluding to the rabbinic discussion relating to Adam and Eve being created as a single body with two faces and then separated *(Erubin* 18a, *Ketubot* 8a, *Megillah* 9a, *Shabbat*, 95a, *Berachot* 61b, *Sanhedrin* 38b, *Genesis Rabbah* 8:1, 18:2, and 22:2; Jerusalem Talmud *Berachot* 9:1 and many other sources).

posteriorly and transformed into a woman. Observe that they grow hair in the pubic region because of the moistness of the ovaries and in the axillae because of the moistness of the breasts. Because their front was reversed posteriorly, women became feeble and weakened just like man to his posterior. Even though all his organs are complete and he is stout-hearted and valiant, he cannot show his heroism immediately when he weakens. So, too, although women are strong and aggressive, in the end they weaken because of the nature that they received which is reversed from men. The male is strong in aggressiveness and valor because his sex organs[174] are in front of him. It is for this reason that the testicles in men are called the important organs or *principalis*.

I had to discuss these matters at length to show that these four organs are the major ones and they are: the liver, the brain, the heart, and the testicles. Although there [may be] fatal perforations in other organs, only these are called major organs.

Completed is the *Sefer Hanimtzah*, Praise to the Lord, Master of all that exists.

This splendid heavenly work was completed on Wednesday, the fifth of Marcheshvan in the year 5356 [1596]. Printed in Salonika by Abraham, the son of Don Shlomo Akara.

---

[174]Literally: utensils.

BIBLIOGRAPHY

by Jacob I. Dienstag

ספר הנמצא

ביבליוגראפיה של הוצאות, תרגומים ומחקרים

א. ספר הנמצא — מקור ותרגום

שנ"ו 1595

1] זה **ספר הנמצא** למאור הגולה הרמב"ם ז"ל עם הקדמה מאת שלמה עקרה. בתוך **פירוש מגלת איכה** לר' שמואל בן חביב. שלוניקי, שנ"ו [1595]). דף נט, א—ע,א. תאור ע"י י. מהלמן **גנוזות ספרים** (תשל"ו), עמ' 79, מספר 54.

תר"ט 1849

2] Polak, Gabriel [Jacob], 1803-1869

Notiz uber das Sefer ha-Nimza von Mose b. Maimun. *Literaturblatt des Orients*, X, no. 18, 19 (May 5, 12, 1849): pp. 273-279, 293-298. Hebrew text with introduction and notes in German. A note on this introduction by D. Holub, ibid. 11 (1850), pp. 169-171.

תרי"א — 1851

3] **ספר הנמצא**... להרב משה בן מיימון... עם הקדמה מאת המוציא ואיזה אמרות מושכלות בסופן להחכם... צבי הירש עדעלמאן איש חן טוב. בספר **בן גרני**... אספתיו אני... גבריאל ב"ר אייזיק פאלק. אמסטרדם: בדפוס אלמנת... דוד פררפס כ"ץ, תרי"א 1851, עמ' XVI-I.

Reviewed by F [Frankel]. *Monatsschrift fuer die Geschichte und Wissenschaft des Judenthums* 2 (1853), 75.

147

תשט״ו — 1954

4] **ספר הנמצא** להרמב״ם. **סיני**, 36, חוברת ד׳ (טבת, תשט״ד — 1954): רא־ריא.
עם הקדמה מאת י.ל. מימון.

5] **ספר הנמצא** להרמב״ם. **בהר״מ במז״ל; קובץ תורני־מדעי**, בעריכת י.ל. מימון.
ירושלים: מוסד הרב קוק, תשט״ו/1954, עמ׳ ז־יז.
עם הקדמה מאת י.ל. מימון.

תשכ״ז — 1967

6] **ספר הנמצא**. בתוך מחקרו של דוד מרגלית, חבורים רפואיים שיוחסו לרמב״ם
ולרמב״ן. **קורות**, ד׳, חוברת ג־ד (סיון תשכ״ז/1967): 208־217.

1970

7] **ספר הנמצא. בדרך ישראל ברפואה** מאת דוד מרגלית. ירושלים: הוצאת האקדמיה
לרפואה, תש״ל/1970, עמ׳ 190־197, 212־213.

1971

8] **ספר הנמצא** להרב... משה בן מיימון... עם הקדמה מאת המוציא ואיזה אמרות
מושכלות בסופו להחכם... צבי הירש עדעלמאן איש חן טוב. בספר **בן גרני**... אספתיו
אני... גבריאל ב״ר אייזיק פאלק. ירושלים: ״קדם״, תשל״א/1971, עמ׳ XVI-I.

צלום מדפוס אמשטרדם תרי״א/1851.

ב. מאמרים ומחקרים

9] דוידזון, ישראל, 1870־1939
מבוא **לספר שעשועים** לר׳ יוסף זבארה. ברלין: הוצאת אשכול, תרפ״ה/1925, עמ׳
ע־עא; 155־168.
השוואה בין **ספר הנמצא** והספר **בתי הנפש** לר׳ יוסף זבארה.

10] זק״ש, שניאור, 1815־1892
מימוני. **התחיה**, חוברת א׳ (תר״י/1850; דפוס צילום: ירושלים: הוצאת תשני,
תש״ל/1969), עמ׳ 38.
״ספר הנמצא ה״מויחס להרמב״ם בטעות.״

11] זק״ש, שניאור, 1815־1892
תוספות לשני המאמרים הנ״ל. **היונה**, תרי״א, ברלין (דפוס צילום: ירושלים:
הוצאת תשבי, תש״ל), 89־90.
וכבר מויחס להרמב״ם ג״כ ס׳ קטן בשם ״ספר הנמצא״... שם נמצא הרבה
מהבלי גזרות הכוכבים [אסטרולוגיה] וזה לבד מספיק להראות כי לא יצא הס׳ הזה
מבטן הרמב״ם, כי האדם הזה לא הוליד את הבל מימיו. וכבר הוכחתי במקום אחר
גם מפנים אחרים שמיוחס אליו הס׳ ההוא בטעות. ושם... נמצא דעות הראב״ע
והרמב״ם מעורבין אלו כאלו, כי מחברו, הבלתי נודע, השתמש בדברי שניהם (עמ׳
89־90).

12] זק״ש, שניאור, 1815־1892
על דבר **ספר הנמצא** המיוחס להרמב״ם ז״ל. **כרם חמד**, ח׳ (תרי״ד/1854): 23־34.
חוזר על השערתו שהספר לא יצא מפרי עטו של הרמב״ם.

[13 זק"ש, שניאור, 1815־1892
על דבר מדרש הנעלם. **ישרון**, א', מחברת ג' (תרי"ז/1857): 94־95.
שהפסקא בספר הקבלי **מדרש הנעלם, לקוח מספר הנמצא.**

[14 זק"ש, שניאור, 1815־1892
דברים עתיקים. **ישרון**, א', מחברת ג' (תרי"ז): 87־94.
אגרת לגבריאל פולק, מוציא לאור **ספר הנמצא,** ובקורת על דבריו של צ.
עדעלמאן בספר זה.

15] Holub, David, 1818-1890
Das allegorische Recept des Maimuni. *Literaturblatt des Orients*, XI, no.
11 (March 16, 1850), pp. 169-171. Note on the introduction to the *Sefer ha-
Nimza* by G. Polak, which appeared in this journal, X (1849), pp. 273-279,
293-298.

16] Steinschneider, Moritz, 1816-1907
Catalogus Librorum Hebraeorum in Bibliotheca Bodleiana. Berlin: P.
Friedlaender, 1852-1860, col. 1933-1934. Reprints Berlin: Welt-Verlag, 1931;
Hildesheim: Georg Olms, 1964.

17] Steinschneider, Moritz, 1816-1907
Hebraische Uebersetzungen. Berlin: Bibliographischen Bureau, 1893, pp.
274-275, note 1196-1197; p. 771, note 87. Reprint Graz: Akademische Verlag,
1956.

ג. ציונים ביבליוגראפיים לכתבי יד

18] Freimann, Aaron, 1871-1948
Union Catalogue of Hebrew Manuscripts and their Location, vol. 2. New
York: American Academy for Jewish Research, 1964, no. 6358.

Book III

TISHAH PERAKIM MIYICHUD

NINE CHAPTERS
ON THE
UNITY OF GOD

INTRODUCTION

The *Nine Chapters on the Unity of God* attributed to Moses Maimonides was published in Hebrew in 1950 by Georges Vajda in the periodical *Kobetz Al Yad* (Jerusalem: Mekize Nirdamim, 1950 New Series), vol. 5 [15], pp. 105–136. Three years later, Vajda published in French, in the *Archives d'Histoire Doctrinale et Littéraire du Moyen Age* (1953), vol. 28, pp. 83–98, an analysis of this work that he called a pseudo-Maimonidean treatise.

Vajda clearly proves the spurious nature of the *Nine Chapters* by showing that it is an abbreviated adaptation of the kabbalistic *Ginnat Egoz* of Rabbi Joseph Gikatila (also known as Siciliano), which was published in Hanover in 1615. The *Nine Chapters* is clearly a kabbalistic work or was profoundly influenced by Kabbalah. Many passages are borrowed from the *Book of Creation (Sefer Yetzirah)*. The combination of the letters that comprise the Tetragrammaton and the isopsephies *(gematria)* differ significantly with the subject of Divine names in Maimonides' *Guide of the Perplexed*. Further, the constant repetition and belaboring of the same points is evidence that the *Nine Chapters* was not written by Moses Maimonides. Maimonides writes in short, clear language and does not repeat himself. Any seeming repetition turns out, on closer scrutiny, to be a clarifying or qualifying phrase that modifies or adds to what he originally said.

Vajda discusses by whom and when the *Nine Chapters* was written and why it was attributed to Maimonides. He considers it unlikely that Gikatila wrote it and suggests that Meir Aldabi may have been the author. Vajda dates the composition of this work to the year 1300. He suggests that the *Nine Chapters* was attributed to Maimonides in order to strengthen the position of the kabbalists who were attempting to justify their legitimacy as sacred scientists. Be that as it may, the *Nine Chapters on the Unity of God* was almost certainly not written by Maimonides.

The first chapter serves as a general introduction and emphasizes that the way to know and understand the incorporeal, incomparable, and incommensurable one God is through His creations and by one's intellectual perceptions. The second chapter deals with the existence of the Creator and His Oneness from which all existences emanate, while Chapter 3 touches on rational understanding. Chapter 4 deals with the nonchanging nature of God and chapter 5 deals with reward and punishment. The sixth chapter addresses the efficacy of prayer. Chapter 7 describes the Tetragrammaton and the benefits of prayer in the Hebrew language. The final two chapters deal with the names and cognomens of God.

Although the *Nine Chapters* has been wrongly attributed to Moses Maimonides, it is nevertheless an important work of historical interest and is, therefore, published together with two other works on the unity and existence of God attributed to Maimonides.

Georges Vajda's Hebrew Introduction

Hebrew manuscript 767[1] of the National Library in Paris contains (fol. 55b–65b) a treatise on theology. The treatise is

---

[1]Vajda states it is a composite of the work of three or four copyists, written in the fourteenth century, perhaps in the East. See the *Catalogue des Manuscripts Hébreux et Samaritains de la Bibliothèque Impériale*, pp. 125–126.

divided into nine chapters and each chapter into many paragraphs marked by Hebrew letters. The superscript attributes
the treatise to Moses Maimonides.[2] However, it is known that
one does not entirely rely on the copyists in such matters.
Actually, even a superficial reading is sufficient to show that
these items are not by the author of the *Guide of the Perplexed;*
rather they come from the spirit of a kabbalist. Evidence[3] to
support this [thesis] comes not only from expressions borrowed
from the *Book of Creation*—found even in [the writings of]
philosophers such as Rabbi Solomon Ibn Gabirol, Rabbi Joseph
Ibn Tzaddik, and Rabbi Abraham Ibn Ezra—but also from
speculations on Divine names, their combinations, and
isopsephies [*Gematrias*] such as "*ha-elo-him*" [the Lord], which
has the numerical value of *teva* [nature] and "*ado-nai*" [the
Lord], which has the numerical value of "*hechal*" [the
Sanctuary]. Nevertheless, lacking here are the characteristic
views of the meditative Kabbalah of the thirteenth century and
beyond, such as the teaching of the "countings,"[4] the explanation of evil by virtue of "the reversé side,"[5] and more.

Let us briefly summarize the contents of the treatise.

Chapter I. Introduction. The Deity. The way to know Him through
His creations and by intellectual perception. Understanding His
proper Name. The difference between His Oneness from all the
unique types.

Chapter II. The existence of the Creator and His Oneness. Emanation of all existences from the Primordial Emanator. The simplicity of the First Cause and the composition of resultant

---

[2]Vajda states, "One should note that the text is not beyond all doubt, but I
cannot present a better one."

[3]Literally: witnesses.

[4]The ten *sefirot* or countings are wisdom *(chochmah)*, understanding *(binah)*,
knowledge *(da'at)*, kindness *(chesed)*, might *(gevurah)*, glory *(tiferet)*, victory
(netzach), majesty *(hod)*, foundation *(yesod)*, and royalty *(malchut)*.

[5]Literally: the other side; kabbalistic expression for the Devil or Satan's
camp. Much of evil is the mirror image of good, rooted in the same traits. The
reverse side is sometimes called the left side and is the mirror image of the
right side. However, there is only one good and one evil.

[existences] of substance and form that prevent one from attributing[6] oneness to existences other than the Divine.

Chapter III. The three existing levels of creation (the three worlds).

Chapter IV. The non-changing [nature] of the Creator. The consonance of this view with the creation of the world from nothingness. The unity of the four descriptions: alive, able, wise, will.

Chapter V. Reward and punishment do not cause a change in the Divine Will, but everything happens according to those who receive (action of the "crucible"). Sins that defile the pure soul are those that distance a person from his Creator.

Chapter VI. The purpose of praying to the unchanging God is to purify the soul of man.

Chapter VII. The One Name of God. The benefit of the Hebrew language[7] in prayer.

Chapter VIII. Explanation of the names *Y-H-V-H*, *Eh-yeh*, *(Y-H-V) Y-ah*.

Chapter IX. Explanation of the cognomens *Elo-him, Ado-nay, Shad-dai, (Y-H-V-H) Tze-Va-ot*.

This summary suffices to show that the structure of the *Nine Chapters* is logical and simple.

Only in Chapter VII is there a combination of two unrelated topics which somewhat disturbs the order. After the Introduction (Chapter I), Chapters II-VI are based on rational introspection, the style of most religious philosophers[8] in the Middle Ages, while the proposed theme of Chapters VII-IX has its source in the teaching of Jewish Kabbalism.

Regarding the sources of the treatise, it is clear that an important portion of the *Nine Chapters* is nothing more than an abbreviated adaptation from the book *Ginnat Egoz* of Rabbi Joseph Gikatila (published in Hanover in the year 5375).[9]

---

[6]Literally: connecting or relating.
[7]Literally: holy tongue.
[8]Literally: believing utterers of views.
[9]1615. Gikatila is also known as Siciliano.

There is no fundamental difference between the teachings of that book *Ginnat Egoz* and our treatise. However, the anonymous author abbreviates endlessly in places where Rabbi Joseph is verbose and where the latter testifies about himself (*Ginnat Egoz*, p. 4, 73): "I repeat and reiterate out of fear so that the readers not err because the topics are extremely subtle." Not only that, but the *Nine Chapters* also omit most of the combinations [of Divine names] that are an important part of the original. It seems clear that the aim of the editor was to disseminate the teachings of Rabbi Joseph Gikatila and to present his views as classical philosophy not at variance with the ideas of the philosophical sages.[10] I cannot decide whether the editor of the treatise intended to attribute it to Moses Maimonides. I do not think so[11] because there is no hint of such an intent in the chapters themselves (while in one of the forged letters to Rabbi Abraham, son of Maimonides, which is included in our manuscript before "the chapters," the forger refers to himself as the author of the *Mishneh Torah* and the *Guide of the Perplexed* without any hesitation). On the other hand, it is possible that he attributed the *Nine Chapters* to the author of the *Eight Chapters* in order to include in his [Maimonides'] teachings something he [Maimonides] never taught nor thought. It was difficult to conceive that Rabbi Moses [Maimonides] omitted from his authentic works that which was so dear to the spirit of the later kabbalists,[12] just as the *Pirké HaHatzlachah* [Chapters on Eternal Bliss] were attributed to him because they did not find in his [writings] a sufficiently satisfying view of prayer, and other topics.[13]

I list briefly the parallels between the *Nine Chapters* and the book *Ginnat Egoz*:

[10]Literally: research scholars.
[11]Literally: my mind is not leaning in that (direction).
[12]Literally: people of mysticism.
[13]Vajda points out that the real connection between Maimonides and mysticism is discussed in the treatise of A. Altman: *Das Verhältnis Maimonis zur jüdishen Mystik. Monatschrift der Geselschaft der Wissenschafts des Judentums* 1937, pp. 305–330.

Nine Chapters	**Ginnat Egoz**
Chapter 2:1	Page 73 Column a
Chapter 3	The section on unity beginning on page 73
Chapter 5:4 until the end of the chapter	Page 74 Column 3–4 (Here is the only place in the *Nine Chapters* where the text is longer than that in the *Ginnat Egoz*.)
Chapter 8: 1–23	Page 4–5; 8, Columns 3–4; 9, Columns 4–10
Chapter 9:1	Page 11 Column 2
Chapter 9:2	Page 5 Column 4—Page 6 Column 1
Chapter 9:3	Page 11 Column 2
Chapter 9:4	Page 13 Column 4—Page 14 Column 1
Chapter 9:5	Page 13 Columns 3–4
Chapter 9:6	Page 13 Columns 2–3
Chapter 9:7–9 and 14	Page 17 Column 1
Chapter 9:10	Page 15 Column 4—Page 16 Column 1
Chapter 9:12–13, 15	Page 17 Columns 2–4
Chapter 9:16–18	Page 18 Side 2

It is consequently clear that a significant part of the subject matter of the *Nine Chapters* is derived from three sections of the *Ginnat Egoz*: the section on existence, the section on cognomens at the beginning, and the section on the unity at the end. That is, the parts of the composition whose spirit and views are not as alien to philosophy as is the remainder of the book.

Concerning the rest of the text [of this work], I was not able to find definite sources for it. Would those people more scholarly than I come forth to fill this void? The first three chapters resemble Chapters 1–4 of the *Laws of the Fundamental*

Principles of the Torah [*Yesodei Hatorah*] in the *Yad Hachazakah*[14]
both in style and in content, if not always in views. It appears to
me that in at least one place the words of the author oppose the
views of Maimonides (Chapter 2:6): "The important commandment of believing in the existence [of God], and so on," while
Maimonides in the *Laws of the Fundamental Principles of the Torah*
1, explains the first of the ten commandments, as a positive
commandment [*Mitzvat Asseh*]). Although there are certain
points of similarity with the *Guide of the Perplexed:* Chapter 2:14
and the *Guide*, Part 1, Chapter 59, the two views are quite
different; Chapter 3:7 (end of the paragraph) and the *Guide*,
Part 3, beginning of Chapter 9: "The corporeal element in
man[15] is a large screen and partition that prevents him from
perfectly perceiving abstract ideals."[16]

Concerning the dissemination of the treatise, I have no ideas.
Perhaps Rabbi Meir Aldabi, the renowned compiler (middle of
the fourteenth century)[17] copied most of it in his book *Sheviley
Emunah* and, as was his custom, did not cite the source. Such
literary theft provides a *terminus ante quem* for the *Nine Chapters*.
If we are not mistaken in regard to attributing it to the book
Ginnat Egoz, we can consequently conclude that it was com-
posed by the editor between 1300 and 1340.

It is possible to use the book *Sheviley Emunah* to correct and
complete the text of the sole manuscript [of the *Nine Chapters*]
in many places, although there is [no] urgency to apply
excessive zeal to this task because Rabbi Meir Aldabi not once

---

[14]Literally: the mighty hand; term used to describe Maimonides' *Mishneh
Torah*.

[15]Literally: matter.

[16]Literally: the detached intellect. Detached intellect is Maimonides' explanation of angels. Human beings consist of two distinct creations: matter and
intellect. We can conceive of matter without spirituality because we can see it
in creation: stones, earth, etc. But there is also a creation of intellect without
a body, not seated in "matter" and that is an angel. We cannot conceive of this
creation because we do not see it. Our concepts are limited to our five senses.

[17]Vajda suggests that one can refer to N. Brill, *Jahrbücher* II, pp 166–168;
M. Steinschneider, *Hebraeische übersetzungen* 16–17, 24–27; Y. Zonah in
Encyclopédie Juive II, 162–165.

[but often] misappropriated the copied text by changing the
order of things and even the formulation of several paragraphs
by adorning the style, by additions and by deletions. Who today
knows the authentic picture of the formulation that he had
before him?[18]

Here below I present for the reader a table of the similarities
between the *Nine Chapters* and the book *Sheviley Emunah* (Regio
D'Taranto 5319).[19]

Nine Chapters	Sheviley Emunah
Chapter 2:1–10	Page 5 Column 1:5—Column 3:10
Chapter 3:2–6	Page 16 Column 4:29—Page 17 Column 1:18
Chapter 3:7	Page 17 Column 1:34—Column 2:2
Chapter 3:9–13 (and no others)	Page 17 Column 2:2–26
Chapter 4:[20]	
Chapter 5:2–15	Page 8 Column 4:10—Page 9 Column 3:22
Chapter 6:1–2	Page 9 Column 4:17–31
Chapter 6:11–14	Page 10 Column 1:28—Column 2:19
Chapter 6:17	Page 10 Column 1:19–26
Chapter 7:1	(Compare Page 10 Column 1:30–33)
Chapter 7:3	(Compare there, lines 33–39)

---

[18]Literally: that was opposite his eyes.

[19]That is, 1459.

[20]Vajda states that for Chapter 4 he found no similarity, in the true sense
of the word, in Aldabi's *Sheviley Emunah*. However, it is clear that Rabbi Meir
Aldabi knew the text and drew from it. Part of the first paragraph was copied
in *Sheviley Emunah*, page 10, column 2:20–21, compare there to page 17,
column 3:30ff.

Chapter 7:12	Page 12 Column 3:3—Column 4:13
Chapter 8:1–5 (first half)	Page 12 Column 4:13—Page 14 Column 3:9
Chapter 8:5 (second half)–24	Page 13 Column 2:38—Page 14 Column 3:9
Chapter 9:1–11	Page 14 Column 3:12—Page 15 Column 2:21
Chapter 9:13–15	Page 15 Column 1:36—Column 2:21
Chapter 9:18	Page 17 Column 2:26–38.

The style of the manuscript itself is not among the very best and the responsibility perhaps lies not only with the copyist but also with the author. I have corrected the inconsistencies of spelling and have restored the scriptural passages and the Divine Name[21] (which is habitually written *Y-Y-Y*) to their traditional formulations.

Georges Vajda
Paris, Iyar 5710[22]

French analysis by Georges Vajda

Hebrew manuscript 767 of the Bibliothèque Nationale de Paris[1] contains (fol. 55 v° to 65 v°) a small theological opus whose superscript attributes it to Moses Maimonides. The text

---

[21]Literally: the one Name.

[22]That is, 1950.

[1]It is described in the *Catalogues des Manuscripts Hébreux et Samaritains de la Bibliothèque Impériale*, pp. 125–126. The script appears German but in view of the content of the work it is quite likely that it was written in Italy. I will not venture to date it with assurance. The writing, I believe, does not permit one to date it later than the first part of the fifteenth century. The filigree is of little help in clarifying the problem. At folio 43, I believe that I recognized Briquet no. 14.515 (certified about 1432) but another resembles 15.310, which places us at about 1538!

is divided into nine chapters, each subdivided, in turn, into numbered paragraphs.

A rapid glance is sufficient to convince us that it is not an authentic work of Maimonides.[2] It is clearly a kabbalistic production or was profoundly influenced by Kabbalah. This fact is proven not only by the passages borrowed from *The Book of Creation (Sefer Yetzirah)*, which one also finds in many Jewish theological nonkabbalistic works (but never in the authentic works of Maimonides), but also and above all by the combination of the letters of the Tetragrammaton Name of God and the isopsephies *(gematria)*, which clash completely with the ideas expressed on the subject of Divine names in the *Guide of the Perplexed*.

More is involved here than the argument of silence and theoretical considerations. Comparison of the texts shows that the *Nine Chapters* owe a large part of their doctrine to a well-known kabbalistic work, the *Ginnat Egoz* of Joseph ben Abraham Ibn Gikatila.[3]

---

[2] "In the name of the Creator of Heaven and Earth, I begin [to transcribe] the Nine Chapters on the Unity [of God] composed by Rabbi Moses, son of Maimon, of blessed memory." I edited this text (the title of the original is *Tishah Perakim Miyichud*) with a brief introduction in Hebrew in *Kovetz Al Yad*, Minora Manuscripta Hebraica, V (XV), Jerusalem, 1950, pp. 105–108 (introduction), pp. 109–137 (text). The superscript set aside, nothing in the body of the text supports this claim, contrary to the immediately antecedent section in the manuscript that awkwardly suggests a Maimonidean origin. The remainder of the latter text is one of the forgeries fabricated in order to draw Maimonides, in a posthumous way, into the camp of the esotericists. See the article by G. Scholem, cited in note 14.

[3] Concerning this Spanish kabbalist, born in 1248, died after 1305, one can consult S. A. Horodetzky, *Encyclopedia Judaica*, Vol. VII, col. 408–411, and G. Scholem, *Major Trends in Jewish Mysticism*, 2nd ed, New York, for passages referring to Joseph S. V. Gikatila. The *Ginnat Egoz (Orchard of Nuts*, title borrowed from the Song of Songs 6:11 comprising an allusion to the kabbalistic methods of exegesis used in the treatise), printed in Hanau in 1615, belongs to the works of the author's youth, having been composed in 1274. Joseph Ibn Gikatila therein abundantly uses the notions of the Arabic-Jewish philosophy, received through Abraham Ibn Ezra and Maimonides (perhaps also Ibn Gabirol), which he adapted, it goes without saying, to his own speculations of kabbalistic inspiration.

The elements of the *Nine Chapters* are borrowed from this work, nearly all originating from the first two parts and from the last part that deal respectively with the Tetragrammaton, the various names of God, and Divine Unity (or Simplicity).[4] The general theme of the small opus itself is identical with that of *Ginnat Egoz* which enunciates it in the following words: "Our intention was to make the statement, 'The Lord *(Y-H-V-H)* is One,' the selfsame structure of our book."[5]

However, we are very far from dealing with a simple summary of a kabbalistic work. Without dealing with the parts of the text that were not derived in a literary manner (we will detail this point later), the material that was borrowed is here rethought and organized according to a totally different plan, even exactly the opposite of the arrangement of the source. In the latter, the metaphysical assertions are embedded in kabbalistic speculations (except for the last part, exploited in the first part of our treatise) and the account is one of overwhelming verbosity, which is moreover deliberate.[6]

The *Nine Chapters* are constructed according to a well-equilibrated plan, notwithstanding several prolixities and stylistic imperfections in the details. The transitions therein are managed with care, and the philosophic and kabbalistic elements are judiciously separated. The first six chapters are assigned to the philosophic and the last three to the kabbalistic although there are certain mergings of the two classes of thought—the kabbalastic speculations, as a matter of fact, extending to the entire composition.

It appears from this general insight that the *Nine Chapters* has its place among the quite numerous works in Jewish literature that, beginning from the second half of the thirteenth century, attempt to synthesize or harmonize the two great currents [of

---

[4]The table of concordance was constructed in the introduction to the printed text, pp. 106ff. We will complete it in that which follows.

[5]*Ginnat Egoz* 72d. This statement is the declaration of the Jewish faith, Deuteronomy 6:4, literally: "Hear O Israel, the Lord our God, the Lord is One."

[6]"I allow myself to use repetitions and restatements, lest the readers go astray, because the problems are very penetrating" (fol. 4c).

thought], which, together with talmudism from thence forward, nourish Jewish thought of the Middle Ages: Greco-
Arabic philosophy and Kabbalah.[7]

Each of these works, for the most part little studied, has its
own structure and needs to be examined separately. The one
that presently occupies us [*The Nine Chapters*] does not place
rational speculation and mystical traditions (which it simply
calls "tradition of the revealed Law," *Kabbalat Ha-Torah* VII, 1)
as adversaries, one against the other, but emphasizes that the
latter surpasses the former in profundity; it considers them as
two expressions of the same truth and makes them cooperate in
the establishment of the belief in the Unity of God, the
condition and assurance for the salvation of man.

Before approaching the analysis of the text, it is incumbent
upon us to consider two preliminary questions.

By whom and when was our treatise written? Why was it
attributed to Maimonides?

To the first of these questions there is only a partial answer.
Until one becomes more fully informed, there is nothing to
specifically identify the author of the *Nine Chapters*. It appears
very unlikely that Joseph Ibn Gikatila himself undertook to
offer this enlarged summary of his *Ginnat Egoz*, reducing, for
the most part, the kabbalistic speculations, because he also takes
a more negative position in regard to philosophy in his later
works than he does in this book [written in] his youth. By
contrast, we have a *terminus ante quem* that allows us to arrive at
a rather precise approximation as to the date [of composition]
of our text. In effect, this text seems to be one of the numerous
sources pilfered by the compiler, or rather the plagiarist, Meir
Aldabi in his *Sheviley Emunah (The Paths of Faith)*. This writer
worked in the middle of the fourteenth century.[8] Knowing the

---

[7]Vajda studied two among them: (1) *La Conciliation de la Philosophie et de la
Loi Religieuse* . . . of Joseph ben Abraham Ibn Wakar, in *Sefarad* IX, 1949,
pp. 311–350; X, 1950, pp. 26–71, 281–323; (2) *Judah ben Nissim Ibn Malka
Philosophe Juif Marocain*, (Paris: Larose, 1954).

[8]See the comparative table in Vajda's edition where he also gave the
bibliographic references concerning Meir Aldabi and remarked that numerous allusions in his book show that he knew passages from the *Nine*

date of the composition of the *Ginnot Egoz*, one cannot be far wrong in placing the date of the redaction of the *Nine Chapters* at about 1300.

Why the attribution to Maimonides?

In truth, it could be nothing more than the act of the scribe whose copy, until the present, is the only one to have preserved the *Nine Chapters*. (The copyist could also have mechanically reproduced the text from his model.) But even in that case, the problem remains.

Before attempting an answer, let us consider the relationships, both external and internal, between our text and the well-known authentic works of Maimonides.

Because of the title, our treatise immediately reminds us, on the one hand, of the *Eight Chapters*, a celebrated ethical précis that is part of the commentary of Maimonides on the *Mishnah*[9] and, on the other hand, of the *Dissertation on the Unity (Ma'amar Hayichud)*, also attributed to the same author.[10]

In addition, there is a certain relationship between the plan of the *Nine Chapters* and that of the theological précis with which Maimonides began his *Code of Laws*,[11] and it is clear that

---

Chapters aside from those he transcribed nearly literally. The borrowings about which we are concerned comprise both texts found in the *Ginnat Egoz* as well as others that do not appear therein. It is thus certain that Meir Aldabi took his extracts from the same text edited by Vajda and not from the larger treatise of Ibn Gikatila.

[9]Bibliographic indications by G. Vajda, *Jüdische Philosophie* (Berne: Bibliographische Einführungen in das Studium der Philosophie 19, 1950), 16:30–33, p. 21.

[10]This small work, written in Arabic, as was the preceding one, was preserved only in the single Hebrew version published by M. Steinschneider (*Maamar ha-Jichud*, Berlin, 1846) with a valuable annotation in Hebrew and a summary in German. The authenticity of this text seems doubtful to me but this is not the place to deal with it.

[11]This work (*Mishneh Torah*) begins with the "Fundamental Rules of the Revealed Law" (*Hilchot Yesodei Ha-Torah*) that, in a fashion accessible to nonphilosophers, exposes the doctrines of Maimonides relative to God, to cosmology, and to prophethood. The general resemblance is established between the first three sections of the *Nine Chapters* and the first four parts of the text of Maimonides whose admirable style and structure cannot be simply

the third chapter of our text used, after Ibn Gikatila, Chapters II to IV of the Maimonidean exposé.[12] Similarly, the fourth chapter, whose equivalent I have not found in the *Ginnat Egoz*, is closely inspired, as we will see, by certain passages of the *Guide of the Perplexed*. In all these cases, however, one notices displacements of emphasis and modifications of perspective, which we will deal with in their place.

By contrast, at least two passages in our text discretely, but resolutely, take a position against Maimonides.[13]

In order not to be contemptuous of the general character and the intention of the *Nine Chapters*, which we believe to be an essay that presents the essential doctrines of the *Ginnat Egoz* in a form acceptable to readers who are not initiated into esotericism, but nevertheless not radically opposed to it, let us conjecture about the motive that led to the inscription of the name of Maimonides on the frontispiece of the text.

In an epoch where no Jewish teacher could permit himself *not* to take a position in regard to Kabbalah, whether in opposition, whether in adherence, or whether at least rendering homage to it in the form of a respectful mention, it is difficult to conceive that the greatest Jewish philosopher would have avoided this obligation. Moreover, for the souls who see in

---

imposed as models on every similar exposé. One must admit from a formal point of view that the *Nine Chapters* remains inferior to this model.

[12]The beginning of the "Dissertation on the Unity" (ed. cit. p. 1) very distinctly also formulates one of the cardinal theses of the *Nine Chapters*: Divine immutability implies immutability of Divine actions. But the similarity ends there and the conclusions derived from this principle are totally different on all sides.

[13](1) II, 6: The belief in the existence of God is not a positive commandment because it is not proper to give notice of an order without the subjugated knowing who is giving it. Also the Decalogue begins with an affirmation ("I am the Lord, thy God," Exodus 20:2), and not with an order. However Maimonides considers this verse as a commandment of the Law, *Hilchot Yesodei Ha-Torah* 1, 10. I did not recognize this opinion in the *Ginnat Egoz*.

(2) Ibn Gikatila reproaches Maimonides for placing in the same plan the Tetragrammaton Y-H-V-H and the "I am" *(Eh-yeh)* of Exodus 3:14 (*Ginnat Egoz* 9 c–d against the *Guide* 1, 63). Our text (VII, 20) recapitulates this criticism without specifying the addressee.

Kabbalah the crowning of the sacred science, the work of Maimonides appeals imperiously as a complement or rather a kabbalistic completion.[14]

The composition of the treatise is, as we have said, quite firm and there is consequently no inconvenience in following the order of the text to extricate the doctrinal contents.

The first chapter (which is qualified in the seventh chapter) is a general introduction—one could say a plan.

The basis for the faith is that there exists a Being that precedes all beings and that bestows existence upon them consecutively from nonexistence and that carries them all.

One arrives at this belief by means of the comparison of all the beings. After having surveyed the series "of the carriers and the carried," one is led to the Unique Being upon Whom all beings depend.

These truths are evident from meditation of the Tetragrammeton name *Y-H-V-H* that designates the Divine Essence, whereas all the other names applied to God only translate the different aspects of His activity.

God is incorporeal, incomparable, and incommensurable.

---

[14]Concerning the genuine relationship between the thinking of Maimonides and mysticism, see the excellent study by M. Alexander Altmann, *Das Verhaltnis Maimunis zur jüdischen Mystik*, in *Monatschrift der Gesellschaft und Wissenschaft des Jüdentums*, 1937, pp. 305–330. A kabbalistic legend has Maimonides converting to Kabbalah in his old age. See the Hebrew study by M. G. Scholem, *From Philosopher to Cabbalist (A Legend of the Cabbalists on Maimonides)*, in *Tarbiz* VI, April 1935, pp. 90–98. See also several indications on the generally favorable attitude of the kabbalists of the second half of the thirteenth century in regard to Maimonides by the same author, *Tarbiz* II, 2, 1934, p. 204 (n.2). The question should, moreover, be corrected with slight variation in detail. Let us add that another apocryphal Maimonidean work, perhaps, because of a similar preoccupation, figures among his works. It concerns a fragmentary writing, "Chapters on the Beatitude" (*Perakim be-Hatzlachah, De Beatitudine Capita Duo R. Mosi ben Maimon adscripta*, edit. H. S. Davidowitz and D. H. Baneth, Jerusalem, 1939) where one finds a spiritualist doctrine of prayer whose absence would make itself felt in the pages as a great exaltation, but imprinted with intellectualism that Maimonides consecrated to this subject at the end of the *Guide*. It is, moreover, possible that this small opus was the work of Maimonides' son Abraham, himself a fervent follower of mysticism, inspired by Moslem sophistry and not at all by Kabbalah.

One cannot attribute to Him wisdom, power, life, and will as well as other attributes; nothing in the world can provoke differentiation in Him.

Moreover, one must explore with the greatest care why one should support these theses, because belief comes only after science.

Having established these theses, man becomes firm in the conviction that God is separate from everything that is not Him (that is one of the meanings of the Unity), that He is also One, in the double sense of uniqueness (absence of a second) and simplicity (unalterable indivisibility).

This verity is perfectly expressed in the scriptural text, "Hear O Israel. . . ." Nevertheless, one must understand well the sense of the Unity proclaimed in this formulation, since the term has multiple connotations. It does not refer to numerical unity, but to the absolute separation of the Unique from all that which is not Him.[15]

When the soul also recognizes the "unified" God, it also finds itself unified and from its performance there results a perfect delectation, because it discovers truths of an intellectual order with which it feels an affinity because it, too, originates from the source of intelligence.

Meanwhile, in attempting to achieve this lofty goal, a barrier is erected between man and God. But to the extent that the former progresses in the understanding of the truths, the barrier recedes and the subject draws nearer to God. It is in this sense that one states: God is close or far; knowledge brings God near, ignorance distances Him.

The barrier, or as one can also state, the screen, between man and God, is anthropomorphism, the admission of a similarity, whatever it may be, between the Supreme Being and something

---

[15]It appears from now on, and all that follows testifies to the same sense, that among the three connotations of the unity described below is separation or absolute "alterity" which most intrigued the author of the *Nine Chapters*, as it perhaps also already [intrigued] Joseph Ibn Gikatila. For the distinction between numerical unity and absolute unity, see the references in *Juda ben Nissim*, p. 71, n. 2–5, to which it seems proper to add now A. J. Festugière, *La Révélation d'Hermès Trismégiste*, IV, Paris, 1954, pp. 18–31.

else. In proceeding on a *path of negation*, man progressively diminishes the thickness of the screen, but if he, a material being, believes that by his research he will penetrate even the essence of God not otherwise distinguishable, he is nothing but a blasphemer.

Beginning from this first part of the *Nine Chapters*, one discerns the complexity of the thought these [chapters] are trying to formulate. The goal is clear for man in his sensual condition to draw close to God, as much as is possible. The path that leads to this end is metaphysical analysis which concludes with the abaliety of beings falling under the hold of the experience of the aseity of their first principle. But this approach, which could be purely philosophic, is not entirely so. First, it transposes a meditation on a scriptural text on the plan of rational thinking, the declaration of the faith of Israel, and even a mystical meditation whose object is the ineffable Name of God. Furthermore, even the rational approach in a certain sense inscribes itself in the framework of a rather theological preoccupation, that of safeguarding Divine Simplicity in all its purity, a negative path and refusal to discriminate in God, the "essential" attributes.[16]

As to particulars, the initial paragraph already reveals, merely by its vocabulary, the diversity of inspirations that animate the doctrine taught in our pamphlet.

By their general appearance, these few lines appear to be intimately connected with the statement found at the beginning of the *Fundamental Principles of the Revealed Law*. But the atmosphere is totally different on both sides.[17] According to

---

[16]The Maimonidean inspiration is here manifest; see the *Guide* 1, 53 (translation of S. Munk, p. 212 ff.) and *Guide*, I, 56 (p. 228). For the theme of the *incognoscibility* of God (underlined in IV, 12 and VIII, 22 by the formulation "the apprehender is greater than the apprehended"), see *Juda ben Nissim*, second part, chapter 1, *God*, especially p. 69, n. 1.

[17]To convince oneself completely, it is helpful to place the two texts in apposition. See p. 170.

Maimonides, "knowing that there exists a First Being who confers existence on every existing being" is the "ultimate fundamental principle and the pillar of *all sciences*." In the initial paragraph of our text, every cognitive term is absent: "the beginning of *faith* and the beginning of *trust*" are coupled words from our *Nine Chapters*, which strangely remind us of the beginning of a contemporary celebrated kabbalistic treatise,[18] if we are not totally mistaken, and which awaken two resonances at the same time, that of a fideistic tradition in Jewish theology[19] and that of one of the stages of spiritual life

Hilchot Yesodei HaTorah 1:1 [Fundamental Principles of the Torah]	Tishah Perakim 1,1 [The Nine Chapters]
"The fundamental principle of all principles and the pillar of all sciences is to realize that there is a First Being who brought every existing thing into being. All existing things, whether celestial, terrestrial, or in between, exist only through His true existence."	"The beginning of faith and the beginning of trust is that there exists a First Being who preceded every existence. It is He that confers existence on all things that exist since they did not exist [previously] and it is He who carries them all."

In the Maimonidean text, note that the beginning ("The fundamental principle . . . sciences") in Hebrew is composed of four words whose initials produce the acrostic Y-H-V-H; this is not an accident. On the other hand, "the fundamental principle of all principles" (in turn, compare the "Song of Songs") is not followed by a complementary name. It should be understood as the ultimate foundation of religion at the same time that metaphysics, taken in its pure state, is coincident for Maimonides.

[18]*Emunah* (faith) and *bittachon* (trust). We are envisioning the *Sefer Ha-Emunah veha-bittachon*, falsely attributed to Moses ben Nachman (Nachmanides), whose [real] author is the kabbalist Jacob ben Sheshet. Compare G. Scholem, *Major Trends*, 2nd ed. p. 355. I hasten to add that except for this terminological comparison, I see no point of analogy between the two writings. But the coupling of the words, not at all ordinary, and the fact that they begin one with the other, poses a problem that I cannot resolve.

[19]Upon which Maimonides is not dependent and for whom the term "faith" has a purely intellectual sense. See our summary remarks which are entirely provisional, *Quelques aspects du problème de la foi et de la raison dans la philosophie juive du moyen âge*, in *Revue de la Pensée Juive*, n° 1, October 1949, pp. 100–115.

according to the most "authoritative" book of piety in the Jewish literature.[20] On the other hand, the final part of the paragraph that enunciates a constantly recurring theme throughout the treatise,[21] is a literal citation from the *Book of Creation*.[22]

God carries, that is to say, maintains, everything.[23] This assertion is the point of departure of Chapter II. One is only explaining this formulation when one asserts that God bestows existence to those things over which He is their Sovereign Master. It is not that God has need of man. If He created him, it is by grace in order to teach him the paths by which he can gain eternal life. Under these conditions, man can only take upon himself the yoke of [His] Kingdom and serve with zeal in accommodating his will to that of his Master. Thus will be realized the benevolent design of God in this regard. First one believes in the existence of God and then one obeys Him. This belief is not an imposed commandment but a matter of understanding. Once this conviction of the existence of a Sovereign Being who orders and who prohibits is acquired, the precepts can be presented to the believer.

At the very outset is the interdiction of serving "other

---

[20]Compare G. Vajda, *"La Théologie Ascetique de Bachya Ibn Pakuda"* (Paris, 1947), chapter V, *L'Abandon*, pp. 60–85.

[21]See II:1, 15; VII:10; VIII:2; IX:17.

[22]Compare the two recensions printed in the first edition, *Sefer Yetzirah* IV, 2, Mantua 1562, and the *Commentaire* by Sabbatai Donnolo, D. Castelli, ed., p. 52.

[23]This and what follows are derived from the last chapter of *Ginnat Egoz*, the "Chapter on the Unity" (fol. 72d–74a). It is quite probable that "The Book of Creation" was not the only work to suggest this manner of expressing divine sovereignty, but here we are dealing with one of the traces of the influence of Ibn Gabirol on Kabbalah. See *Fons Vitae* V, 31, p. 315, 20–21: "Unitas est retentrix omnium et sustinet omnia," and the entire chapter 57 of book III (pp. 205–208, III, 39–42 in the Hebrew summary of Falakera); Ibn Gabirol, *La Source de Vie*, French translation by F. Brunner (Paris, 1950), *Livre III*, pp. 169–171; see also p. 43.

Addendum: There is a lot to say about the theme "God carries the universe." L. Zunz arranged a long list of texts illustrating it, which one could augment at will. *Die Synagogale Poesie des Mittelalters*, 2nd ed., Frankfurt, 1920, pp. 509–511. See also *Juda ben Nissim*, pp. 125–126.

gods."[24] This epithet should not lead us into error. The matter is not to juxtapose with the one God gods who are not such, save in the thinking of their followers. A more profound etymology makes us understand that the intention of Scripture is to indicate the complete dependence of these entities on another Being besides themselves.

Indeed, the comparison of beings teaches us that they are ranked according to a hierarchical order in which each lower level reveals a complexity (the text says *thickening*), an increasing opacity in comparison with higher levels. "According to the measure of the multitude of intermediaries, the opacity increases and decreases the unity. . . ."[25] The First Cause, simple essence, "has no carrier or maintainer but Himself." The caused, although it has essence, is composite because it does not exist by itself but by its form.[26]

---

[24]Exodus 20:3. The exegesis that follows was in part inspired by the commentary of Abraham Ibn Ezra on this verse. It is useless to emphasize that the etymology which will be proposed is purely theological.

[25]See *Fons Vitae* V, 20 (Hebrew summary V, 26), especially p. 295, 6–9: *"quia forma quae fuerit propinquior primae formal spirituali, illa errit subtilior et occultior; et a contrario quia quae forma magis accesserit ad formam corporalem ultimam erit spissior et manifestior."* See *Fons Vitae* IV, 14, pp. 242, 7–245, 4 (Hebrew summary IV, 22). The doctrine of progressive "thickening" according to the measure of the descent on the causal ladder is also clearly enunciated by Joseph ben Shalom Ashkenazi, kabbalist from Catalonia (first quarter of the fourteenth century) in his commentary on *The Book of Creation* 1, 10.

[26]Here again we recognize the teaching of Ibn Gabirol, III, 6, p. 90, 24: *"essentia primi factoris non habet formam"* (Brunner, p. 69; see also p. 63, n.1), but on the other hand "the form completes the essence" (IV, 3, p. 217, 4), it "constitutes the essence of that in which it resides and confers upon it its existence" (IV, 11, p. 235, 24–25, Hebrew summary IV, 17). Many other passages are cited in the *Index* of Baeumker, p. 441. The insufficiently nuanced terminology in our text harms the clarity of his thinking a little. God, pure essence, has no form. But everything except God is composed, in the mind of Ibn Gabirol, followed by the redactor of the *Nine Chapters*, of form and matter. It is the same ambiguous term in Hebrew, *etzem*, which means both *essence* and *substance*, which is used in speaking of the noncomposite essence of God and of matter, and which is intelligible and sensible in the circumstance of all the other beings that exist and subsist in form [as well as essence]. This imprecision is also not without effect on the gabirolean vocabulary; see Baeumker, *Index*, p. 434.

It follows from these considerations that God possesses the exclusive privilege of integral Unity (simplicity), that He is the efficient cause inasmuch as He confers existence, that He is the formal cause inasmuch as He maintains it, and that He is the final cause inasmuch as to Him there leads the chain of the degrees of existence that maintain themselves separately, one from the other.

Opposite the One God, the universe is of increasing multiplicity. To safeguard the absolute separation between them, it is important to know the hierarchy of beings. Clearly inspired, as we have already remarked, by Chapters II to IV of Maimonides' *Fundamental Rules of the Revealed Law*, the second chapter delineates the structure.[27] This hierarchy is not only ontological (composition, increasing "thickening") but also cognitive. No creature, irrespective of its status in creation, can reach a complete understanding of the Deity; the screen that separates God from the created becomes more impenetrable the more material the creature is.

But does not this universe, created opposite the One God and consequently immutable, precisely call into question His immutability? If the actual existence of the world follows nonexistence, may one not ask about the motive for this change of state that can only be correlative to an unexpected radical change in the will of God?

Chapter IV answers this difficulty and judges it to be simply specious. What in effect is changed? It is the passing of the power to act. Well now, reflection shows us that when it relates

---

[27]The corresponding passages in the *Ginnat Egoz* (last chapter and fol. 32d–33a) are unburdened of kabbalistic speculations. It suffices to cite in one word the described schema: three worlds, intelligible (the "ten intellects"), astral and sublunar, God remaining outside the system. For a historical insight into these speculations, see *Juda ben Nissim*, second part, chapter III, *Cosmologie*, above all pp. 94–98. The movement of the spheres, actioned by their desire to know the Creator and their eagerness to serve Him, is illustrated in III:9 (but not, if I am not mistaken, in the *Ginnat Egoz* where all the rest is abridged) by a phrase from *The Book of Creation* (I,5): "to His word, they hurl themselves like a tempest and (run to) prostrate themselves before His throne."

to God, none of the causes of actualization can be invoked. The
body is the indispensible substrate of the passage of the power
to act. God is incorporeal. He has need for nothing, therefore
nothing completes Him and no obstacle hinders Him that He
would have to surmount to attain a perfection which He did not
previously have. There is no other motive from that time to the
temporal production of the world at one moment rather than
another, other than His will.

But was there then not at least a change of will?

No, because such a change postulates duality of the subject
and His will, which is not the case for an incorporeal intelligence.

Certainly, the other attributes of essence, life, power, wisdom, and will do not allow themselves to be differentiated in
God. This truth is condensed in the liturgy in the following
formulation: "*Y-H-V-H* (is) king, *Y-H-V-H* reigned, *Y-H-V-H* will
reign."[28]

We have just demonstrated that neither the action of creation
nor the predication of attributes overshadows Divine Simplicity. Are we nevertheless able at the same time, asks Chapter V,
to reconcile this with the religious doctrine of retribution? God
rewards the good and punishes the wicked. Is the Divine Will

---

[28]The substance of this chapter (of which I have not found corresponding
texts in the *Ginnat Egoz*) is drawn from Maimonides: see the *Guide* I, 53 and
II, 18 (pp. 138–143) and *Hilchot Yesodei HaTorah* II, 10. The scriptural
demonstration of paragraphs 9–12 is a fabrication of the author who might
nevertheless have reminded himself for the last proof (Isaiah 43:7: "all that is
called by My name I created for My glory . . .") of the *Guide* II, 13 (primarily
pp. 92–93 in Munk). What is even more important is that the Maimonidean
statements are exploited from the perspective suited to the author. The
problem for Maimonides was to demonstrate the rational possibility of the
"newness" of the world. He showed that this ["newness" of the world] was not,
contrary to what is claimed by the supporters of eternity, incompatible with
the immutability of God. [It is here that the Divine immutability is put in
question because of the fact, not at all problematic, of the creation of the
world]. In reality, in the emanatist system of our writing, the Divine
immutability is the profound motive of the adventicity of the universe, once
acknowledged that the process of emanation was set into motion by an act of
[His] will.

not compelled to modify Itself depending on the behavior of man?

Certainly not! A unique force can faultlessly cause opposite effects depending on the nature of the receptive subject: the sun blanches linen but tans the face of the washer; through the action of fire, wax melts but clay hardens. Diverse materials react differently to fireproofing. These analogies, and above all the last, allow one to comprehend how the unique Divine Force is, if one can so state, the *crucible (masref)* within which pass the various actions of men. Even if the consequences of these actions also vary, this does not at all affect the operation of the *crucible*, which is unique, but only the diversity of materials submitted to the test. In this manner we can understand the numerous biblical locutions which, if interpreted literally, might persuade one to believe in frequent modifications of Divine Will provoked by the fluctuations in human attitudes.

The "Thirteen Attributes" (Exodus 34:6–7), the love that God is said to hold for certain men, the resentment that He supposedly nourishes against others, His proximity and His remoteness, the purity and the defilement of man—all this phraseology refers to this single truth: tested by a unique force, the various actions of men engender salutary or disastrous consequences without a single alteration in the probing force itself.[29]

We might perhaps say that morality is heteronomous: it is the expression of an immutable order, which is the will of God.

---

[29]The doctrine reported in this chapter was inspired by the conclusion of *Ginnat Egoz* (fol. 74a–b) where one finds more particularly the theory of the "crucible," and the *Guide* I, 53, especially the portion corresponding to the translation of Munk, pp. 207–208, where the example of the multiple actions of fire serve to illustrate the thesis according to which "the diversity of actions does not imply the existence of diverse ideas in the agent," and by consequence the indistinction of the essential attributes in God, a problem treated here in a slightly different context, at the end of Chapter IV. The example illustrating the double action of the sun seems to have been borrowed from Ibn Ezra (commentary on Ecclesiastes, introduction) who used it in the solution of the problem of evil.

But, simultaneously,[30] the freedom of human options engenders from itself the consequences of its actions.[31]

Meanwhile, a new and no less serious problem arises in Chapter VI. If, in order to safeguard Divine immutability, one has to accept a sort of automatism of sanctions in which God has no part, are we not backed into a corner to refuse all efficacy and even all significance of prayer? To whom do the good supplicate, "forgive us, our Father" since, by virtue of impurity, we must of necessity perish because everything is fulfilled according to our actions? Moreover, God does not change as a result of our supplications.

Since we cannot do otherwise, we employ the resources of the human language. The liturgical formulations, moreover, have no other sense than the proclamation of the sovereignty of God, of His providence, of His justice, and no other effect but the purification of our souls. Besides, if we omitted imploring for Divine forgiveness and demanded our subsistence, we would lose the sentiment of our culpability and would forget the benevolence of God on our behalf. Our souls, purified through praying or, more exactly, by the effective abandonment of evil that the words mean in simple translation, bring us closer to God. Accordingly, God does not undergo any change because of the act of our prayers: all depends on the worshiper,[32] on one's purification and one's actual improvement.

Beginning with Chapter VII, the method changes. Until now, we allowed ourselves to be governed by reason; henceforth, the notions of the "tradition of the revealed Law" serve as our guide, the goal remaining the same—knowledge of the Divine Unity.

Knowing God, at least to the extent of our present sensual condition, is to distinguish Him from all other created beings. For this purpose, revelation furnishes us a means that all the efforts of philosophies were powerless to provide us: the name

---

[30]Literally: in contact with this order. (Fred Rosner)

[31]There is no discussion [literally: question] of the role of freedom in *Ginnat Egoz*, so clearly emphasized in the *Nine Chapters*.

[32]Latin: *orant* meaning the worshiper.

of God, His proper name, the one that designates His essence, not one of the circumlocutions that the philosophers could never surpass, "cause" or "agent."

In fixing his intention on the Great Name of God, man, knowing before Whom he finds himself, simultaneously progresses in the path of perfection; his oration is not purely verbal; his purified soul is able to join the celestial hierarchies who only understand prayers pronounced in language adequate for thought. It is in this manner that one should comprehend the talmudic teaching (*Shabbat* 12b): "The ministering angels do not understand the Aramaic language at all."[33]

Diligent meditation, deeper and deeper into the Great Name, greatly intensifies the desire that nourishes the soul to adhere to its Creator to the point of no longer being separated from Him. It is in this sense that Scripture commands: "Thou shalt cleave to Him" (Deuteronomy 13:5).

The two last chapters of the pamphlet expose the ostensibly traditional views of the Divine names. In reality, they consist of a summary of the speculations of the first part of *Ginnat Egoz*, the "Treatise of Divine Names."[34]

---

[33]The reasoning of the author appears to be the following. The Hebrew language furnishes us with the proper name of God that, one might say, permits one to identify Him, if not to know Him intimately. It is, therefore, only in this language that one can address oneself to God in an adequate manner, that is to say to pray correctly, and in that way, to join the celestial hierarchies. Thus understood, the chapter possesses its own internal unity and does not limit itself in juxtaposing two themes as I unjustly declared in my Hebrew introduction, p. 106, lines 1–2.

[34]Here is the detail of the corresponding sections:

Nine Chapters	Ginnat Egoz
V111:1–23	fol. 4–5, 8c–d, 9c–10
1X:1	fol. 11b
1X:2	fol. 5d–6a
1X:3	fol. 11b
1X:4	fol. 13d–14a
1X:5	fol. 13c–d

(*continued on p. 178*)

The Tetragrammaton *(Y-H-V-H)* is an exclusive title that expresses the plenitude of the essence and the subsistence of God. Tradition rightly says that these coexisted in God prior to the birth of the world.[35] The other Divine names, "peri-phrases" or "cognomens" connote one or another aspect of Divine activity, derived from this Great Name, just like in the ontologic order, the totality of beings proceeds from the essence of the Creator.

The Divine names are graded in a hierarchal sequence. Beneath the Tetragrammaton is the "I am" *(Eh-yeh)* of Exodus (3:14); next is *Y-ah* which is short for the Tetragrammaton, then *Elo-him*, *Ado-nai*, *Shad-dai*, *Y-H-V-H* (read *Ado-nai*), *Tze-va-ot*, and *Elo-him Tze-va-ot.*[36]

The Tetragrammaton expresses existence. Immutable exist-

1X:6	fol. 13b–c
1X:7, 9, 14	fol. 17a
1X:10–11	fol. 15d–16a (cf. 36a)
1X:12–13, 15	fol. 17b–d
1X:16–18	fol. 18b (cf. 45a–b)

The two references in parentheses concern the figured texts in the second part of *Ginnat Egoz*.

[35]This [statement] refers to a passage, often explained by theologians and kabbalists, in the treatise *Pirké Rabbi Eliezer*, chapter III: "Before the creation of the world, there was only the Most Holy and His sole Name: (I borrowed this translation from Munk, *Guide* I, 61, p. 271; the entire chapter in Maimonides should be reread to comprehend intelligently the portion with which we are concerned). Concerning the topic of the "Chapters of Rabbi Eliezer," one can refer to B. Heller, *Encyclopedia Judaica*, article *Aggadische Literatur*, Vol. 1, col. 1030 sq.

[36]This list is not exhaustive because we will shortly encounter an observation relative to *El* that has the same sense as *Elo-him*, "Lord." *Ado-nai*, "Master," is the substitute for the Tetragrammaton whose prohibited pronunciation, was given up to oblivion. Two interpretations of *Shad-dai* are later proposed in the text. The two last names: "Master (or) God of Hosts," after the Bible, became the common patrimony of the Jewish and Christian liturgy. The exegetes of our days are far from concurrence on the philologic interpretation of *Y-H-V-H* and of *Y-H-V-H Tze-va-ot*. A list, already outdated, of recent works [can be found] in *Biblica* 34, 1953, *Elenchus Bibliographicus*, p. 147 ff.

ence is also proven by the fact that the twelve possible permutations of the four letters that comprise it cannot be interpreted in any other way but that of existence. This is not the case with any other Divine name.[37]

Eh-yeh, first derivative of the Tetragrammaton symbolizes the procession of all things beginning with Divine Essence. The *Book of Creation* (I, 13), which reestablishes the constitution of the universe in the six permutations of the three different letters of the Tetragrammaton *(Y-H-V)*, teaches precisely the same truth because the numerical value of the two groups of letters is identical.[38]

The knowledge of this eminent Name, which is, however, inferior to the Tetragrammaton,[39] is the supreme degree achieved by Moses, privileged prophet among us. The mystery of the Great Name that expresses the essence of God was withheld[40] from him because if he had been granted this perception, he would have possessed the complete comprehension of the Divine Essence, but the perceiver is superior to the perceived object.[41]

Y-ah symbolizes the Divine government of the world.[42]

---

[37]In *Y-H-V-H*, the Jewish esotericists discern the root *H-Y-H*, "to be." It is for this reason that they designate it as the *shem hawayah* which simultaneously means "the name composed of the [Hebrew] letters *Yod-He-Vav-He*" and "nomen essendi." Since this name includes three different letters, the number of combinations (one of the fundamental procedures of Kabbalah) of these is twelve. But none of these combinations (the text gives the list) coincides with a Hebrew word that one can attach to another root. Consequently, for the kabbalist, the totality of the permutations of the Tetragrammaton is central to existence. By contrast, if one takes a Divine name such as *El= aleph lamed*, these two [Hebrew] letters, when inverted, give *lo*, "no," that is to say the negation even of existence, thus of divinity, as it is described in VIII:13.

[38]*Aleph* (1) + *He* (5) + *Yod* (10) + *He* (5) = 21; *Yod* (10) + *He* (5) + *Vav* (6) = 21. Isopsephy *(gematria)* is another essential method of Kabbalah.

[39]Here intervenes the second criticism directed at Maimonides (*supra*, note 13).

[40]Literally: forbidden (Fred Rosner)

[41]See *supra*, note 16.

[42]The *Ginnat Egoz* (fol. 10b, lines 2–3) thus recapitulates the doctrine relative to the three names *Y-H-V-H*, *Eh-yeh*, *Y-ah*: "these three names constitute the mystery of the *nomina essendi* within which are included (the)

Elo-him speaks of the Divine action that manifests itself in nature.[43]

Ado-nai expresses the Sovereignty of God in the world.[44]

Shad-dai connotes autarchy and, according to others, the superiority of the Divine decree compared to astral determination.[45]

Since the designation *Y-H-V-H Tze-va-ot* is not attested to in the Pentateuch, it is later than Moses. It expresses the Sovereignty of God over the three worlds.

The triple "Holy" of the vision of Isaiah (6:3) conveys the separation of God from the totality of creation composed of the three worlds that He carries.[46]

*   *   *

Let us cast a retrospective glance at this already lengthy, but by no means exhaustive analysis.

Our little treatise fully merits its title. It effectively scrutinizes Divine Unity in its triple aspect of unity, simplicity, and sepa-

---

Primordial, (the) Adventitious, and (the) Governmental," that is to say God Himself, God the Creator, and God the Provident.

[43] IX, 1–6. Following *Ginnat Egoz* which it recapitulates, our text delivers a meticulous esoteric analysis of the name under consideration, which is too long to expound here. Let us only retain two instants. *Elo-him* is the only Divine name used in the narrative of creation, which clearly shows that it expresses demiurgic activity, if one can so state. The numerical value of these letters is 86, equal to that of H-T-B, *ha-teba*, "nature."

[44] IX, 8–12. (Paragraph 7 forms the transition between the successive study of the two Divine names; this is also the case with paragraph 16; the effort of the composition is visible.) Here there intervenes another isopsephy, famous in Kabbalah: *Ado-nai* has the numerical value of 65 = *H-Y-K-L*, *hechal*, "the sanctuary," that is to say, the sensible receptacle, the pronounced form of the ineffable Name.

[45] IX, 13–15. The first interpretation is that of Maimonides (*Guide* I, 63, pp. 284–285, according to *Pirké Rabbi Eliezer*, Chapter III); the second, which the *Nine Chapters* cite rather as a reminder without welcoming it with great conviction, has Abraham Ibn Ezra as its author.

[46] IX, 17–18. For the theme of carrying, see notes 21–23. For ideas on the philosophic exegesis of the *Trisagion*, see *Juda ben Nissim*, p. 96, n. 3 and p. 97, n. 4 and for the whole see pp. 95–98.

ration. The first aspect is, in truth, only superficially discussed, undoubtedly because the previous theological work was sufficiently examined in depth. Simplicity, which removes from God any composition, even a purely conceptual one of the attributes of essence, signifies in the philosophic plan the radical opposition between pure man-caused essence, which subsists by itself, and the increasing complexity of the caused, which subsists only by its form (Chapter II). In the theological plan, Divine immutability serves to place in relief the pure grace of the voluntary act of creation (Chapters II and IV), as well as the freedom of responsible man undergoing the test of the unalterable Divine order (Chapter V), and possessing in prayer a method of introspection and simultaneously a means of verbal externalization of renouncement of sin (Chapter VI).

Separation, the third aspect of unity, is also presented according to the two plans: rational understanding throughout the habitual cosmologic schema (Chapter III), and more profound penetration by meditation on the Great Name and exact comprehension of the value of the other designations, not only of the inaccessible and incomprehensible essence, but of Divine manifestations and activities (Chapters VII-IX).

The God of philosophers, essence subsisting in His aseity and in the indistinction of His attributes, point of departure of the emanation and ultimate foundation of the reality of the hierarchal multiplicity; the God of voluntary creation, author of the moral order, object of mystical aspirations and, nevertheless, radically *other*, of the esoteristic Jewish piety—such is the diptych that is offered to us by the *Nine Chapters on the Unity of God*.

In spite of the mystical climate in every doctrinal exposé, one senses a breath of intellectualism blown into it. Knowledge is the indispensable preamble of belief, even though spiritual life is concerned with "faith and trust." Salvation is gained by knowledge, even though the former finds itself simultaneously surpassed and completed by mystical meditation of the ineffable Name of God unknown in His essence. Even obedience to the Divine law may only be the consequence of an authentic intellectual conviction. We here recognize constants of the

Arabic-Jewish theology, such that they are manifest, despite all
the diversity of philosophic positions and spiritual attitudes, in
[the writings of] Saadia, Bachya, and Maimonides. In this
regard, it seems to me, our treatise rests well in the line of early
theological speculations. If this line is, nevertheless, inflected in
the sense of Kabbalah, it refers there to a strongly moderate
esotericism, not at all theosophic. No more than in the *Ginnat
Egoz*, there is no allusion here to the great theses of "classic"
Kabbalah: interior life of the unknown Deity blossoming forth
in the ten *sefirot*,[47] more or less radical dualism of good and of
evil, and theurgical function and efficacy of benevolent acts.

It remains reserved for others who are tentatives of harmo-
nization to confront and to reconcile a richer and more
luxuriant Kabbalah with philosophic thinking inspired by
neoplatonic-peripateticism. Above its particular plan, the *Nine
Chapters* nevertheless represent an essay by no means negligi-
ble, and we do not believe that we toiled in vain in bringing
them to the attention of medievalists.

---

[47]Literally: countings. These ten countings are: wisdom *(chochmah)*, understanding *(binah)*, knowledge *(da'at)*, kindness *(chesed)*, might *(gevurah)*, glory
(tiferet), victory *(netzach)*, majesty *(hod)*, foundation *(yesod)*, and royalty *(malchut)*. The latter seven are incorporated in the liturgical service of the
counting of the Omer between Passover and Pentecost. (Fred Rosner)

NINE CHAPTERS ON THE UNITY OF GOD

In the Name of the Creator of Heaven and Earth, I Begin the Nine Chapters on the Unity [of God] Composed by Moses Maimonides, of Blessed Memory.

Chapter I

1. The axiom of our faith and the foundation of our trust[1] is that there is an Eternal Being[2] who preceded all that exists and that it is He who caused all other things to exist from nothingness, and it is He who maintains[3] their existence.[4]

2. The recognition of the existence of The Eternal and establishing it as a truism is an important commandment and is a basic and fundamental principle of our faith. The Torah depicts this matter and states: "Know this day, and lay it to thy

---

[1]See Maimonides, *Mishneh Torah, Yesodei Hatorah* 1:1.
[2]Literally: First Being.
[3]Literally: carries.
[4]Compare to the *Book of Creation* [*Sefer Yetzirah*] 24:42.

heart [that the Lord, He is God in heaven above and upon the earth beneath; there is none else]."[5] This is the first fundamental principle that a person should recognize and the foundation upon which his faith should be built.

3. Specifically, a person should have knowledge of everything in creation individually and examine each vis-à-vis each other. By such critical examination, they will form a composite that will establish for him the existence of a single Being from whom all other beings originate[6] and He is responsible for[7] them and there is no other beside Him. And if a person examines all the things that exist,[8] he will understand their purpose.

4. All these things about which we spoke become clear to a person who comprehends and examines the verity of His Great Name, may He be praised, and that is the name referred to as "His exclusive name" [*Shem Hameyuchad*] whose [Hebrew] letters are *yod, hey, vav, hey*. This is the name that demonstrates and testifies to His truth, and He has no other name that testifies about Him, for all [His other names] are appellations that describe His activities.

5. This Being has no physical body or substance or limit or measure[9] and He is not comparable in any way to all other beings that exist in the world. All beings have finiteness[10] in relation to Him but He is not finite in relation to them. None of them have any attributes that can be compared with Him or to allow a person to compare Him with any other being.

6. Similarly, the Exalted One[11] does not possess scientific knowledge, ability, life, and willpower [as separate attributes] because these attributes imply differences from one another,

---

[5]Deuteronomy 4:39.

[6]Literally: hang.

[7]Literally: carries.

[8]Literally: the carriers and the carried.

[9]God is incorporeal, immutable, and eternal. See Maimonides, *Yesodei Hatorah* 1:11.

[10]Literally: have measure, size, or proportion.

[11]Literally: may He be exalted.

but He never changes because there is nothing in the world that can cause Him to change.[12]

7. A person should explore and carefully examine[13] all these matters and search out the foundation upon which each principle is based, and should do this by cognition because faith is not established save after cognition.

8. When these principles become an integrated, organized body of understanding,[14] a person will appreciate[15] that the Exalted One is separate from all other existences and likewise that He is One and there is no other unto Him and He is not composed of multiple parts but is One regardless of which vantage point man views Him from. When a person understands the manner in which the Exalted One is separated from all other existences, he will be able to profess the Unity of God to the exclusion of all other existences.

9. Behold it is written in the Torah: "Hear, O Israel, the Lord is our God, the Lord is One."[16] There are many things in the world that are called singular but these singularities are composed of many units. For example, a man is called a singular [person] but he has 248 limbs, each of which is different from all the others. How, then, can one call something singular if it is composed of many units?

10. I, therefore, state that a person must separate in his mind this Oneness [of God] from other singularities and must understand what the Unity of God is when it is stated, "the Lord is One." He must understand that this Unity [of God] is not related to numbers but He is One because He is singular in relation to all other existences, because the Almighty cannot be classified within the concept of numbers.

11. When a person thoroughly comprehends these fundamental principles one by one and establishes them as truths, his soul will rejoice and his intellect will rise up in the joy of what

---

[12]Were His actions changeable, He would be mutable.
[13]Literally: introspect; pay attention.
[14]Literally: when a person becomes attached to these matters.
[15]Literally: find in his mind.
[16]Deuteronomy 6:4. Vajda erroneously cites 6:5.

he has achieved, because his soul is occupied with intellectual pursuits and is drawn to them because the source of intellect flows from Him.

12. As long as a person is not worthy to grasp[17] these matters, it is as if there is a wall between him and his Creator. As the person begins to investigate these matters one by one and to understand their foundations, the barrier becomes ever smaller and the soul becomes ever closer to the Exalted Creator.

13. Behold, it is written in the Torah: "the Lord is FAR from the wicked,[18] and the Lord is NEAR to all those that call upon Him."[19] Since He is incorporeal, how can He be close or far? Rather, what is meant is CLOSE to the soul in terms of knowledge and understanding [of His Unity] and FAR from the soul in terms of the barrier and the folly if the soul has no knowledge of the verity of the Exalted One.

14. In this manner a person can weigh in his mind the depth of the understanding of those who achieved this understanding by distancing the Exalted One from any thought of comparison to other existences. One can only understand Him by distancing from Him all things that attempt to measure Him, in order to call Him truly One.

15. How? If a person does not distance from the Exalted One[20] any type of rational comparison,[21] there is a large and strong barrier and a screen separating that person from Him. But when the person begins to distance corporeal matters from the Exalted One and distances a movement,[22] he approaches [God] by one step and achieves one level of understanding. These are called the ways of negation.[23]

16. Do not think that one can understand the Exalted One by probing and investigating the quality and substance of His

---

[17]Literally: reach.
[18]Proverbs 15:29.
[19]Psalm 145:18.
[20]Literally: from Him, may He be exalted.
[21]Literally: ways of the imagination.
[22]That is, avoids thinking of God in human terms of finiteness, measureability, corporeality, and so on.
[23]Whereas God is incorporeal.

verity because such an approach is not possible. Rather, it is abusive and blasphemous to probe into a matter that no being other than the Exalted One has the faculty to comprehend and even more so for any intellect that is composed of matter.

17. We will, in due course,[24] explain all these fundamental principles with the help of God. May the Lord our God be gracious to us and show us the path to follow and the deeds we should perform. May He enlighten our eyes with the light of understanding Him, and may He purify the eye of our intellect to comprehend His verity.

Completed is the first chapter.

Chapter II

1. The very first commandment at Sinai commanded us regarding the truth of His existence, may He be exalted, so that we know that there is a Unique Being who rules over all who exist because He maintains them. And He is King in that He caused them to be.[25] There is nothing in all who exist that can compare to Him, may He be exalted, because the Exalted One maintains them and they are all maintained by Him.[26] The matter of Him carrying them means that He maintains them.[27]

2. The essential feature of this matter is that a person should first know that he has a Creator who created him and causes him to exist, not because the Exalted One needs him since He has no need for anything, but because the Exalted One wishes to bestow kindness upon him and to teach him ways through which the world can prosper.

3. Since one will know that he has a Living and Eternal

---

[24]Literally: in the future.

[25]Alternate version: He created them from nothingness.

[26]Literally: carried by Him. The meaning here is that they were not created once and now exist by themselves. Rather, their continuance is itself an act of creation, dependent upon God's continued will that they be.

[27]In his *Sheviley Emunah,* Aldabi here adds: "therefore He is responsible for existences, may He be blessed, as well as for everything else besides He that exists."

Creator who maintains him and sustains him and gives him an abundance from His goodness and bestows His kindness upon him, [it follows that] the person should accept upon himself the yoke of His kingdom and acknowledge before Him all that He has done for him in terms of kindness and all the goodness that He has bestowed upon him.

4. When a person recognizes[28] the truth of the existence of his Creator and accepts upon himself His kingship, it is proper for him to hasten to His servitude and to His wishes and to avoid[29] that which He does not want.[30] If he does this, he will receive the good reward[31] and through him the purpose of creation will be fulfilled because he was created for that reason, as God has said: "Everything that is called by My name, I have created for My glory, I have formed it, yea, I have made it."[32]

5. In accordance with this cardinal principle it is written at the beginning of the commandments: "I am the Lord, thy God,"[33] that is to say, believe in your heart the truth of My existence and then you can accept the yoke of My kingship because the acceptance of the yoke of kingship is not possible until the belief in [His] existence is established.[34]

6. The important commandment of believing in the existence [of God] is not mentioned in the Torah in the form of a command as are all the other commandments. The reason is that it is not appropriate to command something until the listener knows who the commander is and believes in his heart that he exists. Therefore, in this commandment, He tells us: "I am the Lord, thy God," and it is not stated in the form of a command but in the form of belief.

---

[28]Literally: reaches the knowledge.

[29]Literally: distance (himself).

[30]Aldabi here adds: "and the research scholars have written that the only person who can serve the Cause of Causes [God] is a respected prophet or a distinguished scholar who acquired wisdom." This statement appears to be taken from *Hovot Halevavot* or from the *Sefer Ha'olam Hakatan* by Z. Tzadik (Edition of Horowitz 21:14).

[31]Eternal bliss.

[32]Isaiah 43:7.

[33]Exodus 20:2.

[34]Aldabi here explains the remainder of the scriptural verse.

7. After having taught us the truth of His existence and the ways that He conducts the world, He began commanding us and informing us that there is nobody besides Him that is worthy of being served, because all existences other than Him came into existence by His word alone, and it is not proper to include in one's faith in Him and one's acceptance of the yoke of His kingship any of His servants, so as not to equate the honor of the Creator with the honor of the creations.

8. He, therefore, juxtaposes this commandment to the truth of His existence because to worship other than Him belies the truth of His existence. For this reason[35] He first commanded us: "Thou shalt have no other gods before Me."[36]

9. Let it not enter your mind from the statement "other gods" that other gods exist besides Him. Rather, they are "gods" in the eyes of those who worship them. Similarly: "And the men pursued them."[37] It is written "other gods"[38] meaning after them,[39] that is to say, gods who are drawn after others who have no power on their own, but their existence is dependent on something other than themselves. He who has no existence on his own but from something else is not worthy to be served, nor should one swear in his name. However, servitude is appropriate to the One who carries and maintains all powers that are interrelated. The goal is to reach His testimony and He has no one that carries Him and has no one that maintains Him.[40]

10. According to this essential principle, a person must search and examine the existence of all creation besides Him in a scientific manner. And when he understands their existence and their essence becomes clear to him, and he perceives the

---

[35]Literally: And on this matter.

[36]Exodus 20:3.

[37]Joshua 2:7. They did not actually pursue them at all as they were hidden in Jericho, but they "pursued" them according to their belief that they had fled the city.

[38]Hebrew: *acherim.*

[39]Hebrew: *acharayim.*

[40]Aldabi here adds: "may His name be blessed and His remembrance be exalted."

matter correctly, only then will he seat the Creator on His heavenly throne.[41]

11. How? All the beings that exist in the world besides Him, may He be exalted, are interdependent and interrelated and their existence and "powers" are drawn from one another. Ultimately, all creation flows from the One who emanates power to all.

12. Therefore, a person has to assess [all] beings individually and to understand that the greater the number of intermediaries between that being and the Creator, the greater the complexity of the being, and accordingly the greater the unclarity and the closer the being in that chain is to the Creator, the greater its clarity and comprehendability.

13. For instance, there is an item considered one thing that consists of ten levels.[42] Thus, this one item consists of ten things that are ten powers, which it receives from the ten levels that are between it and the Original Cause.

14. In this manner you can understand that the increase in unclarity and decrease in unity are proportional to[43] the increase[44] of intermediaries, and the decrease in clarity and increase in unity are proportional to the decrease in intermediaries.

15. Therefore, how can one distinguish between the Cause and the thing it has caused to be[45] since the Cause is in essence a simple thing. Know that the First Cause is a simple essence that has no carrier nor maintainer besides itself, but the thing it caused to be, although it has essence, also has a carrier and a maintainer outside itself, and its maintenance is its form. Therefore, it follows that the First Cause is simple essence that has no second matter, but the caused has an additional matter

---

[41]Literally: His fixed place. Hebrew: *mechono*. Compare the *Book of Creation*, Chapter 1, 40:4. The meaning is: only then will he establish God as the King of all creation.

[42]Hebrew: *maalot*, also translated as virtues, steps, degrees, and so on.

[43]Literally: according to.

[44]Literally: multitude.

[45]That is, the result, all creations of the Creator.

that is the affirmation called form. Thus, the Cause is only essence and the caused has essence and form.

16. According to this approach[46] it is clear that there is nothing besides Him, may He be exalted, that one can appropriately and truly call One because there is no existing being that can escape from being essence—even if it is the purest essence—without the essence also having something else besides itself to maintain it, and the latter is called form next to the essence. Therefore, the Exalted One alone is essence while all other existences are essence and form.

17. In this manner the Exalted One is called the Doer, the Shaper and the Purpose [Giver]; the Doer in that He brought into existence all activities at the beginning of everything; the Shaper in that He maintains all the activities that He created just as form is the maintainer of the essence; and Purpose [Giver] because all the levels that follow one after the other and which are maintained one by the other, all have the purpose of reaching back unto Him and there they end because He is the maintainer of all forms and the Purpose of all purposes.

18. From these matters that we have explained, a person should know that among all existences besides Him, may He be exalted, there is nothing that can truly be called One because all existences other than Him include at a minimum two things, which are called essence and form.[47]

Chapter III

1. You need to understand[48] the matter of "levels" and then you will be able to differentiate between Him, may He be exalted, and everything else besides Him; because one who

---

[46]Literally: this matter, subject, or topic.

[47]One must distinguish between essence and form. Water is the fusion of oxygen and hydrogen. Its *essence* is made up of these two elements but its *form* is water. Hydrogen and oxygen, in turn, are also a form of *sub-essences* such as atoms consisting of protons, neutrons, and so on.

[48]Literally: to know.

does not understand the ways of "differentiation" cannot understand His precise Oneness, may He be exalted, because when he nears the truth of his Creator and his soul approaches the perception of the One who brought it forth. . . .[49]

2. How? Know that all existences besides Him, may He be exalted, can be divided into three levels. The first level is the World[50] of the Intellect which is a simple essence. Its maintenance, which is its form, depends upon the Creator, may He be exalted. This is the highest of the three levels.

3. The uppermost world, which is the World of the Intellect, is the one that perceives Him, may He be exalted, with an exceptionally great perception and nothing hinders its perception except the great concealment of the Creator, may He be exalted. There is no being besides Him that can reach a precise understanding of His existence since it is truly outside of Him.[51]

4. Therefore, although the uppermost world[52] achieves a great perception, it does not perceive His ultimate truth, may He be exalted, because His being created[53] hinders [complete] perception of the Primordial Being[54] and nothing created can attain the [proper] perception of this matter.[55]

5. In the uppermost world, there is nothing corporeal at all, other than the essence of the intellect, which is undressed matter. There is no physical substance or body there at all and there does not exist either jealousy or hatred or rivalry but only the perception of His truth, may He be exalted. There is also no change at all there because their intent requires it since they are an essence, Intellect, simple and pure.

6. These forms exist forever through the will of their

---

[49]The remainder of the sentence seems to be missing. Compare chapter 1:11–12.

[50]The manuscript omits *world* but it is found in Aldabi's *Sheviley Emunah*.

[51]Aldabi here adds proof from Scripture: Exodus 33:18, 20.

[52]The World of the Intellect.

[53]Hebrew: *chidush*, literally: novelty.

[54]Hebrew: *kadmon*, an epithet of God. Aldabi renders: "the Creator, may He be blessed, who is the First Being."

[55]The Aldabi version differs slightly.

Creator, may He be exalted, and do not change from form to form and from matter to matter. These are the ten levels, one above the other, not levels of place but levels of perception, since a level of place is not appropriate for something that has no physical body.[56]

7. Below this world [of intellect] is the world of the spheres and all the hosts of the heavens and the array of the stars. This world is the world of matter but its substance is clear, clean, and pure and it perceives Him with a great perception, but not like the uppermost world because its substance hinders greatly for it is an existence of matter, and matter is a great barrier between the perceiver and the perceived.

8. There are nine constellations, one above the other, seven of which correspond to the seven heavenly bodies called Moon, Mercury, Venus, Sun, Mars, Jupiter, and Saturn. The eighth is the constellation of the Zodiac and the ninth is the constellation of Aravot.

9. These constellations and the planets therein are all alive. They have intellect and knowledge and perceive Him, may He be exalted, and are aware of themselves and of others. They exist without termination by the will of the One who brought them into existence, even though they are composed of substance and form because their substance does not change from that with which they were endowed at the original creation.[57] All constantly strive to perceive Him, may He be exalted. Similarly, they too do not have among them jealousy, hatred, or rivalry because there is nothing in them that would cause these things. Rather, all are in agreement in a common purpose and that is to [properly and completely] perceive His knowledge, may He be exalted. They rejoice and exult to do the will of their

---

[56]Aldabi phrases the sentence in the positive: a level of place is only appropriate for someone who has a physical body. He also cites the ten levels of the world of angels.

[57]An organic being changes by the nature of its creation. However, the heavenly bodies or planets were created immutable and change only by the will of God.

Master, and they pursue His words like a storm wind and bow down before His throne.[58]

11. Below[59] this world is the world of composition and separation. This is the lower world in which there is one substance, which takes four forms and separates to become four fundamental substances,[60] which are fire, air, water, and earth.

12. These four fundamental substances assume a form and undress the form according to the movement of the constellation by virtue of the World of Intellect, because from there forms emanate throughout the lower world by means of the movement of the constellation.

13. These fundamental substances do not have a soul nor knowledge and they do not perceive themselves nor anything else. They do not have independent movement but [their activity] is derived from the power of the constellations called *chayot*,[61] which are alive and perform activities with the four fundamental substances according to the will of their Creator during their movements. All things that occur in the lower world occur by virtue of His word, may He be exalted, through the movement of the constellations.

14. The gradation of the three worlds[62] was made clear to you, one above the other and the superiority[63] that each has over the one below it and how the maintenance of all existences is dependent upon the Creator, may He be exalted, and that He is One, simple[64] in all possible aspects in which you will

---

[58]*The Book of Creation*, Chapter 1:5.

[59]Paragraph 10 is omitted by error, but there is nothing lacking in the text.

[60]Literally: heads. Compare *Keter Malchut*, Davidson edition, p. 89, line 115. See also Genesis 2:10.

[61]The highest rank of angels. See the *Treatise on the Unity of God (Ma'amar Hayichud)*, attributed to Maimonides, where he discusses the ten levels of angels: *chayot, ophanim, erelim, chashmalim, seraphim, malachim, elohim, bnei elohim, cherubim, ishim*. In that treatise, the various planets and constellations, as well as the four elements, are discussed.

[62]The uppermost world, the world of the spheres and the heavenly beings, and the lower world.

[63]Literally: benefits or prerogatives.

[64]Not "complex."

examine Him. There is no second part within Him because whatever has something else in it has the possibility of change [and God is immutable].

Completed is the third chapter.

Chapter IV

1. The Being without beginning[65] created all creation from the verity of His existence in which He is immutable because He has no [physical] body and does not need anything besides Himself, for everything that is mutable changes for its own sake and everything that changes has someone over it[66] who performs the change.

2. One might ask: Did He not change? Indeed, the creation of the world testifies that He is subject to change[67] for who coerced Him to create a world where there was none? The creation of the world is thus testimony that His will is changeable to create now what He did not wish to create previously.

3. The matter of these types of questions, as to whether a person can ask them, [is problematic]. The reason is that the first problem that relates to the transformation from potential to actual is only applicable to someone who has the potential but cannot convert that to action, either because of lack of the means through which the resultant [action] is accomplished[68] or because of restraints or hindrances. However, in regard to the Exalted One,[69] who hindered Him prior thereto?[70] Until the time of creation, there existed nothing that could assist Him other than Himself.

4. Therefore, one cannot say about Him, may He be exalted, that He went from potential to actual when He created all

---

[65]Literally: the Earliest or Primordial Being.

[66]The end of folio 57 and the beginning of folio 58 in the original manuscript are not clear.

[67]If not physical, then in thought and mood.

[68]Literally: arranged, amended, corrected, improved.

[69]Literally: Him, may He be exalted.

[70]Prior to His creation of the world.

creations because nothing was added to Him at the time of the
creation that He had previously been lacking. Also, there was
no hindrance that prevented Him from creating the world until
now, and therefore the step from potential to actual [creation]
was not due to restraints or hindrances.

5. I have thus explained that the matter of this question does
not apply to Him since there was no hindrance until now to the
creation of that which He created and which exists. This
question was extended after His will, but if a person would ask
in relation to this matter: why did He not create His world until
now,[71] we would tell him that His wisdom or His will thus
decreed and there is none who can grasp the depth of His will.

6. If one would further ask, since you asserted that His will
has so decreed, this means that he now developed the will to
create the world since previously He had no hindrance and
therefore He had a change in will.[72]

7. Know that a change in will is only applicable to one whose
will and he are two [separate] things, such as the body of a
person and his will are two. But regarding He who is a detached
intellect, He and His will are one and the same. There is no
second part or being to Him; how can He have a change in will
since He Himself is the will? Therefore, one cannot say about
One who is the essence of will and nothing else, that He has a
change in will since they are not two.

8. Therefore, we cannot say about Him, may He be exalted,
that such a will is the will that was extant before He created [the
world and then there was another will] because it is the selfsame
will, which is the simple extant essence in that He and His will
are not two things to allow one to say that the will changed in
essence.

9. Thus, this question is clear to every intelligent person that
He, may He be exalted, did not have a change in will at the time
that He created the world. Rather, we should reply to the
questioner: Thus His will decreed, and there is no one who can

---

[71]Why did His will appear at this time, not earlier or later in the eons of
Eternity, but precisely now?

[72]This means that He is unstable or subject to change!

know Him. The prophet testifies to this [truth] when he states: "Who has measured the spirit of the Lord? Or who was His counselor that he might instruct Him?"[73] The explanation of this verse is as follows: Who calculated the depths of His will, may He be exalted, and who can understand it?[74] The phraseology "who has measured [*mi ticken*]" is the same expression as "quantity of bricks [*tochen levenim*],"[75] and the term *spirit* in this context means desire and will as it is written "all that he has by the spirit with him,"[76] that is to say, all that is by his will. Similarily, "a fool spends all his spirit"[77] refers to his desire and his will.

10. Therefore, there is no one who can comprehend the intent of "who has searched out the Spirit of the Lord? Or who was His counselor that he might instruct him [*yodee' enu*]?" The [Hebrew letter] *nun* of *yodee' enu* is soft,[78] that is to say, who can understand His intent, may He be exalted, in the creation of the world and know why He created it now and not previously, and why He created the world with this design and with these dimensions?

11. The prophet addresses these two questions, the first is the question of His change of will and the second relates to the bringing forth from potential to actual. Concerning the matter of the will, he asks: "Who has measured the spirit of the Lord?" And concerning the going from potential to actual he asks: "With whom did He take counsel and who instructed Him,"[79] that is to say, can you imagine that the Exalted One was previously lacking something that prevented Him from creating the world, or that He previously had a hindrance that He has now set aside in creating the world? That is not so, because it is written, "With whom did He take counsel and who

---

[73]Isaiah 40:13.

[74]Literally: grasp it.

[75]Exodus 5:18.

[76]1 Chronicles 28:12.

[77]Proverbs 29:11.

[78]Without the *dagesh* punctuation. If it had a *dagesh*, it would mean "He would make it known [to others]." Without the *dagesh*, it means "He will know it."

[79]Isaiah 40:14.

instructed Him," that is to say, who made the world with Him, may He be exalted, or who assisted Him to create the world now more so than previously and brought it forth from potential to actual? Was He then previously lacking something that hindered Him and was He then able to overcome His deficit at the time of creation to create the world? That is impossible. Therefore, the prophet asks: "With whom did He take counsel and who instructed Him?" that is to say, who transformed it from potential to actual? Because anything transformed from potential to actual has something besides itself that transformed it.[80]

12. It is thus apparent that this question flows from[81] His will, may He be exalted, and concerning His will He has already alluded to us that He has no need of anything that He created, as it is written, "Everything that is called by My name I have created for My glory."[82] He created everything for glory and not for need. Everything flows from His constant wisdom that does not change. We do not have the power to grasp the depths of His knowledge and, of course, the lower forms [of creation] because even if all things that exist besides Him cannot grasp the intent of His knowledge because His wisdom is the essence of His truth, the perceiver would be greater than the one perceived, and this is one of the impossibilities in the nature of existences.[83]

13. If you would further ask: How can you say about Him, may He be exalted, that He is One since we find four things in Him separate one from the other! If the Exalted One were lacking any one of them, He would be lacking in perfection and it is not appropriate for the Creator of the world to be lacking [any] one of them. The four things that are separate, one from the other are: life, ability, wisdom, and will.

---

[80]Who is responsible for the transformation.

[81]Literally: extends, stretches, follows; that is, it is again a question of defining His will.

[82]Isaiah 43:7.

[83]Here there may be an error in transcription of the text. Perhaps the author means that the upper forms of creation, that is, the planets and the angels, cannot grasp the depths of His knowledge and certainly not we human beings, the lower forms of creation.

14. Know well that the term wisdom, when applied to Him, also refers to the matter of life, so that if one perceives oneself as both alive and wise it is because if one is not alive one cannot perceive, and if one is not wise, one cannot perceive. Thus, alive and wise are one matter. When we say that He is wise, we mean that He perceives Himself and the essence that perceives is the same as the perceived because the Exalted One is not two things, that which perceives and that which is perceived, such as a [human] body and its wisdom that are two things: the body is perceived and the wisdom is the perceiver. Behold, wisdom and life are one and the same[84] in Him, may He be exalted. Therefore, it is written *God lives*[85] and it is not written *by the life of God*[86] because life is not something separate from Himself such as "by the life of Pharaoh"[87] . . . [88] "and he swore by Him that lives forever."[89]

15. Likewise, neither ability nor will exists as attributes of the Creator, may He be exalted, if we study Him critically because He and His ability are not two things such as the body of a person and his ability, with ability ruling over the body. Since the Exalted One is not corporeal, He does not have ability ruling over Him. It should thus be clear to you that the Exalted One does not have ability over Himself because *Himself* and *His ability* are a single thing. The same applies to will: just as one cannot say that he rules over Himself, so does he not have will over Himself because His will and *Himself* are not two independent things as we have explained, but one and the same.

16. It is thus clear that all four things mentioned are not separate attributes of Him, but all are one and that is the Creator Himself, may He be exalted. These are all the matters that are clear to anyone who has the intellect to appropriately understand the truth.

---

[84]Literally: one matter.

[85]Hebrew: *chai Hashem.*

[86]Hebrew: *chey Hashem.*

[87]Genesis 42:16. See Maimonides, *Mishneh Torah, Hilchot Yesodei HaTorah* 2:10.

[88]Three or four letters in the original manuscript are not clear here.

[89]Daniel 12:7.

17. Behold, you can know from the matters explained in this chapter that the Exalted One does not change, in that He brought forth everything that bodily exists. In this regard it is stated: "God[90] reigns, God reigned, God will reign [eternally],"[91] that is to say, previously, at present, and in the future, God is His name, and His beings are called existences, and He never changes in any respect.

Completed is the fourth chapter.

Chapter V

1. Many things make man imagine that the Exalted One has changes of will. For instance, in the matter of reward and punishment, when He rewards the good [people] it is a matter of good mood[92] and when He punishes the evil [people] it is a matter of another mood. Thus, there exist [in Him] at least two moods, one for good people and one for the evil.

2. A person should carefully consider these matters and then it will become clear to him from them that they testify to the contrary that from all vantage points the Exalted one is One and has no aspect of change at all. Most matters that occur in the world in the area of reward and punishment testify that they derive from a single entity.

3. How? Behold, you may observe any of the natural bodies that does not live and does not act through will but from its nature[93] from which its varying and different powers are

---

[90]*Y-H-V-H*, the Tetragrammaton name of God.

[91]Part of the Hebrew liturgy.

[92]Literally: will. The problem presented in this paragraph is that when God punishes and causes pain to those who transgress His will, does it not mean that they put Him in a bad mood and in His anger or frustration, He strikes them? Likewise, the reward of the good people is a reflection of His good mood. Is God, therefore, like humans, not a perfect unity but a complex entity, not the *echad* described above?

[93]For example, plants that change color or water that freezes into ice do not make this change as a matter of conscious will. The word *nature* is lacking in the original manuscript.

derived. The cause for the difference in the activities is that they all relate to a single power. For example, the sun blanches linen cloth but darkens [the skin of] the washer; it melts wax, fat, and pitch but congeals clay and brine; it causes plants to grow but diminishes moisture. It has within it all these [contradictory] attributes [to whiten and to darken, to melt and to congeal] because it has a single attribute and that is the power of heat.

4. The basic principle in this matter is that fire[94] refines all natural things and probes them because it is one power. When things are probed by one power, we know that the nature of all is not equal: one congeals and one dissolves, one blanches and one blackens, one increases and one decreases. Behold, fire explores all these with one power. If this power were to change for each and everything, we would never understand the ways[95] of the changes that are explored as to how this one becomes white and this one becomes dark, and this one becomes dissolved and this one becomes congealed, and this one grows and this one deteriorates.[96]

5. In this way you can know that the Exalted One, because He is a unity, examines all humanity as they pass through the crucible. They are separated one from the other and each receives reward according to his deeds. The righteous are determined to be righteous and the wicked are found to be wicked. The Exalted One, He remains as One and examines all existences in this manner.[97]

6. Concerning this matter it is written: "And I will bring the third part through the fire, and will refine them as silver is refined, and will test them as gold is tested."[98] Behold, you thus know that there are not two types of [divine] moods, one for the righteous and one for the wicked. Rather, the crucible is One

---

[94]Aldabi's *Sheviley Emunah* has *sun* instead of *fire*.

[95]The word *ways* is lacking in the manuscript.

[96]In other words, it is the flax that is different from human skin and wax from clay—not that fire or sun have two changeable characters.

[97]The unique divine force or power is compared to a crucible through which pass all the actions of human beings.

[98]Zechariah 13:9.

and the righteous and the wicked pass through it. The righteous become blanched like silver and the wicked become blackened like iron. Thus, the two are separated from each other because the crucible examined them, but it remains one power.[99]

7. It is in this manner that you are to understand the Thirteen [Divine] Attributes[100] for, far be it from the Exalted One to be subject to varying characteristics, character changes are coincidences of body. Rather, the matter of the Thirteen [Divine] Attributes are the rules of reward and punishment governing all humanity. All are examined and tested in that the Exalted One is the crucible but remains as the unchangeable One. All of humanity pass through this crucible and one who deserves mercy [receives] mercy and one who deserves grace [receives] grace. Everyone receives the reward earned by his deeds and according to what he deserves, and not because the Exalted One wishes to take vengeance on one and wishes to reward the other. Rather, His will remains as a Single Unity and those who pass through the crucible are examined on the basis of their merits.[101]

8. Thus, the Thirteen [Divine] Attributes are the crucible of all humanity in that the Exalted One remains as a Unity and when they pass through the very same crucible, one is found to be white and the other black, one deteriorated and the other growing, one congealed and the other melted. But had they all been equal, they would certainly all be white or all black or all congealed or all melted.

9. But if the crucible were to produce varying changes[102] we would not know why the examined are separated one from the other; we would say that this one became white because the crucible changed and made him white and that one became

---

[99]See note 97.

[100]Vajda points out that Aldabi's *Sheviley Emunah* adds here: "and similarly the rabbinic Sages said that wherever the expression *Elo-him* is used, it refers to the attribute of judgment, and wherever the term *Y-Y* is used, it refers to the attribute of mercy."

[101]Literally: by themselves, or automatically.

[102]Literally: many changes.

black because the crucible now changed and made him black, because if the crucible had not changed, both would have been white or both would have been black. If that were so, we would not be able to understand[103] the different results, why these are white and these are black.

10. However, since the crucible remains with its one power without change and it turns one to white and the other to black, we know with certainty that the one was fit [by its constitution] to become white and the other was fit [by its constitution] to become black. Likewise,[104] Reward and Punishment [are meted out] in this manner in that the Exalted One remains the unchangeable One and the righteous and the wicked[105] pass through the same crucible. When one changes from the other, we know that the righteous and the wicked are not equal in their deeds because they passed through the same crucible[106] and the righteous one came out like gold as it is written: "He has tried me, I come forth as gold"[107] but the wicked one was reduced to ash, as it is written: "Behold, the day [of judgment] comes burning like a furnace, and all that do wicked and all that do evil shall be stubble, says the Lord of Hosts, that it shall not leave them root or branch and the day that comes shall set them ablaze."[108] And it is also written: "And you shall tread down the wicked, for they shall be ashes under the soles of your feet."[109]

11. Who caused this one to be gold and that one ash,[110] had not both passed through the same crucible? It is their deeds. Therefore, you cannot say that the Exalted One[111] wishes to take revenge on this one and to reward the other. Rather, each

---

[103]Literally: know.

[104]Aldabi's *Sheviley Emunah* omits *likewise*.

[105]Aldabi renders: and the souls of the righteous and the wicked.

[106]The text varies somewhat in *Sheviley Emunah*.

[107]Job 23:10.

[108]Malachi 3:19. The last part of the sentence is cited out of order.

[109]Malachi 3:21.

[110]The original manuscript has *dust* (Hebrew: *epher*) instead of *ashes*. (Hebrew: *aphor*).

[111]Literally: He, may He be exalted.

of them brought upon himself[112] either his light or his grave.[113]

12. Behold, you now realize[114] that the Exalted One does not change in relation to the righteous and the wicked. Rather, everything is according to the moment and the deeds of every individual in the world. There remains no doubt in this matter because it is clear and pleasantly explained.[115]

13. As a result, what is the meaning of that which is written in the Torah: "Yet I loved Jacob, but Esau I despised?"[116] Know that this is [semantic, the language of] parable and imagery, in that they passed through the crucible and the Torah speaks in the language of human beings, because not everyone is able to sense the subtlety of these subjects. That the Torah speaks in the language of human beings is accepted, whether it is for good or for bad.

14. In this manner [one should also interpret the following scriptural passages]: "for every abomination to the Lord which He hates they have done unto their gods"[117] and similarly "thou shalt blot out the remembrance of Amalek"[118] and similarly "thou shalt not save alive any soul."[119] Far be it from the Exalted One to change and to become their enemy and wish to seek retribution[120] from them because of His anger. Rather, the Torah speaks in the language of human beings. The main point, which is self evident from these things, is that the Exalted One is informing us that when these nations passed through

---

[112]Literally: brought in His hand.

[113]Thus, in *Sheviley Emunah,* which here adds several phrases. The manuscript, however, has "his light or his garment."

[114]Literally: you learned.

[115]The manuscript is somewhat illegible here.

[116]Malachi 1:2–3. The problem is the word *despised.* If reward and punishment is an automatic process, void of moods and emotions, the terms love and despise have no place in the scheme of things.

[117]Deuteronomy 12:31.

[118]*Ibidem* 25:19.

[119]*Ibidem* 20:16.

[120]Literally: payment.

the crucible, their judgment was to be destroyed and lost, not because the Exalted One wished to take vengeance from them but their nature was such that when they passed through the crucible they became ash. Therefore, He said: "thou shalt not save alive any soul."[121]

15. From all these things about which I have aroused you, you should syllogize all other passages in the Torah concerning the terms *friend* and *foe* vis-à-vis the Exalted One because all is [written in the Torah] in the form of analogy. The appropriate judgment when the righteous and the wicked pass through the same crucible[122] is that the righteous are there surnamed *friend* the same as when they are called *gold* and the wicked are termed *enemy* in the same manner as they are referred to as *ash*.

16. If this be so, then that which is written: "The Lord is far from the wicked"[123] and "the Lord is near unto all those that call upon Him"[124] seems to imply great changes from His being near to being far. Know that He is not *"here"* in distance nor *"far"* in distance. Nor is He near in terms of loving this one and far in terms of being an enemy to that one. Rather, the matter is as we will explain.

17. You already know that the Exalted One[125] is a simple, pure and refined intellect and the intellectual soul of man emanates from Him as it is written: "and He breathed into his nostrils the breath of life."[126] All who breathe breathe from their spirit, and since the soul of man emanates from Him, [his breath] is holy, pure, refined, and undefiled[127] and it is near to Him, may He be exalted.

18. Since this soul was placed in man [by God], man is obliged to follow it and to pursue holy and pure attributes so that he cleave to his Creator. But if he commits transgressions and defiles himself and is therefore guilty because of the impurity

---

[121]Deuteronomy 20:16.
[122]Literally: one crucible.
[123]Proverbs 15:29.
[124]Psalm 145:18. Compare Chapter 1:13 of this treatise.
[125]Literally: He, may He be exalted.
[126]Genesis 2:7.
[127]Hebrew: *nabar*. See also Psalm 18:27 where the same word is used.

of his deeds, those transgressions become like a partition between the soul and its Creator, because the Exalted One is holy, and the soul became impure, and that which is holy cannot tolerate the proximity of that which is defiled,[128] as it is written: "Thou that art of eyes too pure to behold evil and injustice."[129] The sins of this soul have distanced it from its Creator as we explained. It is far from Him because it is defiled. The Exalted One does not come close nor distance Himself nor change. Rather it is the soul that distances itself from Him through its defilement and it is the soul that causes the separation between it and its Creator in that the sins of the soul are like a partition that divides them as it is written: "Your iniquities have separated between you and your God."[130]

19. Thus, it is clear that when it is written: "The Lord is far from the wicked"[131] it does not mean that the Exalted One distances Himself or comes close. Rather, the change from distant or close is on the part of the soul depending on whether it is pure or defiled. In this way a person can understand the judgment of Gehenna and their time as our rabbinic Sages, of blessed memory, said: the measure of judgment is according to the defilement of the soul until the time that its shortcomings are fulfilled and it rises from defilement to purity.

20. From all these matters that we have explained, you should know the secret of the Exalted One being *close* or *distant*. For there is no manner of change in Him. So, too, for the terms[132] *beloved* and *enemy*; so, too, for the terms *reward* and *punishment* in that the Exalted One does not change in any manner of change that exists in the world.

---

[128]Literally: cannot look at something that is defiled.
[129]Habakkuk 1:13.
[130]Isaiah 59:2.
[131]Proverbs 15:29.
[132]Literally: the way or path.

Chapter VI

1. You should take cognizance of an extremely difficult question. The question that has been asked is: Since the Exalted One[133] does not change in any manner, and does not love this one and hate that one, but all is according to the state of the soul when it passes through the crucible, what benefit is there in our prayers and supplications [to Him]? If we are *ashes* how can we pray so that He will decree that we become *gold* since everything is dependent upon the defilement of the soul or its purity? Therefore,[134] what benefit is there in our praying, "Forgive us our Father?" We know that we are defiled and justice dictates[135] that we be destroyed and lost because our deeds cause [the outcome] and everything is according to deeds.

2. Similarly, what benefit is there in crying out [to God] in our troubles since He does not change after supplication from that which preceded the supplication?[136] If we were to say that He changes after prayer from that which preceded the prayer,[137] this would be a great change and there could not be a greater change than that.

3. The answer[138] to this question is extremely subtle and is as follows:[139] you already know[140] that our rabbinic Sages of blessed memory interpret [the passage], "Return, O Israel, unto the Lord thy God"[141] to mean: "Great is penitence for it reaches up to the very Throne of Glory."[142] How is this possible? You already know that the soul which is holy originates from a pure

---

[133]Literally: He, may He be exalted.
[134]The original manuscript omits *therefore*.
[135]Literally: from judgment.
[136]The first part of this paragraph is missing in Aldabi's *Sheviley Emunah*.
[137]The last phrase is missing in the manuscript.
[138]Literally: dissolution or untying or loosening.
[139]The manuscript renders: and it is pure.
[140]The manuscript renders: I already know.
[141]Hosea 14:2.
[142]*Yoma* 86a; *Pesikta de Rav Kahana* 163b. The passage links *return,* that is repentance, *unto the Lord,* meaning it reaches up to the throne of God.

source. However, since it became defiled through deeds and became distanced [from God], were it not for its ability to return and become pure, the world would be destroyed. Therefore, our Sages said that "penitence reaches up to the Throne of Glory," that is to say, even though the soul became defiled and distanced [from God], it can return to the state whence it came, which is the Throne of Glory, the source of all souls.

4. Our prayers[143] and supplications are not offered so that the Exalted One should change from will to will. Rather, each prayer that we pray dismantles one partition between us and Him. When we supplicate, "Hear our voice" or "Be gracious and have mercy upon us" or "Answer us, our Father," we are using terms that enable us to pacify our minds in that we pray with the terminology and language employed [and understood] by human beings. Were we to pray not using human language, in what language would that be? That is to say, the order of the prayers we utter is designed to cleanse our souls, when we are engaged in accepting the yoke of His Kingdom upon ourselves and in recognizing that the Exalted One rules over everything. Then the soul becomes united with Him and develops an intense desire to perceive the Exalted One.[144] If it was previously defiled, it is now transforming [from defilement to purity] by its engagement in His praises, His thanks, and His perception.

5. When a person prays, "Answer us," he is testifying that he has a Creator who observes all His works, whether for good or otherwise. Even though he utters the prayer in human language, he thereby gives a crown to His Creator, may He be exalted.[145] Similarly, when he says, "Forgive us," he thereby testifies that he has a Creator who can bestow goodness upon the good and will exact punishment from the wicked.

6. When a person prays to his Creator for sustenance and

---

[143]Paragraphs 4 to 10 are slightly different in Aldabi's *Sheviley Emunah*.

[144]See Maimonides, *Mishneh Torah, Hilchot Yesodei HaTorah* 2:2.

[145]He acknowledges that God rules the universe and all therein.

maintenance[146] he is testifying that the world has a Creator who carries everything and who maintains everything and who rules over all. One does not ask for nourishment and maintenance save from the Master who rules over servants. Thus, in regard to all these matters, although the Exalted One does not change from will to will and from subject to subject, they testify to His greatness and His virtues, may He be exalted.

7. Thus, all types[147] of prayer and supplications and the various forms of praise [to God] all [serve to] purify the soul and transform it from defilement to purity. Because when it is occupied in offering praises to the Exalted One, it is testifying that everything is in His hand, when it asks Him for forgiveness, it is testifying that He rewards and He punishes and that all is according to one's deeds. When it asks for nourishment and maintenance, it testifies that it is He who nourishes and sustains all. In all events, as it is engaged in prayer it is purifying and sanctifying itself.

8. Therefore, prayers are of great benefit to man. Although the Exalted One does not change, the soul proceeds and draws ever nearer [to Him] when it is praying before Him and bears testimony to Him, may He be exalted. Thus, the [prayer], "Forgive us and pardon us" being uttered in human phraseology brings the soul[148] ever closer to purity during prayer. Supplications are equally beneficial and they, too, are a form of[149] prayer.

9. Were we not to say, "Forgive us" or "Pardon us" and if we did not ever mention these things, we would not sense [the evil] when we did wicked things. However, since we are always ashamed of our sins and ask for forgiveness and pardon[150] for our transgressions, we will not intentionally repeat our wicked behavior, for the one who sins and has remorse is not equal [in wickedness] to one who sins and has no remorse.

---

[146]Literally: food and livelihood.
[147]Literally: matters, subjects, topics.
[148]Literally: it.
[149]Literally: from the topic of.
[150]The manuscript has "supplications," not "pardon."

10. Similarly, if we did not pray and ask for sustenance from Him, we would forget the benevolence of the Creator who maintains us and who feeds and nourishes everyone. However, since we always ask Him for nourishment and sustenance, we are ashamed if we sin and we are embarrassed by our iniquities and we repent. The soul becomes ever purer and draws closer [to God] and thereby the Exalted One is revealed [to us] by the removal of the partition [separating us], and He bestows [His] goodness upon us.

11. In this way [one can understand] the various prayers and supplications that we constantly pray before Him, may He be exalted. Even though He does not change, the soul proceeds to draw nearer [to God] when it is engaged in praise and thanks, and yearns to [achieve] perception of the Exalted One. Then the prayers are accepted, the sins are forgiven, and sustenance is provided[151] because the souls draw near [to God] through prayer and through penitence if they had become distant; and they become pure if they were defiled.[152]

12. From all these approaches that we have mentioned,[153] we may learn that prayer is the pillar of the world. He who prays and supplicates and praises the Creator, may He be exalted, with truth and devotion, cleaves his intellect [to Him in recognizing] that He gives in abundance, and He is One and accomplishes actions. It is written, "And I will magnify Myself and sanctify Myself,"[154] and when he says, "May God be magnified and sanctified," he is glorifying Him.[155] Were we not to pray, we would forget the Creator of everything, may He be

---

[151]Literally: prepared.

[152]The manuscript adds here: "In these ways the matters of prayers and supplications are pillars of the world, for without them one would forget the Creator of the world, may He be exalted and may His name and His remembrance be exalted." Vajda suggests that this sentence should be deleted because it represents a poor variation of paragraph 12.

[153]Literally: which we have stirred.

[154]Ezekiel 38:23.

[155]The last two sentences are missing in the manuscript but can be found in Aldabi's *Sheviley Emunah.*

exalted, and we would not know whether we have over us a Master who rules over everything and gives to everything that exists its appropriate needs, and we would be oblivious to the conduct of the world as it is written, "They have belied the Lord and said 'It is not He.'"[156] However, as long as we pray, although everything is in His hand,[157] we will not cease to ask Him for forgiveness and pardon and sustenance and maintenance.

13. Our rabbinic Sages, of blessed memory, enunciated an essential principle when they said "one who has sinned and confesses but does not abandon it [the sin], even if he prays all the days and all the nights [of his life], he is not forgiven. The matter can be compared to a man immersing himself [in a *mikveh* or purifying body of water] but with a dead rodent in his hand. As long as the dead rodent is in his hand, the immersion is of no avail[158] even if he immersed himself[159] in all the waters of the world."[160] They here allude to the fact[161] that all forms[162] of prayers are not phraseologies of His will, may He be exalted. Rather, the prayers serve as an opening for the soul to confess that it has sinned and to separate from its sins.[163] In this way it rises from defilement to purity and it comes[164] closer to its Creator and He, may He be blessed, does not change.

14. It is also written, "And God saw their deeds that they had returned from their evil ways."[165] It is not written that He saw their sackcloth and their fasting. Thus, prayers are dependent

---

[156]Jeremiah 5:12. The last phrase, including the scriptural quote, is missing in *Sheviley Emunah*.

[157]The manuscript renders: our hands.

[158]The term *to him* is missing in the manuscript but is added here by Vajda.

[159]The phrase "if he immersed himself" is missing in the manuscript.

[160]*Taanit* 16a.

[161]The text differs slightly in the manuscript.

[162]Literally: matters.

[163]That is, refrain from repeating the sins.

[164]Literally: is found.

[165]Jonah 3:10.

upon the purity of the soul, and after it becomes purified, He replies and becomes merciful as it draws nearer to Him.

15. Therefore, from all these matters, it may be learned that the essential [effect] of prayer is totally dependent upon the one who prays because prayer is of no avail without cleanliness and purity of the soul. And it is written, "Rend your heart and not your garments, and turn to the Lord your God."[166] Similarly, "This is the fast that I have chosen; loose the fetters of wickedness, to undo the bonds of the yoke."[167] [These scriptural verses] inform us that all prayers and supplications and fasts are all dependent on the purity of the soul and as long as it is not pure they are of no avail [and that purity is brought about by abandoning sinful deeds].

16. You have thus learned that the Exalted One does not have a change in will in the matters of prayers, supplications, and outcries. Rather, everything depends upon the one who prays. When he purifies his soul and repents from his wickedness, his soul draws closer to its Creator. Included therein are [the prayers] "Hear our voice" and "Have mercy upon us" and "Answer us, forgive us for we have sinned" and "Pardon us, for we have transgressed." All these and their like are dependent on the purity of the soul when it repents from its wickedness.

17. The reason we adopt the phraseology [of prayer] to Him even though He does not change, and we say "Forgive us" when everything is dependent upon us, is because the Torah uses the phraseology of human beings. Anyone who sins against his friend, asks him for forgiveness. In order to assuage the mind of the general public, we say all these matters in common[168] understandable language so that the human mind does not become confused before it knows the fundamental principles. Otherwise, the result would be the closing of the gates of prayer, and no person could pray. That is why the Torah speaks to us in human terms.

---

[166]Joel 2:13.

[167]Isaiah 58:6.

[168]Literally: close, perhaps meaning close to Hebrew, the holy tongue.

Chapter VII

1. You need to understand the Oneness of our Creator, may He be exalted and praised, in terms of "Receiving of the Torah," now that it has been clarified in intellectual terms.[169] When you know this, your mind will be at ease because you are praying in a language you understand. The benefit of prayer and its acceptance all depend on the language so that the one close to the kingdom [of God] understands what his lips utter, and comprehends those things about which he is praying.

2. The essential feature of these matters is that a person should learn to differentiate between the Creator of everything, may He be exalted, and all other creations. When he separates Him in his mind, then he is able to reach his goals because he knows before whom he worships and who can be trusted to reward his activities.

3. One can reach [an understanding of] these matters through traditional teachings,[170] if one studies diligently and intensively His holy Torah that was transmitted to us. Through it[171] we can understand all physical perceptions that can be reached by intellect, which is [composed of form and] substance. Then will we perceive Him, may He be exalted, in terms of His Torah, with a complete understanding.[172]

4. Philosophers are divided in that they were stirred to call the Exalted One by a recognized name that teaches and testifies about the essence of His truth, may He be exalted. They searched but they did not find [such a name]. Some of them[173]

---

[169]The point the author is making is: now that we have established the Oneness or Unity of God by a rational or philosophical approach, we should examine its parameters and learn its fine points by studying what He has taught us in His holy Torah. It is not clear why the author brings in the "language of prayer" in this introductory paragraph.

[170]Hebrew: *kabbalah*. In this context, it does *not* mean the mystical teachings generally referred to as Kabbalah, but is better translated as *tradition*, meaning the handed-down interpretation of Torah.

[171]That is, by studying the Torah.

[172]*Sheviley Emunah* renders: with the correct perception.

[173]Philosophers.

called Him "The Cause" and others called Him "Doer" but neither group's "names", although each cites proof to support its contention,[174] reflect the essence of His truth because they are only cognomens, not [His real] name.

5. But His holy Torah teaches us that He has a singular name which reflects the essence of His truth alone without being associated with anything else, only to teach a truthful teaching about Him. This is the peg upon which everything depends.[175] When a person knows the true meaning of His Great Name, his soul unifies and cleaves to its Creator and all its prayers are accepted and all its desires are fulfilled as it is written, "I will set him on high because he has known My name; he shall call upon Me and I will answer him; I will be with him in [his] trouble; I will rescue him and bring him to honor."[176] And it is also written, "The Lord is near unto all them that call upon Him; to all that call upon Him in truth."[177] In the matter of truth there is a secret in the explanation of the secret of His Great Name, may He be exalted. And it is written, "He will fulfill the desire of them that fear Him; He will hear their cry and will save them."[178]

6. In this way it becomes clear that he who devotes himself to studying His Great Name is assured that his soul is bound in the heavenly chain, and all his desires are fulfilled because he prays and understands in his heart that which he utters with his lips. When he uses pure language, he stands before his Creator like one from whom all the partitions and all the separations and channels have been removed, and like one who stands "Face to Face" [with his Creator]. One is speaking and the other listening, because this soul is proceeding to purify itself.[179]

---

[174]Literally: their words or their things.

[175]This is an analogy to the center peg of a tent. All other pegs and strings depend on its stability. Even the tent itself depends on this one peg.

[176]Psalm 91:14–15.

[177]Psalm 145:18.

[178]Psalm 145:19.

[179]There is no go-between or channel between the one who prays and God. They stand *face to face*. See Deuteronomy 5:4.

7. Our rabbinic Sages, of blessed memory, allude to a great fundamental principle when they state that if one petitions for one's needs in Aramaic, "the Ministering Angels do not heed him because the Ministering Angels do not understand Aramaic."[180] Is it possible for an angel who is all intellect and nothing is concealed from it—not to understand Aramaic and every other language in the world? But the explanation of this matter is as follows: It is known that whoever petitions for his needs in Aramaic is not praying in language close to Him, may He be exalted, and he cannot concentrate on the truth of his Creator since he is not praying in the sacred language[181] in which the clarification of His Great Name and His truth can be manifested, and since he cannot express[182] ["The Name" in Hebrew], his soul is not bound up with "The Heavenly Chain," which is the world of the Ministering Angels. Therefore, it is not appropriate that the Ministering Angels should pay heed to his words because the Ministering Angels are not accustomed[183] to Aramaic but to the sacred language because they are holy and use an acceptable[184] [?] language above all other languages. In this case, the one who prays in Aramaic is mixing one type [of language] with another type[185] and one pays no heed to his words.

8. With all this, the virtue of the Hebrew language teaches us that this language is all intellect, just as the world of the angels is all intellect. For anyone who does not use something that is intellect, the detached intellectuals—who are the Ministering Angels[186]—do not pay heed to him, not because they do

---

[180]*Shabbat* 12b.

[181]Hebrew.

[182]Literally: have intention.

[183]A marginal note in the manuscript says, that is why it says "understand Aramaic but are not accustomed to it" and it does not say "know [Aramaic]."

[184]Literally: possible. The meaning is unclear.

[185]The person is trying to ascend to heavenly heights ("The Heavenly Chain") which is one type (of holiness) and he approaches it with another type (of language). Therefore, we pay no heed to him.

[186]Angels are referred to as detached intellects. Humans are a combination of body and intellect, whereas angels are pure intellects without bodies.

not know it but because [Aramaic] is not a proper language that they should come close to when compared with the sacred tongue.

9. Although one can say that Aramaic is preferred over all languages other than the sacred tongue, it is not esteemed when compared to the sacred language. If this [Aramaic] language is not esteemed, how much less so are all the other languages [insignificant alongside the sacred language].

10. Thus, there is no language that can reach the level of the sacred language. All this is due to the use of the sacred tongue in designating His Great Name, may He be exalted, which is the secret of the Great Singular Name that teaches His Truth, may he be exalted. Therefore, anyone who clarifies this and uses his intellect diligently and intensively to comprehend His Great Name, may He be exalted, will understand in his mind the Truth of the Creator of the world: that He, may He be exalted, carries [everyone and everything] but is not carried, and that He surrounds[187] but nothing surrounds Him.

11. When a person frees his mind to understand the significance of His Great Name, may He be exalted, the more he expounds and searches, the more his soul longs for and desires to cleave to its Creator and is not able to separate itself from Him, to the point that it is constantly cleaving to Him. It is in this respect that it is written, "And unto Him shall ye cleave."[188]

12. These matters are the secret[189] of the world. Although we have alluded to some of them, it is not proper to reveal in a book all that can be revealed, because they should only be revealed to those who are constantly engaged in studying such books,[190] not to those who review it lightly in their free time, but only to one who frees himself from all other activities and occupies himself with them [exclusively].[191]

---

[187]Encompasses.
[188]Deuteronomy 13:5.
[189]Alternate translation: furnace.
[190]Literally: who constantly stand on the book.
[191]The text in *Sheviley Emunah* differs somewhat.

Chapter VIII

1. The Exalted One commanded us in His Torah to declare His Oneness twice daily. This [declaration of] His Unity is to be accomplished by our recitation of the verse: "Hear, O Israel, the Lord our God is One."[192] How is the matter of the Unity?[193] Know that it is the mystery of His Singular Name[194] which is called the Tetragrammaton[195] and is made up of the four [Hebrew] letters *Yod, Heh, Vav, Heh.*[196] This Great Name demonstrates the truth of the Exalted One in that there is no other thing at all mixed in with Him except the demonstration of His truth,[197] as it is written, "I am the Lord, that is My Name,"[198] that is to say, that which is implied by the Tetragrammaton is My name,[199] that is My truth and My essence.

2. Therefore, this name is called the Singular Name because it alone has been singled out and separated from all other expressions[200] in the world that are used to refer to Him, may He be exalted. There is no expression in the world that is not included in this name and it carries all expressions and is the essential [cause] of their existence, just as the Exalted One carries all things that exist and He is the essential [cause] for the existence of all things.

3. The Singular Name that we utter is always singled out in the Torah to call Him [by that name].[201] About Him it is written

---

[192]Deuteronomy 6:4.

[193]This phrase is lacking in *Sheviley Emunah.*

[194]Hebrew: *shemo hameyuchad,* variously translated as His Singular Name, His One Name, His Unique Name, His Individual Name, His Name of Unity, and so on.

[195]Literally: name of four letters.

[196]*Sheviley Emunah* adds a phrase about the virtues of the letters of the Tetragrammaton here.

[197]The *Yod, Heh, Vav, Heh* has no other components.

[198]Isaiah 42:8.

[199]*Sheviley Emunah* omits "My name."

[200]Literally: languages, tongues.

[201]The meaning of this sentence is unclear both in the original manuscript and the slightly variant reading in Aldabi's *Sheviley Emunah.*

at the beginning of the Decalogue, "I am the Lord, thy God,"[202] that is to say My truth[203] shows that this name is a matter of existence and being and nothing else. The expression *being*[204] includes all the existences in the world in that they are carried by the [*Divine*] *Being* but all the existences do not include the expression *being* because the Exalted One is the truth of existence and being.

4. Some of our rabbinic Sages, of blessed memory, stated:[205] "before the world was created there was only He in His name."[206] How pleasant is this subject to any person with intellect. When they said[207] of the Exalted One that "He was" they meant that He is the truth òf His name. If they did not say "was," how could one say that this is the fundamental [cause] of existence and being? When they said, "there was only He in His name," their intent was to say that He alone, may He be exalted, existed before the world was created and there was nothing else[208] there besides Him. It should not be difficult for you [to understand] what they meant when they said, "He was in His name" since we already stated that His name testifies only to the truth of [His] existence. The Exalted One exists in the truth of existence and there is none comparable to Him.[209] The prophet has already testified that He and His Name are one and the same[210] when he said, "I am the Lord, that is My name"[211] and it is also written, "That they may know that it is Thou alone whose name is the Lord."[212]

5. This honorable name is the source and wellspring of

---

[202]Exodus 20:2.

[203]*Sheviley Emunah* renders: His truth.

[204]Hebrew: *H-V-Y-H*, a variation of the Tetragrammaton.

[205]*Sheviley Emunah* renders: Rabbi Eliezer the Great stated in Chapter 16 (of Pirké de Rabbi Eliezer).

[206]Pirké de Rabbi Eliezer, Chapter 3. *Sheviley Emunah* renders: He and His Name.

[207]*Sheviley Emunah* renders: when he said.

[208]Literally: no second thing.

[209]*Sheviley Emunah* omits "to Him."

[210]Literally: one thing.

[211]Isaiah 42:8.

[212]Psalm 83:19.

everything and from it flows[213] and emanates all the rivulets
but it itself does not flow from another [source] because it has
no need for anything in view of its truth, which is the essential
[cause] of existence and permanence, in that it needs nothing
beside Him for its existence.[214] This name is the principle[215]
from which flow all the individual cognomens. In all the other
expressions[216] in the Torah, there is no expression that includes the truth of His existence, may He be exalted, because all
other names are cognomens for His actions.

6. This name shows the truth of the Exalted One before He
created the world because it signifies "existence" and there is no
existence without His existence. Just as the Exalted One is not
a created entity *(creatio ex nihilo)* so, too, His Great Name is not
a created entity.

7. The other cognomens such as *Elo-him, Ado-nai Tze-va-ot,
Shad-dai* are all cognomens for His actions and all were created
when the world was created. Since they were created they
cannot demonstrate the verity of the First Being.[217] However,
there are two[218] names derived from the Singular Name that
flow from the One from which they were derived,[219] and
extend power to all other things. These two names are *Eh-yeh*
and *Y-ah.*[220]

8. In this manner we need to make subtle reference to the
order of the characteristics of these matters, one after the other
so that it serves as an opening for every intellectual. He should
motivate himself to seek the hidden aspects of the Torah so that
his soul can cleave to "The Heavenly Chain," and the potential

---

[213]Literally: are pulled.

[214]Literally: permanence.

[215]Hebrew: *yesod*, thus in *Sheviley Emunah*. The original manuscript has *sod*
meaning mystery.

[216]*Sheviley Emunah* renders: names.

[217]The cognomens relate to or are descriptive of His characteristics which
we observe in the manner in which He conducts the world. Before creation,
they had no meaning, being a description of *nihilo* or nothingness.

[218]The manuscript omits the word "two."

[219]*Sheviley Emunah* renders: from the source.

[220]See Exodus 3:14.

of his intellect will be realized in that and he will understand
and comprehend the words of the living God in the way of
truth.[221] This is the mystery of His Names and His cognomens.

9. The honorable and awesome name which is called the
essential name is *Y-H-V-H* and after it is *Eh-yeh* and after it is
Y-ah and after it is *Ado-nai* and after it is *Shad-dai* and after it is
Y-H-V-H Tze-va-ot and after it is *Elo-him Tze-va-ot.* These are the
general cognomens that are derived from the truth of the
Singular Name and all demonstrate the known activities [of
God]. I will allude to them, one by one.

10. The Singular Name, which is known as the essential
name, demonstrates the truth of [His] existence and being. It
also testifies that the Exalted One does not change, neither little
nor much. How? Behold the Singular Name demonstrates
"being." If you try reversing it[s letters] in any direction you
like, you will find that it still demonstrates "being,"[222] which is
not the case for all the other expressions as we will explain.

11. How? The order [of letters] of the Singular Name
demonstrates "being" in all combinations as follows: *Y-H-V-H,
Y-H-H-V, Y-V-H-H, H-Y-H-V, H-Y-V-H, H-V-Y-H, H-H-Y-V, V-
Y-H-H, V-H-Y-H, V-H-H-Y, H-Y-V-H,*[223] *H-H-V-Y, H-V-H-Y.*[224]
Examine closely the usage of this name and you will find that it
signifies "existence" and "being" and does not signify anything
else. Concerning this the prophet said, "I the Lord have not
changed,"[225] in that the truth of His essential name shows that
there is no aspect of change in Him.

12. Therefore, in the ways described above, that He does not
change His Great Name is testimony for them all. Just as He
does not change, His Great Name does not change. This is

---

[221]Euphemism for Kabbalah.

[222]Being in Hebrew is *H-V-Y-H;* compare to the Tetragrammaton *Y-H-V-H.*

[223]Vajda points out that this combination should be eliminated since it is
already cited above as the fifth in the series.

[224]In Aldabi's *Sheviley Emunah,* the order of these combinations differs
somewhat. He also here adds the talmudic passage about the reciting of the
Divine Name (the Tetragrammaton) in the Temple (*Kiddushin* 71a). (Compare also Maimonides' *Guide of the Perplexed,* Part 1, Chapter 62.)

[225]Malachi 3:6.

strong proof.[226] That is why we utter, "The Lord is One," that is to say, no matter which way you turn [the Tetragrammaton], it demonstrates one thing and that is the truth of existence and being.

13. You will not find this to be so in all other languages.[227] Reflect on the matter of *E-L* that is the first of all the cognomens. If you reverse *E-L* you obtain *Lo*.[228] Thereby *E-L* is changed and becomes *Lo* and the former word[229] is not like the latter word.[230] As an example of this situation the prophet states, "They have roused Me to jealousy with a none-god,"[231] that is to say they have denied My Godliness and have reversed *E-l* to say *Lo*. Another example is the scriptural verse, "They have belied the Lord and said, 'It is not He'."[232] If you look into this you will observe that the Singular Name does not change but all the cognomens and other [Divine] names are susceptible to change.

14. We have shown that the cognomens do not testify to His truth but only to His actions.[233] Therefore, you should reflect on the truth of the Singular Name, which demonstrates and which testifies that the Exalted One is immutable.

15. Now that we have noted only one of the million matters which the Singular Name denotes and have motivated persons with intellect to examine each and every one of the matters

---

[226]Literally: great testimony.

[227]Cognomens or Divine names other than the Tetragrammaton.

[228]Reversing the Hebrew letters *aleph* and *lamed* in *E-L* meaning God produces the Hebrew word *Lo* which means "no."

[229]Literally: matter, topic, subject, situation.

[230]*Ibidem.*

[231]Deuteronomy 32:21. The Hebrew expression for no-god is *Lo-el* whereby the two words *Lo* and *el* are composed of the two Hebrew letters *aleph* and *lamed* but in reverse order.

[232]Jeremiah 5:12.

[233]The cognomens do not describe or identify His being—*Him*; they only describe His attributes. As an analogy, one can describe a person as one who distributes alms to the needy and prays in the synagogue three times daily; these are descriptions of his actions but not of him. Likewise, only the Singular Name describes God; all other names describe His actions or attributes.

which the Singular Name denotes, we will return to explain the two names derived from it but we will allude to very little therein.

16. The name that is derived from the truth of the Singular Name and is first among the streams that flow from it is called *Eh-yeh*[234] and it teaches that the existence of all beings is an extension emanating from the truth of His existence, may He be exalted, as it is written,[235] "The Lord (Y-H-V-H) made me as the beginning of His way the first of His works of old,"[236] and it is also written, "And I was (*Ve Eh-yeh*) by Him as a nursling,"[237] *Ve Eh-yeh*, dwell next to Him.

17. The scriptural word *Ve-Eh-yeh* testifies that the mystery of the word *Eh-yeh* is in the first six letters [of the Hebrew alphabet], whose secret is *aleph, bet, gimmel, dalet, heh, vav*.[238] Thus, the scriptural word *Ve-Eh-yeh* is as if it were written "until six letters is the secret of *Eh-yeh*." Therefore, the beginning of the alphabet[239] is the mystery of *Eh-yeh* that is derived from the beginning of the ways of the Exalted One from the truth of the Singular Name.[240] When you understand the mystery of *Eh-yeh*, which is the mystery of *aleph, bet, gimmel, dalet, heh, vav*, reflect about that which is written in the *Book of Creation*[241] about *Y-H-V*[242] being the seal of the six directions[243] whose

---

[234]Hebrew letters *aleph, heh, yod,* and *heh* or *A-H-Y-H*.

[235]Literally: in the manner they said.

[236]Proverbs 8:22.

[237]Proverbs 8:30.

[238]*Sheviley Emunah* adds: "because this and this have the same numerical value, i.e., the sum of the numerical value of the letters *aleph, heh, yod,* and *heh* in the word *Eh-yeh* is twenty-one, which is the same numerical sum of the first six letters of the Hebrew alphabet.

[239]Literally: of its way.

[240]*Sheviley Emunah* here adds several phrases relating to the *gematria* (numerical values) of the names *Y-H-V* and *Eh-yeh* both of which have the numerical value of twenty-one.

[241]*Book of Creation*, Chapter 1, section 13.

[242]The three Hebrew letters *yod, heh,* and *vav* spelling the word *Ye-huh*.

[243]The Sages refer to "six directions or dimensions to describe matter. We refer to matter in "three dimensions," time being the fourth. What we call three dimensions the Sages refer to as the six directions: right, left, front, back, top, bottom. Therefore, all matter or all creation or all *physical* existence is an extension of the cognomen *Eh-yeh*.

mystery is *aleph, bet, gimmel, dalet, heh, vav* as follows: *aleph: Y-H-V*, upward; *bet: Y-V-H*, downward; *gimmel: H-V-Y*, East; *dalet: H-Y-V*, West; *heh: V-Y-H*, South; *vav: V-H-Y*, North.[244]

19. Thus,[245] the whole of creation revolves around the secret of *Eh-yeh* whose own secret is [the word] *Y-H-V*,[246] which is the seal for *aleph, bet, gimmel, dalet, heh, vav*. Therefore, behold, the mystery of *Y-H-V*, which is the mystery of *Eh-yeh,* which is the mystery of the emanation of the existence of all beings from the truth of His existence, may He be exalted. If you understand this, you have a patent opening to delve into the depths of the matters that are demonstrated by the name *Eh-yeh*. We have, therefore, made only minor allusions in order to motivate you to [study] the subject in full.

20. The virtue of *Eh-yeh*, however, is not as great as the virtue of the Singular Name because it does not testify to the truth of the existence of the Exalted One. Thus, you observe that the Singular Name is not pronounced according to its letters, but *Eh-yeh* is.[247]

21. You might ask: what is the [meaning of God's] statement to Moses that my name is *Eh-yeh* [*I am that I am*]?[248] Know that this is the mystery that we mentioned in the matter of *Eh-yeh,* that is to say, I am the One that exists and it is from the truth of My existence that all other existences exist. It is a joint name[249] indicating His existence and existences other than Him.[250] The secret of *Eh-yeh* was given to Moses, our teacher, may he rest in peace, but the secret of the ultimate truth of *Y-H-V-H* was not given to Moses. About this it is written, "And thou shalt see My back, but My face shall not be seen."[251]

---

[244]In *Sheviley Emunah* the last two are reversed.

[245]Number 18 is omitted but there is nothing lacking in the text.

[246]See note 242.

[247]The text varies slightly in *Sheviley Emunah*. One should note that the Tetragrammaton is spelled *Y-H-V-H* but is pronounced *Ado-nai.*

[248]Exodus 3:14. Hebrew: *Eh-yeh asher Eh-yeh.* It is the active manifestation of divine existence.

[249]Literally: partnership name.

[250]*Sheviley Emunah* adds another explanation.

[251]Exodus 33:23.

22. The very little we have revealed by allusion in *Eh-yeh* will suffice.[252] You might ask: How can you say that Moses did not know the truth of the Singular Name whose mystery is *Y-H-V-H*? But I have already informed you[253] that the Singular Name is the truth of the existence of the Creator and if Moses, may he rest in peace, would have perceived the purpose thereof, he would have perceived the essence of the truth of the Creator as it is, and therefore the perceiver would have been greater than the perceived. The Exalted one has already informed us that it is not in the nature of man to perceive this matter. About this it is written, "Thou canst not see My face."[254]

23. After the truth of *Eh-yeh* whose secret is *Y-H-V*, the matter of His governing the world emanates from the mystery of *Y-ah*[255] about which it is written, "If Thou Lord [*Y-ah*] should heed iniquities"[256] and it is also written, "The hand [of God is] upon the throne of the Lord" [*Y-ah*].[257] These [passages] refer to His governing power of the world. This matter is difficult to grasp and it is the mystery of "All that breathes"[258] praises the Lord [*Y-ah*], Hallelujah."[259] This is [also illustrated] in "I said, I shall not see the Lord [*Y-ah*] in the land of the living."[260] This will serve you as a small allusion[261] [on this matter].

24. Therefore, the name *Y-H-V-H* signifies the truth of the existence of the One [God], while *Eh-yeh* teaches that all existences emanate from the truth of the existence of the One, and the mystery of *Y-ah* teaches the matter of His governing the world according to the circumstances therein according to the flow of the maintenance of all existences and their endurance.

---

[252]The text differs somewhat in *Sheviley Emunah*.
[253]Literally: stimulate you.
[254]Exodus 33:20. Vajda erroneously cites Exodus 33:21.
[255]Hebrew word composed of the two letters *yod* and *heh* or *Y-H*.
[256]Psalm 130:3.
[257]Exodus 17:16.
[258]Alternate translation: let every soul.
[259]Psalm 150:6.
[260]Isaiah 38:11.
[261]The text differs somewhat in *Sheviley Emunah*.

This is the secret of, "And the Lord was *(Va-yehi)*[262] with Joseph, and he was [*Va-yehi*] a prosperous man"[263] and, "And it came to pass [*Va-yehi*] in those days,"[264] and, "And the rain was [*Va-yehi*]"[265] and, "And there was [*Va-yehi*] a famine in the land."[266] This is the secret of the existence of all the good and bad [occurrences] among all the existences [that emanate] from the truth of the existence of the One.[267]

Chapter IX

1. The first of the cognomens is *Elo-him*. The [Singular] Name always occurs before the cognomen, such as *Y-H-V-H Elo-him*.[268] The mystery of *Elo-him* is that it is a cognomen by which He is called to indicate the functioning of nature for it is the mystery of creation. Therefore, in all of creation you only find the mystery of *Elo-him*, which is a cognomen for all those actions. From "In the beginning"[269] until "And [the heaven and

---

[262]The Hebrew word *Va-yehi* is composed of the Hebrew letters *vav, yod, heh,* and *yod* or *V-Y-H-Y.*

[263]Genesis 39:2.

[264]Exodus 2:11. Vajda repeats *days.*

[265]Genesis 7:12.

[266]Genesis 12:10.

[267]The author wishes to convey what seems like mutability on the part of God—Joseph was a prisoner and then a successful leader in Egypt; first there was prosperity and then a famine, and so on—are reflections of the mutability of circumstances in the world. See Chapter V which speaks of righteousness and wickedness. This characteristic is reflected in the cognomen *Y-H*. Vajda also sums up the essence of this chapter in the closing paragraph:

   1. The Singular Name *Y-H-V-H* signifies the existence of God as an uncomplex, single, simple entity—a ONE in its fullest meaning.
   2. *Eh-yeh* signifies that all that exists emanates from Him and His Singular Name.
   3. The name *Y-H* signifies that all that occurs in the world—for good or for the opposite—emanates from Him and His Name *Y-H*, and that these occur according to circumstances in the world.

[268]The original manuscript omits "such as . . ." Genesis 2:4 is the first Pentateuchal site where *Y-H-V-H* precedes *Elo-him.*

[269]Genesis 1:1, the opening words of the Torah.

the earth] were finished"[270] you will find *Elo-him* thirty-two times, which is the mystery of the "Thirty-two Pathways of Wisdom," which are the twenty-two letters [of the Hebrew alphabet] and the "Ten Countings."[271] Their mnemonic signs are the twenty-two letters, the six dimensions,[272] and the "Four Fundamentals."[273] All are the "Glory of God"[274] and the mystery, "It is the glory of God to conceal a thing."[275]

2. You might ask: why did not the Torah begin with the name *Y-H-V-H* since it is the first? We have already stated that the name *Y-H-V-H* only demonstrates the truth of the existence of the Creator. Had the Torah begun by relating what is the essence of the glory of the Creator, it would have used the name that testifies thereto, which is [the Name] *Y-H-V-H*. However, since it refrained[276] from relating His essence, may He be exalted, and the essence of His truth, it refrained from [using] the name that testifies thereto. Just as it begins with the activity of creation, it begins with the cognomen that testifies to that activity and it is the one called *Elo-him*.

3. The mystery of *Elo-him* is that it flows from the truth of *Y-ah* and *Y-ah* from *Eh-yeh* and *Eh-yeh* from *Y-H-V-H*.[277] If you remove the secret of *Y-ah* from *Elo-him*, there remains *Elem*[278] and that is the secret of "And God [*Elo-him*] said 'Let there be [*Ye-hi*][279] light'."[280] Reflect in that if one speaks of *Elo-him* it is

---

[270]Genesis 2:1, the conclusion of the account of creation.

[271]The ten *sefirot* or countings are wisdom *(chochmah)*, understanding *(binah)*, knowledge *(da'at)*, kindness *(chesed)*, might *(gevurah)*, glory *(tiferet)*, victory *(netzach)*, majesty *(hod)*, foundation *(yesod)*, and royalty *(malchut)*.

[272]Literally: directions, such as upward, downward, East, West, South, North. See also footnote 243.

[273]Air, fire, water, earth.

[274]Hebrew: *Elo-him*.

[275]Proverbs 25:2. The manuscript omits the second half of the quote.

[276]Literally: kept concealed or kept silent about.

[277]The latter part of this sentence is omitted in *Sheviley Emunah*.

[278]If you remove the Hebrew letters *yod* and *heh* from the cognomen *Elo-him*, there remain the three Hebrew letters *aleph*, *lamed* and *mem* which spell the word *Elam*.

[279]The Hebrew word *Ye-hi* is composed of the three letters *yod*, *heh*, *yod* or *Y-H-Y*.

[really] *Y-ah* about which it is written, "Let there be [*Ye-hi*] light." The mystery of *Ye-hi* is the secret of *Y-ah*. Were it not written "Let there be [*Ye-hi*] light," what benefit would there be in "And God [*Elo-him*] said"?[281] behold *Y-ah* which is included in *Elo-him*[282] and is a form of the cognomen *Elo-him*.[283]

4. In addition,[284] the cognomen *Elo-him* in the mystery of its combinations[285] testifies to the amalgamations of the natures. For example, *Elo-him, Elem, and Y-ah* are [related to] the expression *Me-Almim Alumim*,[286] that is to say in it were blended the natures during creation and all the compoundings were connected and some were mixed with others.[287]

5. In addition, the cognomen *Elo-him* testifies to the stability of the natures on a permanent base, just as *Elem* is [related to] the expression *Yonat-Elem*,[288] that is to say the strength of something and its permanence. This is the meaning of: "whatsoever God doeth, it shall be forever; nothing can be added to it, nor anything taken from it,"[289] because it was made with the cognomen *Elo-him*, which testifies to stability and permanence.

6. In addition,[290] the mystery of *Elo-him* demonstrates that the entire creation occurred with the rule of righteousness,

---

[281]Genesis 1:3; 1:6; 1:9; and so forth.

[282]The Hebrew letters *yod* and *heh* are part of the Hebrew word *Elo-him*.

[283]Vajda points out that Aldabi's *Sheviley Emunah* (page 14d, lines 2–12) here adds: "do not consider it incorrect when the Torah says, "And God *(Elo-him)* said, 'Let the earth bring forth'" [Genesis 1:24] and, "And God *(Elo-him)*, said, 'Let the waters swarm'" [Genesis 1:20]. It states the beginning of the existence of the new existences: "'Let there be *(Ye-hi)* light'" [Genesis 1:3] because the One existence causes the existence of the light, for if there was no existence [of God] there would be no light; a fortiori for the rest. Therefore, it is not necessary to use the word *Ye-hi* [Let there be] anywhere else since He was revealed first."

[284]Literally: yet, still.

[285]The original manuscript renders: His form.

[286]"We were binding sheaves." Genesis 37:7.

[287]*Sheviley Emunah* here adds: "because *Elo-him* has the same numerical value [*gematria*] eighty-six as *ha-teva* meaning *the nature*.

[288]A silent dove. Psalm 56:1.

[289]Ecclesiastes 3:14.

[290]Literally: yet, still.

justice, and judgment because *Elo-him* is an expression that signifies justice and judgment as it is written, "Thou shalt not curse a judge,"[291] and it is written, "For the judgment belongs to God."[292] Concerning this matter, the master of the prophets[293] said, "The Rock, His work is perfect; for all His ways are judgment,"[294] that is to say, the entire creation of them was in thirty-two ways; all were done with the rule of judgment with the secret of *Elo-him* [being mentioned in Genesis] thirty-two times. Its secret is judgment. Therefore, they will exist forever, having been made with the rule of judgment and the scales of righteousness.

7. Thus, we have alluded to very little of the matters that encompass the mystery of *Elo-him* to stimulate the intellectual to think. Let us return to allude to the mystery of the cognomen *Ado-nai* a very little bit. You already know that this cognomen was already mentioned by the patriarch Abraham, may he rest in peace, "O Lord [*Ado-nai*] God [*Elo-him*], whereby shall I know."[295]

8. The meaning[296] of *Ado-nai* is that it is a cognomen for sovereignty and lordship. The fundamental [reason] that necessitated the patriarch Abraham to state it is because in his time all the people[297] of the world denied the existence of the Creator, may He be exalted. Some worshiped the sun and others worshiped[298] the moon, and some the other stars and yet others the various heavenly bodies. Their view and their thinking was that there was no other deity in the world save these.

9. When the patriarch Abraham, may he rest in peace, was born and began to reflect on the conduct of the world and the characteristics of all existences, he perceived that there is a

---

[291]Exodus 22:27. The word *Elo-him* here means judge.

[292]Deuteronomy 1:17. The word *Elo-him* here means God. Vajda thus makes the point that creation has justice and fairness.

[293]Moses.

[294]Deuteronomy 32:4.

[295]Genesis 15:8.

[296]Literally: matter, topic, subject.

[297]The manuscript omits *people*.

[298]*Sheviley Emunah* omits *worshiped*.

Single Creator who created all these beings, and that He is the Master and rules over all of them. He began to call there "on the name of the Lord, the Everlasting God."[299] The meaning[300] of "the Everlasting God"[301] is that He is the Master of the world because the expression *El* means power and sovereignty as in the expression, "Like the mighty mountains of El."[302] Similarly the word Master[303] means power and sovereignty. For this reason he[304] had to call to Him by the essence of the name *Ado-nai* which means Master [*Adon*] of the world, and Abrahamic (teachings) extended[305] to this day[306] that a great nation[307] issued forth from him and follows him and his teachings.

10. Yet you find that we pronounce the Singular Name by the cognomen *Ado-nai* instead of *Y-H-V-H* [as it is written]. This matter is clear since we cannot perceive the ultimate truth of *Y-H-V-H* but we reflect about Him in our hearts and we accept Him over us as a Master in that we know Him in truth to be the Master over everything. Although we cannot comprehend the ultimate truth of *Y-H-V-H*, we accept upon ourselves His Kingship and His Mastery and we call Him *Ado-nai*.[308] This is the secret of "The Sanctuary [*hechal*] of the Lord"[309] because the mystery of *Ado-nai* is *hechal*[310] and in the mystery of *hechal* is the name *Y-H-V-H*, but we read it *Ado-nai*.

11. About these matters [King] David, of blessed memory, said, "O give thanks unto the Lord [*Y-H-V-H*],[311] O give thanks

---

[299]Genesis 21:33.
[300]Literally: matter.
[301]Hebrew: *El olam.*
[302]Psalm 36:7. This citation is lacking in *Sheviley Emunah.*
[303]Hebrew: *Adon.*
[304]Abraham.
[305]Literally: stretched or flowed.
[306]The phrase "to this day" is omitted in *Sheviley Emunah.*
[307]The Jewish people.
[308]*Ado-nai* is a cognomen for the Tetragrammaton and has the same Hebrew derivation as *Adon* meaning Master or Lord or Sovereign.
[309]Hebrew: *Hechal Y-H-V-H.*
[310]The Hebrew words *hechal* and *Ado-nai* have the same numerical value [*gematria*], that is sixty-five.
[311]Psalm 136:1.

unto the God of gods [*Elo-him*],[312] O give thanks unto the Lord of lords [*Ado-nai*]."[313] The reason for these three thanks is as follows: the first thanks is for His firstness and His existence as it is written, "O give thanks unto the Lord [*Y-H-V-H*] for he is good."[314] The second thanks is for His action in creation using the cognomen *Elo-him* as it is written, "O give thanks unto God of gods [*Elo-him*].[315] The third thanks is because He is the Master and rules over everything that He made as it is written, "O give thanks unto the Lord of lords [*Ado-nai*]."[316]

12. Thus,[317] we have alluded very little to the matter of *Ado-nai* from which the intellectual should be stimulated to cite the mysteries included in this cognomen, in the mystery of the Name and its letters. For this is the totality of the secret of *Ado-nai* and other important and profound topics contained therein such as this mystery. We are only drawing one drop from the ocean and casting it into these chapters and we are only placing one mustard seed in the Mediterranean Sea.[318]

13. The matter of the mystery of *Shad-dai* which the patriarchs called Him is also a clarification of[319] the Singular Name, that is to say His existence alone suffices for Him and He has no need for anything besides Himself.[320] The meaning[321] of *El Shad-dai*[322] is that it is a mystery of the [Singular] Name. He who understands the secret of *Shad-dai* will understand the mystery of the [Singular] Name. The secret of *Shad-dai* testifies that it is sufficient for Him to be and to exist. This is the secret[323] why

---

[312]Psalm 136:2.
[313]Psalm 136:3.
[314]Psalm 136:1. The Lord here is the Tetragrammaton.
[315]Psalm 136:2. Hebrew: *Elo-hey Elo-him.*
[316]Psalm 136:3. Hebrew: *Ado-nai Adonim.*
[317]This paragraph is missing in *Sheviley Emunah.*
[318]We have only scratched the surface of this topic. In rabbinic literature, mustard seed is the epitome of tininess, for it is but a speck hardly visible to the naked eye.
[319]Alternate translation: explaining.
[320]Autarchy or absolute sovereignty of God.
[321]Literally: matter, subject, topic.
[322]Literally: God Almighty. See for example Genesis 17:1.
[323]*Sheviley Emunah* here adds *name.*

Abraham "called there on the name of the Lord, [*Y-H-V-H*], the Everlasting God" [*El Shad-dai*].[324]

14. [Because of] all this, the patriarchs had to call Him by this name to inform the people of the world the truth of His Oneness and His Sovereignty[325] before there were miracles and wonders in the world. They called Him *El Shad-dai* until the master of prophets, Moses our teacher, may he rest in peace, came and publicized signs and wonders in the world. Then [the name] *El Shaddai*[326] became concealed. This is what is written. "And I appeared unto Abraham, unto Isaac, and unto Jacob, as God Almighty [*El-Shad-dai*] but My Name is *Y-H-V-H*,"[327] before My name was spread throughout the world. This is the mystery of, "I was not known to them,"[328] that is to say, I was not known and I was not publicized to the people of the world through them because they did not show signs and perform wonders like you [Moses] will later do. Therefore, the patriarchs had to call [God] *El Shad-dai* until Moses came. Then this name became concealed because His Sovereignty, may He be exalted, was publicized and signs and wonders newly appeared in the world.

15. Yet we have seen commentators[329] who interpret *Shad-dai* to mean that He directs and arranges the heavenly system and performs hidden miracles for the righteous, just as miracles are wrought for the pious in every generation. However, the miracles performed by Moses, our teacher, may he rest in peace, were revealed and widely known miracles because they were performed with the power of the Singular Name.[330]

---

[324]Genesis 21:33.

[325]Literally: Godliness.

[326]The last two phrases are missing in the original manuscript.

[327]Exodus 6:3.

[328]Exodus 6:3.

[329]Vajda says it refers to Rabbi Abraham Ibn Ezra.

[330]This is the text from *Sheviley Emunah* because the text in the original manuscript is corrupted here.

Thus, we have alluded a little to the secret of *Shad-dai*.[331]

16. After Moses, our teacher, may he rest in peace, publicized His Sovereignty, may He be exalted, in the world with signs and wonders, and all the people of the world knew that the Exalted One rules over the angels[332] and over human beings[333] as was stated by Rahab the harlot, "For we have heard how the Lord dried up the waters of the Red Sea before you. . . ."[334] And she also said, "And as soon as we had heard it, our hearts did melt, neither did there remain any more spirit in any man, because of you; for the Lord your God, He is God in heaven above, and on earth beneath."[335]

17. After His sovereignty, may He be exalted, was known throughout the world, the prophets after Moses, may he rest in peace, came and chose another cognomen for Him that designates His Sovereignty and Lordship and they called Him by the name *Y-H-V-H Tze-va-ot*,[336] that is to say, the One who rules over all the hosts of the world and who carries the three hosts of the world that exist from the truth of His existence. It is according to these fundamental principles that the prophets, may they rest in peace, called Him *Y-H-V-H Tze-va-ot*.

18. According to these fundamental principles, we will now allude to the matter of holiness which is threefold. Know that the term *holy* means separated and designated to one [person or purpose].[337] It is because there are three hosts in the world— they are the detached mentalities,[338] the heavens and their hosts, and the earth and its produce—that we triple holiness

---

[331]This sentence is missing in *Sheviley Emunah*. The rest of the text also varies in *Sheviley Emunah* except for paragraph 18 which finds its parallel on page 17b.

[332]Literally: upper ones, perhaps referring to the heavens.

[333]Literally: the lower ones, perhaps referring to the earth.

[334]Joshua 2:10.

[335]Joshua 2:11.

[336]Literally: Lord of hosts.

[337]A marginal note in the original manuscript cites "Sanctify them today and tomorrow" (Exodus 19:10).

[338]Angels who are not housed in a body like human beings.

representing the three hosts in the world, that is to say holy and separate from angels, and holy and separate[339] from the hosts of the [heavenly] spheres, and holy and separate from the hosts of human beings.[340] Therefore, *Y-H-V-H Tze-va-ot* is included in holiness so that *Y-H-V-H* is holy and separate from the three hosts. This is what the prophet, may he rest in peace, [meant when he] said, "Holy, holy, holy is the Lord of hosts,[341] the whole earth is full of His glory."[342]

This is the conclusion of the treatise on the Unity [of God] in nine chapters.

Blessed is He who gives strength to the weary.[343]

---

[339]Another marginal note in the manuscript says: So, too, the Aramaic translation of Jonathan ben Uziel: "Holy in the highest heavens, the place of His Divine abode; holy upon earth, the work of His might; holy forever and to all eternity." This passage is recited in the daily morning prayers. See *The Authorized Daily Prayer Book*, J. H. Hertz, ed. (New York: Bloch Publishing Co., 1959), pp. 202–203.

[340]Literally: the lower ones.

[341]Hebrew: *Y-H-V-H Tze-va-ot.*

[342]Isaiah: 6:3.

[343]Isaiah 40:29. This blessing is also part of the daily liturgy. See *Daily Prayer Book, op. cit.* pp. 22–23. Vajda's final footnote states that after the *Nine Chapters* in the original manuscript, there is a listing of seventy names of Israel and seventy names of the Holy One, blessed be He, and a comment about the secret of seventy *alephs*, seventy *bets*, and seventy *gimmels*. In the margin there is a note that is three lines long but is not clearly legible. The explanation is, "Blessed be the glory of the Lord from His place" (Ezekiel 3:12.)

BIBLIOGRAPHY

by Jacob I. Dienstag

תשעה פרקים מיוחד המיוחסים להרמב״ם
ביבליוגרפיה
מאת
ישראל יעקב דינסטאג

א. הוצאות

1] תשעה פרקים מיחוד המיוחסים להרמב״ם. יוצאים לאור על ידי יהודה אריה
ואידה. **קובץ על יד**, ס.ח. ספר ה׳ (תשי״א), קג-קלז.

"בנוגע למקורות המאמר, ברור שחלק חשוב של ט׳ הפרקים אינו אלא קיצור
ועיבוד של ס׳ **גנת אגוז** לר׳ יוסף ג׳יקטילא (נדפס בהאנווא שנת שע״ה לפ״ק). אין כל
הבדל יסודי בין תורתו של ס׳ ג״א וזו של מאמרנו..." (עמ׳ קו).

Reviewed by J.M. Millas Vallicrosa, *Sefarad*, XI (1951), pp. 200-201.

ב. מחקרים

2] Scholem, Gershom (1897-1982)
Kabbalah (1974). New York: Quadrangle/New York Times, p. 64.

3] Vajda Georges (1908-1981)
Le Traite Pseude-Maimonidien: Neuf Chapitres sur l'Unite de Dieu.
Archives d'Histoire Doctrinale et Litteraire du Moyon Age, 28 (1953), pp. 83-
98. Reprinted in *Melanges Georges Vajda...in Memoriam*. Hildesheim:
Gerstenberg Verlag, 1982. pp. 535-550.

ג. ציונים ביבליוגרפיים לכתבי יד

4] Freimann, Aaron (1871-1948)
Union Catalog of Hebrew Manuscripts and their Location, vol. 2. New
York: American Academy for Jewish Research, 1964, p. 139, no. 3378.

5] Zotenberg, Hirsch
    Catalogues des Manuscripts Hebreux et Samaritains de la Bibliotheques
Imperiale. Paris, 1866, no. 767 (11).

INDEX